# MORGAN
## THE LAST SURVIVOR

*by Chris Harvey*

The Oxford Illustrated Press

The Oxford Illustrated Press

© 1987, Chris Harvey

Reprinted 1988

ISBN 0 946609 28 4

**Published by:**
The Oxford Illustrated Press Limited, Haynes Publishing Group,
Sparkford, Nr Yeovil, Somerset BA22 7JJ, England.

Haynes Publications Inc.,
861 Lawrence Drive, Newbury Park, California 91320, USA.

**Printed in England by:**
J.H.Haynes & Co Limited, Sparkford, Nr Yeovil, Somerset.

**British Library Cataloguing in Publication Data:**
Harvey, Chris
  Morgan: the last survivor.
  1. Morgan automobile—History
  I. Title
  629.2'222      TL215.M57
  ISBN 0-946609-28-4

# Contents

# Acknowledgements

It is hard to list the number of people who have helped me with this book on the four-wheeled members of the marque Morgan, but I would like to begin with Peter and Charles Morgan who make them, Jeremy Coulter, deputy editor of *Classic Cars*—with the encouragement of editor Tony Dron—who helped so much with invaluable pictures along with Phil Young. Alex Sully, surely one of the world's great organisers, who moved heaven and earth to provide a wonderful selection of cars for special photography, Barrie Taylor and Zöe Heritage, who started it all by levering me into the cockpit of their 4/4 for the Land's End Trial, and Barry Isles, who helped provide so many contacts.

And as for the Morgan owners who gave so much time and effort to provide their cars for my wife, Mary, to photograph (besides taking so many of the Hilton Press Services pictures while I was busy writing, not to mention processing endless rolls of film, and printing hundreds of pictures), I would like to say to John Allan that I'm glad his fuel injected Plus Eight survived being first registered as a Reliant Scimitar; John Ashton was able, with help from his father, to complete the rebuild of his unique Standard-bodied 4-4 drophead coupé bought — pre-decimalisation — for £17 7s 6d; Jeremy Bagnall-Oakeley can devote so much attention to his Plus Four Plus in company with his 26 other glass fibre-bodied cars; Richard Barclay was able to totally rebuild his tuned series 11; Frank Butler could liberate 2,000 hours for such a superb restoration of his Plus Four; Allan Cameron's four-seater Plus Four Super Sports, which shares a garage with a Big Healey, continues to give him such a rewarding performance; Bob Cragg never sells his Plus Four, nor his 4-4 series 1, so that — after a total of 8 years' rebuilding — his wife does not carry out a threat to go with them; Kevin Donnelly continues to find his Flat Rad Plus Four racer so enjoyable and chuckable; David Hammet wins another cup of tea from telephone linesmen held spellbound by his Plus Eight; Paul Holmes finishes the restoration of his 4/4 4-seater so that he does not have to take the family out in his baker's van; Donald and Cecily Jellyman continue to enjoy their first road production five-speed Plus Eight and TV star series 11; Clinton Jones's Fiat-engined Plus Four remains a passport to a great social life; Pat Kennett, of Panama fame, still storms hills in his Interim model and completes the restoration of his early Plus Four; Brian and Annette Lewis still enjoy new experiences in their ex-Ray Meredith Plus Four competition car; John Orton, a life-long Morgan enthusiast, has many more years with his 8,000-mile series 1, the oldest surviving 4-4 in original condition, and with his ex-Jeff Sparrowe Le Mans Replica; George Parry never has to make another louvred bonnet for his series 1 4-4 which shares a garage with his MG TA of the same year, and that his wife never has to endure another week with a bath full of soaking body timber; Richard Robinson can carry on using his 4-4 4-seater every day; karate teacher John Smith finds enough time to complete the rebuild of his Standard-10-engined 4-4 4-seater to stand alongside his Fiat-engined Plus Four; Stretton Smith's Plus Four four-seater still finds it way to Silverstone; Ray Springthorpe's Plus Eight will always restore pleasure to his motoring; Alex Sully still says his 4-4 is a small boy's best toy; Barry Sumner finds enough time for the odd job of rebuilding his Flat Rad Plus Four despite trialling and racing his other Moggie; Edgar Wallace and Tony Howard keep racing their surviving SLR, once a TOK; and Richard Wheatley always enjoys his very rare Standard-engined Flat Rad coupé, which — almost — shares the same birthday and that his front wheels never fall off again . . .

To all these people, and so many others, notably Jane Marshall of Oxford Illustrated Press and John Haynes of Haynes Publishing, my thanks for waiting even longer than normal for another Chris Harvey car book.

Chris Harvey
Hethe
August 1987

# Colour Plates

# I
# Morgan: The Last Survivor

Morgans have become the last survivors of what was once a popular machine
. . . the traditional open sports car. As such they have gained a fanatical
following because they have always offered, not only inspired styling, and
often sensational performance, but, above all, the most extraordinary value
for money.

It is intriguing to note, therefore, that their design was conservative in
many aspects even when the first Morgan was introduced in four-wheel form
in 1935, all previous production models having been three-wheelers powered
by motor cycle-type engines. Oddly enough, these Morgans were unusually
advanced when the first was seen in 1909 because they had independent front
suspension!

This system, designed by the founder, H.F.S. Morgan, was based
around two vertical pillars with sliding links to the axles on which the front

Where it all started . . . with a
tiller-steered single-seater Morgan
three-wheeler runabout at Malvern
in 1909.

wheels were mounted, was based on motor cycle practice and was later to be adopted by Lancia with their history-making Lambda, one of the first to adopt the integral construction that eventually left only cars like Morgans using the traditional ladder-style chassis.

One of the main advantages of Morgan's suspension was that it allowed the wheels which had to be steered to stay in contact with the surface over which they were travelling at almost all times. This meant that the steering was always much better than that of typical contemporary vehicles which relied on a cart-style solid front axle bouncing from bump to bump and thus spending little time in contact with what were frequently very rough roads.

Naturally Morgans soon started showing well in competition, especially because the chassis could handle more power than many others due to their front suspension. However, with the advent of the Austin Seven, the days of three-wheelers—which cost about the same but offered far less accommodation and stability—were dated and eventually even the conservative Morgan company had to introduce a four-wheeler. It was only natural that this model, called the 4-4 (for four wheels and four cylinders, many previous Morgans having been powered by twin-cylinder motor cycle engines) would be based on the existing three-wheeler practice.

An early Morgan 4-4 (for four wheels and four cylinders) demonstrates the advantages of its independent front suspension in its natural habitat, the Land's End Trial.

In engineering terms it amounted to little more than an extended chassis frame with two wheels at the back instead of one and a more powerful and flexible four-cylinder Coventry Climax engine to haul the extra weight. But although the 4-4 was of a conventional appearance for its day—very much like MG's Midget—its lines were exceptionally well balanced, and it was soon available in four-seater form to supplement the normal two-seater range. Morgan were also able to offer a more luxurious drop-head coupé version without disruption to their normal production of around four four-wheeled cars a week because they were in the unusual position of building their own bodywork and not having to rely on outside sources.

Reliability trials, the forerunners of modern-day rallying, were the most popular form of motor sport at the time, with Morgan 4-4s performing especially well in this medium and making good use of the publicity that resulted. They were also successful in the limited number of circuit races in which they could compete, one intrepid customer, Miss Prudence M. Fawcett, setting the standard in 1938 for never-say-die Morgan enthusiasts by finishing 13th in her first event—the most important sports car race in the world, the Le Mans 24-hour race!

Bliss was a brand-new Morgan 4-4 waiting in the dispatch department at Malvern before the 1939-45 war.

One of the first of the 'curved rad' Morgans poses opposite the works in Pickersleigh Road, Malvern, in 1954.

Brave attempt to modernise a Morgan . . . the Plus Four Plus of 1963.

When supplies of the small Coventry Climax engine dried up in 1939, Morgan were luckily able to switch to a similar unit produced especially for them by Standard, who continued the association after the war. But when the small Standard engine became uneconomical to make, Morgan were able to revamp the 4-4's design in 1950 to take the much more powerful Standard Vanguard unit for a model called the Plus Four.

The strength of the family who owned Morgan was never more evident than when they managed to resist the efforts of Standard to take them over as a short cut to marketing a new Triumph sports car in 1952 aimed at competing with the Austin-Healey 100. Despite this snub, Morgan kept buying their engines because they had become such a dearly-loved part of the English motoring scene, only MG still producing a traditional sports car in any quantity.

And once the MG TF had been replaced by the MGA in 1955, Morgan were left on their own. Following a temporary cut-back in the supply of Standard engines, they introduced as a second line, the smaller—and cheaper—car, now called the 4/4, with a Ford Anglia engine. The Plus Four continued to use the reduced supply of Standard's big four-cylinder power unit from the Triumph TR sports cars. In this form the Plus Four's exceptional power-to-weight ratio brought it many successes in international rallies, frequently with the firm's managing director, Peter Morgan, at the wheel.

A brief flirtation with an alternative all-enveloping modern fixed-head glass fibre body on the same chassis, called the Plus Four Plus, was not well received in 1963 by Morgan's diehard customers—so it was discontinued and the Plus Four remained the top model. A Super Sports racing version of this achieved what was thought to be impossible for a car of such antique construction—it finished 13th at Le Mans in 1962. At the same time, the 4/4 benefited from ever more-powerful Ford engines.

When the Triumph TR range went over to longer six-cylinder engines, Morgan once more managed to revamp the top model in 1967 as a Plus Eight

Morgan charged into the supercar class with the early Plus Eight.

with a Rover V8 engine to produce their fastest car yet, having survived another take-over bid—by Rover! Because of its still simple construction, the Plus Eight was relatively light for such a fast car and proved capable of exceptionally fast acceleration at the expense of what was now a distinctly vintage, very stiff, ride. On smooth tracks, however, the Plus Eight proved to be a front-runner in production sports car racing, often with Peter Morgan's son, Charles, at the wheel.

Then, in 1984, the Plus Four was reintroduced with an Italian Fiat twin-cam engine of two litres capacity like the original Triumph TR2 unit, before development work started on a new Plus Four with British power. In this manner, Morgan were still enjoying long waiting lists into the 1980s with cars which were, in essence, very much like their pre-war machines and still relying on their original design of front suspension which had stood the test of time so well that it now proved ideal for the latest developments in low-profile sports tyres!

# II
# The Early 4-4s

The first four-wheeled Morgan was really a three-wheeler, modified to accept a car-type rear axle. It was built during 1934 around the front end of Morgan's contemporary three-wheeler, the F type, with a Ford 8-hp side-valve engine. This drove through a Meadows gearbox to a Moss rear axle, which was suspended on quarter-elliptic springs. Once it had been established that the engine's power and torque were inadequate for a near 40 per cent rise in weight over the F type H.F.S. Morgan decided to build another prototype with a more suitable unit and car type (or, in reality, cart-type) half-elliptic rear springs.

More than 90,000 cheap four-cylinder engines designed by Coventry Climax had been built by the mid-1930s for use in machines like Triumph's small sports cars. This engine's output in 1,122-cc form (34 bhp at 4,500 rpm with 52 lb/ft of torque at 2,500 rpm) was modest, but it was still around 15 per cent more than Ford's equivalent unit, and sufficient for the four-wheeler's needs.

The first prototype (which was not road-registered, running on Morgan's 094 NP trade plates) was quite rudimentary, with hardly any bodywork behind the scuttle. But the second, built in 1935, clearly defined what every four-wheeled Morgan to follow would look like. It had the same familiar flat radiator as the three-wheelers and substantially similar

H.F.S. Morgan's first production car was a tiller-steered three-wheeler powered by a 10-hp JAP motor cycle engine.

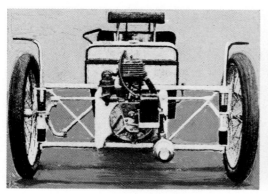

The early 4-4 Morgan carried its badge proudly on a 'flat' grilled radiator.

independent front suspension, but it now had a neat body that followed contemporary sports car lines with cutaway doors and long flowing wings. The world's oldest motoring magazine, *The Autocar,* was quite enthusiastic about this car, saying: 'The Morgan is unusually low in build and looks long and graceful. It is of distinctive design, with a long bonnet, plentifully louvred, and a tail which slopes, streamline fashion, to match the contour of the rear wings.'

Although it had been well-tried on the three-wheelers, the front suspension was distinctly novel—and very advanced for its day—when half-elliptic springs and a solid front axle were still the norm for cars. It was built up around two horizontal tubes, attached to the main frame by a cruciform-braced steel pressing which was further reinforced by gussets at each side. The top tube had diagonal tie bars on each side to stiffen the structure. The ends of the horizontal tubes were each joined by a vertical pillar, providing a mounting for a stub axle which could slide up and down and be rotated from side to side for steering. A heavy, 9.25-inch long, coil spring surrounded each vertical tube above the stub axle, with a bracket for location, and another bracket engaging a lighter spring below the axle line to counter rebound motion. The road wheels were mounted on stepped stub axles which, although adequate for the stresses imposed by the ultra-lightweight three-wheelers, subsequently proved rather fragile on the heavier four-wheeler. This really needed the bell-shaped stub axle it was to receive later. These early Morgan 4-4s also had a notable degree of the positive camber popular at the time and enjoyed delightfully-light steering as a result.

Telescopic shock absorbers, made by Newton, were bolted above the

*Opposite page top:* H.F.S. Morgan prepares to attack the Brooklands hour record in a three-wheeler, supported by his father, the Rev George Morgan (in top hat).

*Opposite page bottom:* The second prototype Morgan four-wheeler built in 1935 established the lines of the traditional roadsters to follow.

stub axle and ahead of the pillar to provide further damping. Steering arms projected forward of the stub axle bracket to be coupled by a ball-jointed track rod, with a drag link on the left-hand side (when viewed from the front) to a steering box just behind the axle line. The geometry ensured a reasonably-agile turning circle of 37 ft, and the steering box was mounted further forward than on many contemporary cars to allow a gently-raked column, on which was mounted a 16-inch diameter steering wheel. It looked very large by today's standards, but proved ideal in conjunction with a ratio which allowed only two complete turns from lock to lock. This plastic-rimmed steering wheel by Ashby also had four springy spokes in the popular contemporary style aimed at cushioning drivers from the shock expected of primitive front suspension systems on poor roads and cart tracks. The Morgan was far better than many of its rivals in this respect because of its independent suspension. Nevertheless, it was considered stiffly sprung, even by the standards of the 1930s when roll was generally countered by making the springs almost solid!

Independent rear suspension was even rarer in 1935, and did not always work very well, so it was not considered unusual that the Morgan had a cheap and reliable live rear axle mounted on 40-inch long half-elliptic springs, with transversely-mounted scissor-type friction dampers made by Andre. Telescopic shock absorbers were rarely used at the back because they intruded too much on already limited body space and hydraulic lever arm dampers simply cost more than the friction versions.

The frame was designed with a close eye to off-road competition. It was based on two Z-section side members which had lower flanges projecting inwards to provide a mounting for a strong, but light, plywood floor. This extended from just behind the engine to just in front of the rear axle. Nothing projected below this smooth sheet of wood, so that the car, which had only 6 inches of ground clearance to give it as low a centre of gravity as possible for maximum cornering ability on the road, could slide over rough surfaces with the minimum of damage. In the event of the wood being splintered, it was easily replaced. Morgan's ingenuity was shown in the way the exhaust system ran from the engine bay, through the left-hand side member (when viewed from the cockpit), and along the outside of the chassis—which protected it from rough ground—but under the running board and wing so that the occupants were protected from the hot pipe and silencer. The outward-pointing top flanges then provided the widest possible, and therefore the most rigid, mounting for the body with this type of chassis configuration. Two conventional U-section girders were used to brace the chassis (based on a 7 ft 8-inch wheelbase and 3 ft 9-inch track front and rear) in the cockpit area, with a deeper one in front of them providing a rearward engine location and support for the vertically-mounted accelerator, brake and clutch pedals. A tube at the back of the chassis also had a dual function linking the side members and providing location for the rear springs. The main leaf of each spring slid through a trunnion slot in this chassis tube from a spring eye formed by a bolt through the sill member to a bracket on the adjacent crossmember. The other cockpit girder in front of that, supported the gearbox. Radius arms extended back from the outer ends of the front suspension's lower horizontal tube to strengthen the bottom tube. The chassis side members were notched to about half their depth at the back to give clearance to the underslung rear axle which passed over their top flanges. As a result, only the springs limited the upward movement of the rear axle, but hardly any rebound was possible, which meant that the Morgan had to have a very hard ride! But, in company with most other cars at the time, the entire chassis flexed and made the car more sinuous than would have been the case with a modern rigid structure.

The four-cylinder in-line engine was not very heavy, so it could be mounted well forward in the chassis. This was necessary, in any case, to provide a decent amount of foot room within the cockpit. Morgan could have bolted the gearbox directly onto the engine, but decided on a remote mounting in the middle of the chassis for three reasons. Had the gearbox been mounted further forward, a much longer propellor shaft would have been needed, which might have whipped badly if it was made in one piece. It could have been divided in the middle for extra support, but that was less efficient and cost more. A forward mounting for the gearbox would also have entailed fitting a complex gear linkage which could not approach the standards of precision that could be achieved with a direct-acting lever for mid-mounted ratios; and again the cost would have been higher. The central location of the gearbox also helped to move more weight to the back for an overall distribution of about 46 per cent front, 54 per cent rear. This was not too much to upset handling badly, but enough to provide decent traction on the typically loose and slippery surfaces used in trials.

The Coventry Climax engine had a good reputation for durability despite essential weaknesses in design which would soon make it obsolete. It was based on well-tried iron castings with a detachable cylinder head, sump finned to aid cooling, and a strong three-bearing crankshaft. But it was a compromise between the side-valve engines typical of earlier years and more efficient overhead-valve engines which were beginning to take over. The inlet valves were overhead, operated by pushrods and rockers, concealed beneath a detachable cover, whereas the exhaust worked off the three-bearing camshaft at the side. This layout resulted in an awkwardly-shaped combustion chamber in which the sparking plugs were sited directly over the exhaust valves, which meant that there was not enough room for water passages to cool the valves properly. But this 'halfway house' engine provided a more sporting performance than the sluggish Ford unit, with all its valves at the side, which was used in the first prototype. This engine also relied on the simple thermo-syphon form of cooling which worked perfectly well under normal open-road driving conditions, but tended to boil over when the car had to climb long hills or became ensnared in heavy traffic. But the substantial exposed radiator held 16 pints of water, which allowed plenty

The four-cylinder Coventry Climax engine used in the early 4-4 Morgans was a relatively-cheap mass-produced unit, but had enough power to give the car a sporting performance.

of time to stop and refill it from a wayside stream or handy suburban tap! Other features of the Coventry Climax engine included a chain drive to the three-bearing camshaft. This chain also operated the dynamo, which could be adjusted through an arc to tension it. A single 'self-starting' Solex carburettor like that used by Standard was fitted along with coil ignition and

a distributor driven by skew gears from the camshaft chain. The engine was available in a variety of sizes based on a 90-mm stroke. Morgan favoured the 63-mm bore variant (which gave the overall capacity of 1,122 cc), with a 6.85:1 compression ratio as used in more powerful versions of Triumph's Southern Cross sports car. The Morgan would be considerably faster, however, because it weighed only 1,500 lb and had a smaller frontal area than the 1,900 lb Triumph.

Triumph used an ENV gearbox, which did not have the benefit of synchromesh, and a 5:1 ratio rear axle from the same source, but Morgan managed to go one better by using components made by Meadows. The gearbox, as fitted to the Morgan, had synchromesh on third and fourth gears, and ratios of 1:1, 1.4, 2.4 and 3.5, which were closer and more sporting

The rolling chassis of the 4-4 was a simple affair with the exhaust running along the side of one rail and the gearbox mounted in a central position, behind the hand-brake lever, remote from the engine.

The 4-4's independent front suspension was delightfully simple, this example—on a Le Mans replica—having been fitted with steering dampers.

than those available from ENV. If the bottom gear proved too high, however, it was worth considering trying to reverse up a hill on its even-lower ratio of 4.52:1—which was marginally better than that available in first gear on ENV boxes—before resorting to seeking a tow from a horse or a tractor!

The gearbox was linked to the engine by a flywheel and Borg and Beck single dry plate clutch running in an aluminium bell housing to which was bolted a 3-inch diameter steel tube enclosing a driveshaft to the gearbox. This tube was then bolted so rigidly to the gearbox casing that the linked units could be mounted on the chassis at only three points: the front of the engine against the cruciform plate, the bell housing on the pedal girder and the rear of the gearbox on the first of the U-section girders.

A conventional propellor shaft with universal joints and sliding splines in the middle then ran back to the Meadows rear axle which was of more modern design than Standard's ENV in that it had a spiral bevel drive rather than worm and pinion, which would, in any case, have been too restricting for trials use.

Cable-operated Girling brakes with 8-inch diameter drums were used all round. A separate handbrake was mounted beside the gear lever on the passenger's side of the transmission tunnel to leave enough room for the driver's legs and feet. Space was at a premium here, drivers having to rest their left foot between the clutch and brake pedal as there was no room to the left of the clutch.

Wire wheels were considered old-fashioned in the mid-1930s because they were more difficult to maintain and keep clean than the steel disc equivalent. They also cost less, and Morgan were happy to fit them to the new 4-4, with two spares carried vertically in the tail. These wheels—along with twin 6-volt batteries for the 12-volt electrical system, mounted either

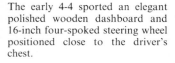

The early 4-4 sported an elegant polished wooden dashboard and 16-inch four-spoked steering wheel positioned close to the driver's chest.

side of the propeller shaft ahead of the axle—helped concentrate weight at the back for maximum traction. Initially, the spare wheels were fitted with knobbly-treaded tyres that could be quickly substituted for the back wheels for trials use by using a Stevenson quick-lift jack. Two of these screw-acting devices were attached to the rearward U-section chassis crosspiece, one on each side of the car. These jacks were wound up or down by a large handle inserted in the head—which protruded through the floor when the seat squab above it was hinged forward. Either side of the car could then be lifted in safety, no matter how loose the surface below, because the jack could not slip away from the chassis. The spare wheels were secured in a tubular bracket each side of the rear crossmember behind the nine-gallon fuel tank, which gave a range of comfortably more than 300 miles.

These 16-inch diameter wheels with their 5-inch wide tyres look tall and spindly by today's standards, but were quite normal and relatively chunky compared to those used by other cars in the 1930s. They were painted in the same colour as the car's body—what was officially British Racing Green (but is now better described by Morgan's in-house designation 'mid-green', black or blue (with black wings)—and they were secured by four studs concealed beneath chrome-plated knave plates.

The body was erected in the time-honoured manner of building an ash frame and hanging steel panels on it. These panels were initially of a very thin gauge, like those on the earlier three-wheelers in which weight was of critical importance. At the point where three thicknesses of metal were lapped over at the top of a door, the total thickness was little more than that of a single sheet of metal used on later cars.

By its very design, room was so restricted in the 41-inch wide cockpit that the rear-hinged doors, which had an internal cable-operated lock, had to be cut away to give clearance for the 'outside' elbows of the driver and

The gearlever, complete with safety catch, was sited under the bottom rail of the dashboard.

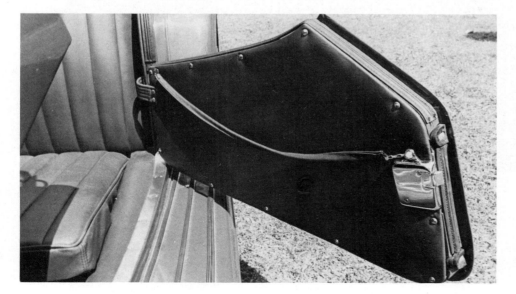

The long, low, doors were opened by a lock operated from a leather-covered chain.

passenger. They shared a leather-trimmed bench seat back, but were separated by a hump in the middle of the squab covering the propeller shaft. In general, they could be seen to be wedged in so tightly that they needed no further location, particularly as they normally wore far thicker clothing to protect themselves from the elements than is normal today! Spirited solo driving would require special preparation . . .

The scuttle was one of the main parts of the body's structure and was reasonably rigid when it had to carry out light aeroscreens. It had a tendency to shake, however, when fitted with the standard full-width metal-framed windscreen, which folded flat for better visibility and less wind resistance—but then offered less protection, of course. A severely-limited amount of luggage could be carried behind the seat back in a compartment shared with the hood irons, and the hood when it was down, which was most of the time. But the flat pane of glass that was used for the windscreen—all that was available in the 1930s—so disturbed the airflow around the car that less wind (and rain) whipped round the backs of the occupants' heads than is encountered with the curved screens on today's open cars. Sidescreens could be fitted to block off the gaps either side of the canvas hood (which gave an overall height of 4 ft 2 ins when erected), but, inevitably in view of the aerodynamics, they promoted severe draughts around the leading edges of the hood at the back of the doors. All told, it was far more comfortable to drive a Morgan with the hood down because rain, in any case, was deflected over the occupants' heads from even quite modest speeds. The hood also had only a very small 'post box' sized rear window—which was fashionable at the time—but which made the interior seem quite claustrophobic by modern standards.

On the cars fitted with two windscreen wipers, the drive from one was taken from the other (operated by an electric motor) through a push-pull bar.

The second prototype 4-4 had two windscreen wipers, each driven by a linkage from a central electric motor attached to the base of the windscreen frame, which, for the record, was 3 ft 8 ins from the ground at its highest point.

A small cubby hole each side of the dashboard surrounded the instruments and switchgear mounted in the middle. A large central

speedometer containing a milometer and trip meter, and a clock, dominated the display, with the vital information of how much petrol was contained in the tank, and the engine's water temperature, on segments of a circular instrument in front of the driver. To the left of the speedometer was a similar

Even the driver's mirror was a work of art, mounted on the fold-flat windscreen's frame.

The bonnet was secured by spring-loaded clips.

Twin spare wheels were mounted in the elegant tail for trials work, with a single rear lamp which also illuminated the number plate.

And the sidescreens were held in place by thumb screws.

instrument recording the dynamo's output and the engine's oil pressure. A rev counter could be fitted, but entailed blocking off the right-hand cubby hole to provide it with a mounting. Costs had to be saved wherever possible, so it was not a normal fitting, the theory being that the exhaust note provided sufficient information on how the engine was revving! In any case, room for personal effects was so limited that some owners were having to resort to stowing personal items in the toolboxes under the bonnet on the scuttle top! Beneath the combined ammeter and oil pressure gauge was a Lucas ignition, charging rate and lighting switch. This operated small sidelights mounted on each front wing and large headlights alongside the radiator. There was no dipping mechanism to avoid dazzling oncoming traffic, but simply a foot operated switch which activated a central driving light as the headlights were extinguished. This gave a broad spread of light, but not much range. Other

Massive headlamps were supplemented by small sidelights mounted on the wings, with a central driving light operating when the main beams were extinguished.

switches scattered about the instrument panel operated items like the electric starter motor on the right-hand side of the bell housing (when viewed from the front of the engine), provided a hand control for the throttle, and enriched the mixture for cold starting. The horn was also worked by a button in the middle of the dashboard and there was another to operate panel lighting.

In its initial form, the 4-4 was priced at 185 guineas (a common unit of currency formerly used for horse-dealing), which when translated to £194. 5s (or today's £194.25) compared very favourably with the £222 asked for rival machines such as the MG.TA which would go into far larger-scale production during 1936.

It was inevitable, however, that there would be some changes before the first 4-4 could go into production, because it was a prototype, and in any case, hardly any two Morgans were exactly alike. Essentially, modifications made to the handful of 4-4s produced in 1936 concentrated on making the car easier to drive, more comfortable and durable. The steering was given a conventional self-centring action by inclining the suspension pillars back from the vertical with the spindle diameter increased from 0.75 ins to 1 inch now that it had to cope with more weight than that of the F-type three-wheeler. Rubber bungs at the bottom of the spindles were introduced at the same time as a better way of absorbing road shock than the very bouncy lower coil springs which had been used before. The suspension's vertical spindles were made easier to maintain by the use of a forged steel hub carrier which had phosphor-bronze bushes at the top and bottom. These could be replaced from time to time to take up wear. The new hub carriers also provided a flat surface onto which the brake back plates could be bolted at four points. This arrangement made the backplates stiffer and the braking much smoother and more consistent as a result. Further improvements included replacing the reduction gear on the steering column with a Burman-Douglas box.

Resonance from the engine and gearbox was damped by rubber bushes in the mountings and tappet adjustment improved by inverting the ball joint between the pushrod and rocker so that the cap took up a position in the top of the pushrod and the ball was attached to the rocker. Lubrication was improved because the cap then retained oil. A little extra power—1 bhp—was obtained by increasing the size of the inlet valves and reshaping the combustion chamber. The engine's cooling was also made marginally better by adopting a thicker tubular-type radiator block, which had a larger-diameter bottom connection from the left-hand side of the cylinder

The four-seater had room for only one spare wheel, but plenty of accommodation under its generous canvas hood.

block when viewed from the front. These later-series units could be readily identified by the movement of the oil filler from the timing casing to a position high up towards the back of the engine. Dynamo bearing life was dramatically increased by giving it a separate driving belt, the generator itself being better ventilated. Costs were reduced at the same time by linking the driver's side wiper to that on the passenger's side so that only one motor was needed.

These changes, phased in around August 1937, were followed a year later by the introduction of four-seater bodywork as an option on the same chassis. The extra room in the back was liberated by repositioning the fuel tank and batteries further back in the space normally occupied by the forward of the two spare wheels. A rear bench seat, 34.5 ins wide with an 18-inch high backrest, was then placed directly over the rear axle on a line

The rear-seat passengers sat, quite literally, over the axle and between the wheel arches.

about 2 ins higher than the front seats. Just over 12 ins of knee-room was then available in what had been the luggage compartment behind the front seats, which normally measured 42 ins by 24 by 17. Headroom in the back when a new extended hood was erected amounted to only 32 ins rather than the 37.5 ins available for the front seat passengers, but it did enable the overall height to remain unaltered at 50 ins. These new rear seats, which cost £25 extra, certainly extended the family appeal of the Morgan 4-4 at a time when MG's T-series cars were made with only two seats, especially as the inevitable weight increase was confined to only 10 per cent at an overall 1,642 lb.

During the following year, 1938, the rear axle casing was stiffened and a new four-star differential adopted. Twin spare wheels continued to be fitted to the two-seaters despite a ban late in the year on 'knobbly' tyres in trials because weight over the rear wheels was so important for such activities. Customers could, however, specify a single spare wheel with slightly reshaped rear bodywork. A delightful new filler was also fitted which allowed one of the new-fangled cans of oil to be inserted in a casing which then drained it into the sump!

A further permutation on the basic chassis followed in 1938 on Morgan's by now traditional August new-model launch date (immediately after the works holidays) when more luxurious drophead-coupé bodywork

*Left and below:* The early drophead-coupé presented a similar frontal appearance to the roadster and four-seater, but had a higher door line and more luxurious hood. Because it had only two seats, however, there was room for twin spare wheels and a sloping tail.

became available as an option for the two-seater. One of the chief features of the new body was the 26-inch wide rear-hinged doors which were not cut away at the top, looking like those normally fitted to a saloon car. They had detachable windows made up of two panes which could be slid either way in a metal frame to give an opening at the front or the back for ventilation (or signalling although semaphore-style trafficators were also fitted behind the trailing edge of the doors), with ventilation flaps in the scuttle. The windows did not have a wind-up mechanism so that a recess could be scooped out of the interior trim to allow elbow room of 44 inches across the cockpit. The lined hood was also much more impressive, folding away for stowage in the luggage compartment behind the front seats. It was also possible to roll back just the front section above the occupants' heads while the rear part remained upright in *coupe de ville* style.

The hood fitted neatly into the well behind the seats, leaving an uncluttered line with framed windows that could be left in the raised position without bowing in a slipsteam.

Along with an altogether more luxurious leather and wood-capped interior, with a bright metal waist strip and proper outside door handles the coupé was made quieter for its occupants by using larger and more expensive Silentbloc metal-and-rubber sandwich bushes for engine and gearbox mountings. Fatter 5.50 section tyres were also fitted on 16-inch steel disc saloon car-style wheels to give a smoother ride than the standard section tyres fitted to 17-inch pressed-steel spoked wheels adopted for the more spartan models. Weight suffered, however, at an overall 1,736 lb.

The coupé was also distinguished by a new radiator grille with vertical plated slats rather than wire mesh used on the normal 4-4s. A choice of two colour schemes was 'recommended,' cream and black, or blue all over, although other finishes were available at extra cost. It was by this degree of standardisation that Morgan was able to keep down the cost of the coupé to £225, only £3 more than an ordinary MG T-series and far cheaper than MG's Tickford coupé. Soon after, the normal two and four-seater Morgans got the Silentbloc bushes and, from March 1939, all cars were fitted with a very similar synchromesh on top and third, and a Moss gearbox as supplies of the

Meadows box dried up. The new gearbox had ratios of 1, 1.34, 2.39, 3.86 (with a 4.47 reverse).

Triumph also produced a 62-mm bore, 6.4:1 compression ratio, twin Solex carburettor version of the Coventry Climax engine for their Southern Cross Special and Gloria Four, giving an overall displacement of 1,087 cc, a power output of 46 bhp at 4,500 rpm (and 56.5 lb/ft of torque at 2,500 rpm). With a higher compression ratio, it was possible to extract as much as 50 bhp from one of these units. Engines such as these were specified at extra cost by customers who wanted to compete in the popular 1,100-cc international competition class until Coventry Climax decided to cash in. They were too small to produce normal engines in large quantities, so Triumph built them under licence. But they could not build enough pure competition units, so they began to offer a 1,098 cc version with balanced bottom end, four-branch exhaust manifold with straight-through Burgess silencer, Solex or Zenith carburation, and magneto ignition. These engines—all individually-built— produced around 55–60 bhp, according to specification.

These engines were fitted to competition versions of the 4-4, called the T.T. Replica (after the Tourist Trophy race) following a successful showing in this event. These special lightweight cars were then developed into the Le Mans Replica—capable of nearer 90 mph than the normal 4-4's 80 mph—being offered at £250 from March 1939. This had special lightweight bodywork with much weight being saved by substitution skimpy cycle-type front mudguards for the normal long flowing wings. The back of the bodywork was also different, with a single spare wheel recessed into a reformed rear panel. The luggage compartment was also panelled over and an enlarged long-range tank fitted with twin fillers for rapid refuelling. Higher ratio gears were used for more restrained high-speed cruising, and other models made with a sloping tail concealing an even larger fuel tank of as much as 24 gallons capacity. In the case of the T.T. Replica an exposed spare wheel was carried on top of the sloping tail. Various other special items—such as rev counters—were fitted to these rare machines.

The Le Mans replica had far more spartan bodywork with cycle-type wings to save weight. This is the ex-Jeff Sparrowe car owned and restored by John Orton.

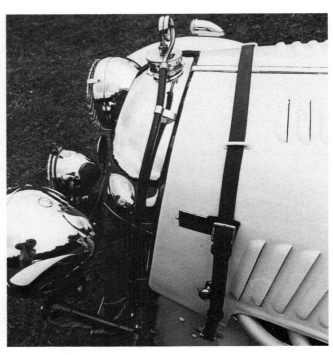

*Above left:* More power was liberated from the Le Mans replica's engine with a four-into-one tubular exhaust system.

*Above right:* The radiator was fitted with an external overflow system and the bonnet held down by a strap.

*Below left:* The wheels of the Le Mans replica were fitted with a quick-release knock-off spinner system for hurried pit stops.

*Below right:* The Standard engine fitted to the later 4-4s bore a special Morgan valve cover.

Meanwhile Triumph, who made the Coventry Climax engine, had been badly hit by a general slump in the motor industry sales and went into receivership in June 1939, leaving Morgan to search for a new engine. At that time, the Standard Motor Company in Coventry were emerging as one of Britain's leading manufacturers. Their cars were typically mundane saloons, although the chief executive, John Black, on the one hand fancied a sporting car to promote a more glamorous image, but, on the other, was loath to risk

heavy losses by involving one with Standard's large scale of production. He compromised to a certain extent by producing hardware—such as engines—for a rapidly-rising sporting car manufacturer in another part of Coventry: Jaguar. These included an overhead valve conversion of his four-cylinder 1,776-cc Standard unit for the Jaguar '1½-litre'. Needless to say, this policy attracted Morgan, and especially because Standard had a superb reputation for craftsmanship (and would soon become the first company to be allowed to make Rolls-Royce engines without direct supervision). The Morgan family heaved a sigh of relief when Black agreed to produce a similar engine for them based on his 1,267-cc Standard Ten unit.

This overhead valve conversion on an existing side valve unit produced usefully more power and torque than the normal Coventry Climax engine without moving the 4-4 into the higher tax bracket (based on engine size) which H.F.S. Morgan felt he could not risk. The new engine produced 39 bhp at 4,500 rpm with 62 lb/ft of torque at 2,500 rpm as a result of having a much more efficient combustion chamber shape. The general arrangement of the engine, with a bore and stroke of 63.5 mm by 100 followed what had become established practice in the late 1930s. It had a line of eight valves (four inlet and four exhaust) along one side of the detachable 6.5:1 compression ratio cylinder head. The valves were operated by overhead rockers and tubular pushrods from a chain-driven camshaft in the right-hand side of the cylinder block (when viewed from the front). The inlet and exhaust manifolds were on the other side, above the sparking plugs. Cast iron was used for ease and economy of construction with a counterbalanced crankshaft running in three main bearings. Modern shell-type bearings were used with steel connecting rods and alloy pistons. A gear-driven oil pump was submerged in the alloy sump. It was worked from the centre of the camshaft by a vertical spindle which extended upwards to drive the distributor. The camshaft was driven by chain from the crankshaft with an external pulley in front of it to work a belt which drove a dynamo and a fan to supplement the water cooling, which still operated on the thermo-syphon principle. The camshaft also drove an AC mechanical fuel pump for the single downdraught Solex carburettor. The engine and gearbox mountings represented a further improvement over those used on the earlier 4-4s in that there was now more rubber. The Moss gearbox—was mounted as before, with its connecting tube now meeting a steel bellhousing containing the flywheel and Borg and Beck clutch with the starter motor under the manifolds.

Morgan had time to install this engine in only a handful of cars—all coupés—before war was declared and the factory went over to munitions work. But within months of peace being declared, Morgans were back on the market with the Standard engine in slightly modified form. It now had a water pump incorporated in the fan housing, which was much appreciated. The compression ratio was also increased to 7:1, which gave the engine 40 bhp with a higher 4.72:1 rear axle ratio.

For a short while, the Le Mans Replica could still be bought. Four were either assembled from spare parts or dusted down from war time storage. But there was no hope of the model going into proper production as there were less than a dozen of the by-now obsolete 1,098-cc Coventry Climax engines in stock.

Initially, all post-war Morgans were two-seaters, because the four-seaters and coupés took far longer to build and maximum production was needed for markets starved of new cars. Minor changes in the bodies established the dimensions at 136 ins in length for the two-seater and 139.5 ins for the coupé with overall heights, hood up, of 52.75 ins and 54.5 ins. The very early post-war 4-4s (by now sometimes described as 4/4s) differed from the pre-war more noticeably, however, in that the positive camber had disappeared and rebound springs in the front suspension had been developed to such an extent that Morgan thought it possible to dispense with the front shock absorbers. Front wheel wobble was also effectively countered by the use of steel and bronze leaf steering dampers connecting the top of each suspension upright to the chassis alongside, but the deletion of the shock absorbers did not work out so well, so they were soon returned. The coupé was also reduced to using 5.00-section tyres in an immediate post-war shortage, but all cars could now be fitted with improved 9-inch diameter front brake drums. Essentially, however, the Morgan 4-4 was little changed—except in price, which had now risen to £455 for the normal car and £506 for the coupé (including 27.5 per cent purchase tax in Britain).

Rolling chassis had been supplied to bodybuilders in the grand old

John Menhinick Ashton's 1947-model 4-4 is believed to be one of three fitted with Standard drophead-coupé bodywork by City Garages, Exeter.

manner, with this practise continuing after the war. It was especially attractive to Morgan because bodybuilding and trimming were the biggest bottlenecks in production. As a result, it is believed that three in particular were bought by City Garages at Exeter in 1947 and fitted with attractive Standard drophead four-seater coupé bodies before the Morgan factory started building their own version again in 1948, when the coupé-style radiator grille was standardised for all chassis. Happily, at least one of these Standard-bodied cars survives today.

Utility cars were also in short supply at the time and another Exeter garage, called Peamore, experimented with producing a Morgan 4-4 estate car. Their prototype had a Ford V8 Pilot-style 'woodie' rear body on the normal Morgan rolling chassis kit, which was sold complete with standard wings, radiator grille and so on. The estate car offered 40 cubic feet of space behind the front seats but failed to find a market because it cost £250 (before painting) for the body alone, putting a finished car into the £800 class with purchase tax.

The Morgan factory also experimented with differing permutations on the 4-4 chassis. The first such vehicle, built late in 1937, had a high-pressure Centric-supercharged 1,122-cc Coventry Climax engine which gave it a similar performance to the Le Mans cars. But thoughts of putting it into production were abandoned when the crankshaft—which had a tendency to whip even in normal adaptations—proved inadequate. There seemed little point in supercharging the 1,098-cc engine because there was no competition class to encourage it.

As a result a 60-bhp 2,228-cc 'flat head' Ford V8 engine similar to a larger model which had begun to dominate pre-war trials, was tried in a 4-4 chassis during 1938. The performance with the considerable torque of this side valve engine proved highly attractive but the project was abandoned because of H.F.S. Morgan's fears that such a car would cost too much to tax.

At the time Morgan was searching for a new engine to replace the Coventry Climax unit, a Ford side-valve unit bored out from 933 cc to 1,021 cc was tried with a high-compression alloy cylinder head, and, as a further experiment, a side-valve standard engine was fitted with an Arnott low-pressure supercharger. Two works cars were also fitted with 10-hp Ford engines, which were slightly lighter than the standard unit. One was the short-chassis 4-4 used by W.A. Goodall in trials and the other driven by Harry Jones. Production of the normal 4-4 continued until Standard decided to adopt a one-model policy in favour of the larger-engined Vanguard in 1950. The performance of the Plus Four which followed was to prove sensational.

# III
# The Plus Four

The Morgan four-wheeler became a much faster car with the introduction of the Plus Four in 1950 due to two factors: the confirmation that the British government would not revert to the pre-war system of taxing cars on a rising scale influenced by engine capacity, and Standard's own engine-building arrangements. Production of the 1,267-cc engine was doomed when Jaguar stopped using their similar unit in 1948. For a time Morgan considered using an 1,172 cc Ford Ten engine, which could be tuned to give a decent

The Plus Four introduced in 1950 was a more substantial car than the 4-4 it replaced, in keeping with its bigger and heavier power unit. This example, the prototype coupé built in 1951, was used as a demonstrator and team car in the Land's End Trial as well as being featured as a road test car in several magazines.

Works manager Jim Goodall takes a first-class award in the 1952 Land's End Trial with another Plus Four, a two-seater which was later converted—with its sister car, registered HUY984—to cowled-radiator bodywork.

performance, before taking the radical step of following Standard's line and going for a much larger engine.

This was the 2,088-cc unit introduced for Standard's new Vanguard saloon, which replaced the Flying Eight, Twelve and Fourteen range midway through 1948. It was also used in the Ferguson tractor which formed the backbone of Standard production, leading to all sorts of ribald jokes . . . but it was a very practical unit, designed with simplicity in mind for a long life and easy maintenance. That is why it was fitted with easily-removable wet cylinder liners—a practical feature that was to endear it to amateur engineers throughout the world because it made it so simple to rejuvenate this extraordinarily tough engine: you just slapped in new pistons and liners, gave it a quick valve and bearing job, and it was likely to be as good as new!

When the engine was revealed in 1947 for future production it had a bore of 80 mm and stroke of 92, giving it a capacity of 1,849 cc although prototypes were of 1,760 cc capacity—which was 100-cc more than the 1,500-cc limit H.F.S. Morgan had set for his cars at the time. He was still wary that the government might revert to the earlier taxation system. Sir

*Below, left and right:* The Standard Vanguard engine, seen here mounted in the prototype cowled radiator bodywork, formed the basis for the later twin-carburettor Triumph TR2 power unit.

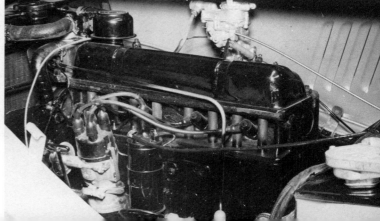

John Black, who had been knighted for war work in 1944, was less suspicious and authorised an increase in bore to 85 mm to give the Vanguard—which weighed a hefty 2,716-lb—a reasonable performance. Equipped with a single Solex downdraught carburettor, it produced 68-bhp at a slugging 4,200 rpm, with no less than 112 lb/ft of torque at 2,300 rpm, which would give a Morgan weighing in at a quoted 1,900-lb (although there is reason to believe that this might be something of an understatement) a startling performance. Capacity reductions to bring the engine within the two-litre competition classes could easily be achieved without extensive work on the cast-iron cylinder block by substituting 83 mm bore pistons and liners. This option was not offered initially, however, as the priority was to get the new car into production at as low a price as possible.

Naturally, this all-purpose engine had a robust crankshaft, with three white metal main bearings of 2.479 inches diameter and an 11-pint sump. With ease of maintenance in mind, the big ends were split diagonally to allow the H-section connecting rods and pistons to be withdrawn upwards through the cylinder bores rather than downwards, which would have meant removing the crankshaft. The camshaft, on the right-hand side when viewed from the front phosphor bronze bearing, ran direct in the crankcase in two other bearings. Like the earlier shaft, it was operated by a duplex roller chain with the distributor and the oil pump driven from the top and bottom, respectively, of a vertical shaft meshed to the camshaft by a skew gear. Another pair of skew gears could be fitted under the distributor to drive a rev counter, although Morgan continued to ignore such luxuries, saying that the engine note was enough reference to what was going on under the bonnet! The camshaft's final function—apart from operating the pushrods to the overhead inlet and exhaust valves—was to drive the well-tried AC mechanical fuel pump. The dynamo was driven by a belt as usual, which now took in not only the radiator fan but—at last—a proper water pump and thermostatically-controlled cooling system. The cylinder liners were seated at the bottom on special figure-of-eight washers, one to each pair of liners, and at the top, against the gasket of the cast-iron cylinder head. The split flat-topped pistons, which were made of aluminium alloy, had gudgeon pins secured by circlips—all basic and well-tried engineering.

Initially, the cylinder head, with its inverted bathtub combustion chambers, had a relatively low compression ratio of 6.7:1. This was quite common in those days because of the difficulties in obtaining good-quality petrol in many countries, including Britain. The cylinder head had eight ports and vertical overhead valves (1.5-inch diameter inlet, 1.28-inch exhaust) returned by more durable double valve springs rather than the single used on the 1,267-cc unit. In fact, the only way in which this engine was modified from its Vanguard installation could be seen in a reshaped inlet manifold to keep the carbuettor upright because it was mounted at a slightly different angle in the chassis.

The changes to the Plus Four went far deeper than the substitution of

The Plus Four chassis followed the lines established by the 4-4, although it was altered in detail and included a three-spoke steering wheel. But the change most immediately obvious was the dramatically-increased footroom liberated by moving the engine forward and the siderails outwards.

one engine for another, although the basic layout remained much the same. Apart from revised gear ratios, the chassis was redesigned to make it stronger and with dimensions that would make the car more comfortable; the suspension was also modified with comfort in mind as well as better handling, the brakes were uprated, and the stub axles were made in a more durable bell shape. The body was also panelled in thicker gauge steel now that there were no problems over power and torque to pull a heavier car.

The most obvious change in the chassis was that the wheelbase was

The rear end of the chassis was much the same as that of the 4-4, other than for the increased track.

*Below:* The Plus Four coupé was a good deal more sophisticated than the earlier bodies with details such as sliding sidescreens and semaphore-style windscreen wipers to give better outward vision.

*Bottom:* The hood of the Plus Four drophead was just as snug—or claustrophobic, depending on which way you reacted to it.

lengthened by 4 ins to 96 ins and the width increased by 2 ins to take the front and rear track to 47 ins, the same amount being let into the cockpit to make that 44 ins across. While these changes were welcome, a total reshaping of the front footwells was even more so. Moving the engine slightly further forward in the longer wheelbase and setting the side-rails further apart liberated no less than 6 ins extra foot-room and 2 ins more leg-room in the pedal area.

At the same time, judicious paring at the bodywork—particularly around

*Left and above:* Soon after the introduction of the Plus Four coupé, it even boasted a 'luggage boot' although, when opened, it appeared to be well filled with the spare wheel . . .

the front wings—contained the overall length of the two-seater to 140 ins (the same as before) and the coupé and four-seater to 142 ins, with overall heights of, open, 46 ins for the two-seater, 47 for the coupé, and 48 for the four-seater, with 52 ins hood up for the two-seaters and 54.5 for the four-seater. This was achieved despite having to accommodate a larger, 11-gallon, fuel tank so that the Morgan's range of more than 300 miles would not be compromised. Something had to give in the four-seater, however, so that got only a 10-gallon tank.

The increased wheelbase improved the ride and handling of the Plus Four, which was made better still by the use of longer and softer front springs, which now measured 12.25 ins. This extra 3 ins was squeezed in by inclining the vertical spindles inwards by 2 degrees, the turning circle remaining unchanged at 33 ft. The 1.375-inch wide six-leaf rear springs were lengthened by 2.75 ins to 42.75 to give more flexibility at the same time. Girling double-acting hydraulic front shock absorbers (with Girling lever-arm dampers at the back) further improved the ride and handling despite the weight of the engine which amounted to around 100 lb more than the 1,267 cc unit. Front suspension maintenance was also made much more convenient by connecting the upper ends of the spindles to copper piping, with a feed from the oil pressure gauge metered by a pedal-operated valve. A depression of the pedal every 100 miles or so while the engine was under full load was now sufficient to lubricate the front suspension and steering. A momentary reduction in the oil pressure reading signified that the system was actually working.

Girling also supplied new hydraulically-operated brakes with two leading shoes at the front which were a vast improvement on the old cable-operated devices although the drums themselves were basically the same at 9 ins all round with a width of 1.5 ins. Dunlop tyres of 5.25-section, on 16-inch pressed-steel wheels drilled to reduce unsprung weight and aid brake cooling (but complete with hub caps), were also standardised on all models.

All the important controls on the Plus Four were placed as near as possible to the drivers' hands. These included a large white switch in the centre of the dashboard for the trafficators now that it was difficult to give hand signals with full-sized doors.

*Below left:* The Plus Four drophead's doors were also railed in wood to match the dashboard, with deep leather map pockets.

*Below right:* Some drophead coupés were even fitted with a heater in the passenger's footwell.

Sir John Black was of the opinion that three forward gears were enough for any car, but H.F.S. Morgan was not, so the Plus Four kept its four-speed Moss box linked to a Borg and Beck single dry plate clutch in the same way as before. Little comment was made at the time, but it now had synchromesh on second ratio as well, and with a higher, 4.1:1, rear axle made by Salisbury. In view of the increase in performance it was amazing that Morgan was able to hold the price of the two-seater to £652 (after purchase tax), and the coupé to £565. Four-seater production—with rear springs uprated to seven leaves—had to be delayed for a year to meet the demand for the two-seaters, the 'family model' eventually making its debut at £597. A prototype four-seater Plus Four drop-head coupé was also built in September 1951.

Once production of the Plus Four in all three standard body styles—two-seater, four-seater and two-seater drop-head coupé—was under way, Morgan was able to improve the general specification in detail. The rebound springs in the front suspension were strengthened during 1952, and following a spate of clutch linkage failures, the diameter of the operating pawl's eye bolt was increased from 0.375 ins to 0.5. The top water hose connection was changed from a single to a double unit during the year, with a new tubular-type radiator replacing the earlier film one. The steering dampers were also modified so that the blades could be renewed without dismantling.

More noticeable was a new badge plate fitted outside the bars of the radiator grille, with changes to the lighting gear as Lucas modernised their range. Double-dipping headlamps were introduced at the turn of the year, with new block lenses soon after and smaller, and neater, sidelamps. The headlamp wiring also used push connectors from this point. Towards the end of 1952, it also became possible to order a higher final drive ratio of 3.73:1

*Above left:* The hood frame of the Plus Four coupé was of substantial construction, keeping the canvas covering taut and allowing it to be rolled back to a sedanca configuration in which the area above the occupants' heads could remain open while the backs of their necks were protected by the rear portion.

*Above right:* The most practical place to carry luggage in the Plus Four drophead was on the platform above the rear axle.

*Below right:* Semaphore-style trafficators were fitted to the early dropheads.

*Below left:* The Plus Four four-seater allowed a decent amount of knees-up legroom even for adults.

for more relaxed cruising (at the expense of top-gear flexibility).

In the circumstances, Morgan were still keen to supply bare chassis for specialist coachwork, notable examples being what is believed to be the only Plus Four saloon, an open car with a conventional luggage boot, and a Ferrari-like fixed-head coupé. The four-seater saloon, built in 1952, had lines following those of a typical pre-war or early post-war limousine, except that it had only two side windows at the back, giving as much light as possible for rear seat passengers. Its constructors, Cooper Motor Bodies, of Putney, South West London, also incorporated a neatly swept tail containing a luggage locker.

Four-seater saloon coachwork was also mounted on a Plus Four chassis by the London firm of Cooper Motor Bodies.

The Plus Four badge was also mounted on a plate outside the flat radiator's grille.

The open car with a luggage boot was built only a couple of miles away by Coach Bodies in Tooting Bec the following year. Again, a four-seater chassis was used with aluminium panels to keep the weight down to around 2,000 lb. A spare wheel was mounted vertically at the front of the luggage locker, protruding through the top and fared in front and rear by rounded metalwork. The whole effect, when the hood was down and concealed by a tonneau cover, was rather like that of the contemporary, but rare, Riley roadster, especially in its wrap-round bumpers. But when the hood was up, it still looked very much like a normal Morgan four-seater. The overall length was increased by about 18 inches, however.

Problems with headlight supplies led to the front of the Plus Four having to be restyled to accommodate flush-fitting units. This is the 'interim' model built in 1953.

The interim model featured forward-hinged doors much smaller than the coupé's rear-hinged examples. The object was to improve the rigidity of what was a considerably lighter rear end to the bodywork.

The interim model also introduced a wider range of colour schemes than had been previously available now that cheaper leathercloth trim was more readily acceptable.

The fixed-head coupé, owned and used in competition by Roy Clarkson, was quite obviously inspired by the Touring-bodied Ferrari coupé of 1951, as were several other specials, including one built by the Belgian firm Oblin on a Jaguar XK120 chassis. The object of these exercises was to qualify competitive machinery for the saloon car classes of international rallies. It was also during this period—early in 1953—that Morgan built another four-seater drop-head coupé on the Plus Four chassis, which was subsequently used by H.F.S. Morgan until his death in 1959.

About this time Morgan began to run into real problems with supplies of items such as upright radiators and exposed headlamps as they were going out of fashion on mass-produced saloons and sports cars like Standard's Triumph TR2. Morgan were forced, for the first time, to restyle their car to keep down the cost. Recessing new headlamp units into nacelles in wings, of more generous proportions which extended right down to a bumper line, was no great problem. But changing the elegant upright radiator took more soul-searching. At first, towards the end of 1953, a painted cowl was used with slats slanted back at a discreet angle. This led to a storm of protest from die-hard Morgan fans, so about a year later, in 1954, Morgan went the whole hog and restyled the nose completely, with curved radiator slats and a neater cowl. The headlights were also raised at the same time to meet new height regulations although they were still recessed in the wings.

The two Plus Four four-seater coupés, which had been retained by the works, were among the first cars to receive this new bodywork. The rear end was modified to incorporate a 'luggage boot' lid which swung down to reveal the vertically-mounted spare wheel occupying most of the luggage area. But Morgan pointed out that the luggage could be carried on the lowered lid! The doors were also made slightly longer to allow easier access to the rear bench and the windows a shade deeper. The hood and frame received obvious modifications, plus an ingenious zip-out panel at the back which improved ventilation when the occupants did not want to lower the hood—which provided shade in a hot climate. This style of bodywork was then produced for the occasional customer over the following three years at an extra £30, including tax, over the price of the normal two-seater drop-head coupé. For the first time, also, a front bumper was fitted to all models, with small vertical over-riders front and rear (although there was no rear bumper bar), the chief reason in this case being to please the American market.

But the overall result was generally considered to present a far happier frontal appearance than that of the 'interim' model . . . few people complained that you now had to lift the bonnet to reach the radiator filler cap. With a water pump, the days of having to refill header tanks from wayside streams was fast disappearing.

Detail improvements included fitting wider, 1.75-inch, brake dums at the front.

Meanwhile Sir John Black had become desperate for a mass-produced sports car to compete in the fast-expanding American market. Its price had to be kept as low as possible to compete with the latest MG T-series car, the TD, so the specification had to be confined to whatever mechanical parts Standard or Triumph were using in saloon cars at the time. This meant that there was only one engine available: that from the Vanguard.

It was also necessary that this car could compete in the international two-litre class, so liners of an 83-mm bore (to reduce the overall capacity to 1,911 cc) became a necessity. Early experiments, during 1952, involved fitting two constant vacuum semi-downdraught SU carburettors, which, with a special rake-type manifold coupling the inlet ports and a cast exhaust manifold with a single inlet, produced an extra 3 bhp, taking the output to 71. Triumph thought this would be enough to give their new car a desired 90 mph top speed, but, in the event it was not enough.

They had been lucky, however, in that they had mounted the large cooling fan directly on to the crankshaft, with a long casting—which ran under a chassis member—to take its ancillary drive belt. This proved to be an excellent damper that enabled the engine to run much more smoothly at high revs. This had not been the intention; mounting the fan in such a way had been done simply to help squeeze the engine as far forward as possible in what would be their TR2 sports car.

As a first stage of increasing the power output beyond 71 bhp, they were able to raise the compression ratio to 8.6:1 because better-quality petrol was now becoming more readily available; the engine's power output was then nearly 80 bhp. After this, tuning was chiefly confined to work on the camshaft and valves. First, the valve lift was increased from 0.36 ins to 0.375, then the timing was changed to give more overlap. This took the power up to 84 bhp. Next, the inlet valves were increased from 1.5 ins diameter to 1.5625, which liberated another 3 bhp. Further developments with the 1.5-inch carburettors' needles and the distributor obtained 90 bhp at 4,800 rpm, despite the compression ratio being lowered a fraction to 8.5:1. Maximum torque was a very healthy 117 lb/ft at 3,000 rpm.

Increasing the engine's power from 68 bhp to 90 was not so simple as that, however, because the unit had to remain utterly reliable. The first problem encountered when the compression ratio was raised was that the cylinder head wanted to go with it; cracks developed around some of the securing stud bosses. The trouble was cured by extending the bolts to the bottom of the block to be screwed into the crankcase, which was much thicker and stronger than the lugs which had been provided further up. This also meant that the water jackets surrounding the cylinder liners were held in compression, rather than under tension, which was a good thing. Cylinder head gaskets continued to give trouble, however, as a result of the bottom gaskets collapsing under the increased stud loading. New figure-of-eight steel gaskets coated in resin solved this problem after production tolerances were revised and special care taken with cleanliness on assembly. In other words, a good seal was vital.

Sustained running at as much as 5,200 rpm—Triumph were to recommend a red line of 5,000 rpm—in top gear was too much for the big end bearings, so indium-coated lead-bronze ones were substituted. This problem occurred when direct top gear was used in such a test rather than the overdrive which Triumph had decided to offer as an option on the TR2, and it persisted when the new bearings were subject to even more strain. The next step was to improve the lubrication system, and the problem was solved only when the crankshaft drillings were modified to spread the oil better in the new bearings, which needed greater clearances.

The connecting rods had not given way at this point, but the big end bolts were increased to 0.4375 ins in diameter as a precaution, with a dowel location system that also helped assembly. Mysterious problems with number one exhaust valve burning out intermittently in endurance tests at 6,000 rpm were eventually traced to the camshaft flexing and were cured by the offending end being made thicker than the other! A lot of development time was spent fiddling with the crankcase breather as well, to stop oil being

A couple of prototype Plus Four four-seater drophead coupés were built in 1951 and 1953, followed by a limited run heralded by this London Motor Show car in 1954.

thrown under fierce cornering. The cooling fan also had to be given a rubber mounting on its boss to stop bad vibrations.

Some months after the TR2 went into full-scale production in 1954, this far more potent engine became available to Morgan for the Plus Four. The first production Morgan to be fitted with one was also the first of the cowled-radiator cars, completed in time for the London Motor Show in October 1953. This engine had been fitted in the Peter Morgan's demonstration, road test and competition two-seater, registered KUY387, earlier that year.

Early Plus Fours fitted with the optional TR2 engine cost only £830, tax paid in the United Kingdom, and as such became the cheapest car on the British market which could clear 100 mph—just! Naturally they had the higher, 3.73:1, rear axle ratio, and—until October 1955—retained the traditional twin spare wheels. But cost control was tight, and road rallies had become far more popular than reliability trials like the Land's End by then, so from that point just one spare wheel became the norm, in a tail that ceased to have double curvature. The rear panel now covered the fuel tank in a single curve before sweeping straight down in a diagonal path when viewed from the side.

The slightly more powerful Triumph TR3 engine was also phased in from October 1955. It could be readily identified under the bonnet by its larger, 1.75-inch SU carburettors, which gave it 95 bhp against the earlier 90, although it had a modified cylinder head and inlet manifold as well. This unit began to appear in Triumph production late in 1955 from engine number TS9350E, but not on every car, as supplies did not seem to be able to keep up with production.

A notable change to the running gear was the replacement of the old Burman worm and nut steering box, which had survived since pre-war 4-4 days, with a more sophisticated Cam Gears cam and peg system, which gave

*Above, left and right:* Experiments early in 1954 resulted in the works Plus Fours registered KUY 387 and HUY 982 being fitted with cowled-radiator bodywork. KUY 387 was re-bodied with the normal bonnet line used on the early 'flat rad' Plus Fours and the interim models, and HUY 982—pictured competing in the 1954 Scottish Rally—received a low-line bonnet which gave it a much squatter appearance. This form of bodywork, which reduced the frontal area, but made maintenance more difficult, was subsequently adopted on the series 11 4/4 the following year, and offered as an option for a short period of the Plus Four chassis.

the same two turns from lock to lock in a more precise operation. A more modern three-spoke steering wheel was adopted at the same time in place of the four-spoke item.

Other changes included replacing the trunnions which located the rear springs with rubber-bushed shackles. This eliminated two greasing points. The seating arrangements were also improved by allowing 2 ins of adjustment at the top of the back rest with a variety of locations at the bottom. To add to the confusion over engines, early in 1956 Triumph developed yet another cylinder head and inlet manifold, combining the best features of the original and the uprated equipment (called the Le Mans because that is where it was first used). The latest head was called the 'high port'—for obvious reasons—and was phased in from engine number TS13051E produced in August 1956, when supplies of the earlier components finally ran out! The power output was then rated at 100 bhp at 4,600 rpm. Exact specifications on Morgans were even more confusing as the original Vanguard engine was still being fitted to a significant number of cars and would continue for another two years.

Triumph also began to list larger-bore, 86 mm, liners and pistons for their TR3A sports model from the summer of 1957 although they were not generally available until January 1959 and were only rarely fitted to Morgans at the time. The advantage of these engines, of 2,138cc overall capacity, was not that they gave noticeably more power—100 bhp at 5,000 rpm—but that they had even more torque (127 lb/ft at 3,350 rpm) which was highly attractive on the American market.

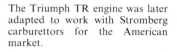

The Triumph TR engine was later adapted to work with Stromberg carburettors for the American market.

By 1957, all Morgan's competitors had gone over to the new all-enveloping bodies, which gave them a superior performance at high speed because they offered less wind resistance. It was difficult, however, to see how a Morgan body could be made more aerodynamic without such fundamental changes, which would have made it heavier and yielded its only advantage in terms of performance: low weight. But it was possible to extend the top of the radiator cowling downwards by three inches to make a

marginal improvement in streamlining. The only problem was that this change made the car look a good deal squatter at the front, so—ever mindful of the protests three years earlier—Morgan offered this restyled nose only as an option from October 1957. Few customers fancied it, so it was dropped during 1958.

Much time was spent that year on reshaping the interior, too. The idea was to liberate an extra 4 inches of elbow room—as a special request from the American market where customers were used to far bigger cars than in Britain. The low-line cowling had been seen to offer a tiny advantage in terms of wind resistance, so Morgan were anxious not to increase the overall width to the detriment of the performance—which was one of the primary reasons for buying a Plus Four, in any case. Something had to give, and it was, not surprisingly, the running boards, which were rarely used by the occupants. A couple of inches was pared off the inside of each and the body sides moved out to make more room in the cockpit. At the same time, careful attention to the lines of the rear panel enabled the fuel tank size to be increased to 12 gallons—a distinct advantage for Plus Four customers—the new bodywork bringing the Plus Four into line with a revised 4/4 introduced in 1955. But with a bumper at the front and overriders at the back, the overall length now became 147 inches.

Other changes included a new dashboard featuring a rev counter as a

*Above left:* The Plus Four badge was mounted on the radiator cowl of the later models.

*Above right:* An ingenious zip-out rear window improved ventilation immensely in the Plus Four drophead coupés.

The new interior introduced in 1958 once again adopted a four-spoke steering wheel.

standard item for the first time. The instruments were grouped in a halter formation over the steering column with one dial incorporating an ammeter, fuel gauge and oil pressure gauge to the left, the rev counter occupying the pride of place directly in front of the driver, and the speedometer, competition-style, to the right. Switches and warning lights were grouped in a recessed square central panel, with a large open cubby hole on the passenger's side.

The wider bodywork then became standard on all Morgans from October 1958, with competition centre lock wire wheels offered on the Plus Four at an extra £32.50. If these wheels were specified, wider, 5.60-15, tyres were fitted as standard, which gave the Plus Four a 2-inch wider rear track—at 49 ins—because they had a different offset. The suspension was also reset to accommodate the new tyres, of a smaller rolling radius, so that ground clearance was not impaired. If the old drilled disc steel wheels were specified, they were now of 15 ins diameter with the earlier 5.25-section tyres.

Aluminium body panels (with an alloy front bumper for American enthusiasts who were not allowed to change the body shape for the standard classes in sports car races) were offered as options at an extra £62.50, although the standard steel scuttle was retained for rigidity. A competition exhaust system was listed at an additional £45, with a finned alloy sump to improve cooling for an extra £27.50, and a higher-pressure electric fuel pump for £10.

Although Triumph had made history by introducing the first mass-produced car with disc brakes—the TR3 of 1956—Morgan had less need to follow suit at first because their Plus Four was lighter. In any case, many reactionary people, Enzo Ferrari included, said that disc brakes were not necessary for competition cars, let alone road machines. By 1959, however, even Morgan and Ferrari had to move with the times and began offering discs on the front from May that year. These 11-inch diameter Girling units had benefited from extensive development work on the TR3A and balanced well with the same manufacturer's 9-inch by 1.75-inch rear

*Below left:* Eventually even Morgan—and Ferrari—had to give in and fit the new-fangled disc brakes at the front; in the case of the Morgan, they transformed the car into a formidable competition machine.

*Below right:* Later examples of the Plus Four had a dashboard with toggle switches to suit the then-predominant American market.

drums. The front calipers, as offered on the Plus Four, were of Girling's latest two-piece pattern, carrying quickly-detachable pads. The total swept braking surface on all four wheels was increased from 198 sq ins to 312. A 0.75-inch diameter master cylinder was used with a separate fluid reservoir as it had been found that a combined cylinder and reservoir did not offer enough capacity. The wire wheels and wider tyres were fitted as standard with the disc brakes, disc wheels being confined to drum-braked models.

At the same time, a competition version of the TR3A engine, with compression ratio raised to 9.2:1 and special inlet and exhaust manifolds, was offered at an extra £42.50. The power output was 106 bhp at 5,500 rpm.

Once a backlog of orders had been met, the new disc brakes were offered on solid wheel models from October 1959 and made standard from September 1960. It was also at this point that a more sophisticated Cam Gears steering box was fitted which gave a variable ratio over its 2.25 turns from lock to lock. Although a slightly shorter drop arm was used with this steering box, less effort was needed to turn the wheel.

The dashboard was also revised to incorporate more modern toggle switches for the panel light and windscreen wipers. A large central toggle switch was also fitted for the direction indicators which had now become a legal necessity in Britian. The actual lights were mounted, at the front, beneath the headlights, and at the back, in the main tail panel alongside the rear lights in the wings.

When Triumph updated the TR3A to turn it into the totally-reshaped TR4 in August 1961, there was still a demand from American dealers for another run of the 'classic' TRs, because they felt that the new model would appeal to a different sector of the market. Triumph, ever ready to meet bulk orders, transferred their old tooling to the Forward Radiator Company in Coventry, who produced another 3,200 of the old cars—now called the TR3Bs—the first 500 of which used the 1,991-cc TR3A engine which had graced the Morgan Plus Four in various states of tune.

Meanwhile, the TR4, for the European market, was fitted with a new 2,138-cc unit (as fitted to the remaining 2,800 TR3Bs). The main difference in the larger-capacity engine, apart from the use of 86-mm bore liners and pistons instead of 83 mm, was that the combustion chambers had chamfered edges. This reduced their 'squish' effect a little, but increased the compression ratio to 9:1 to take full advantage of the better-quality petrol that was readily available by now in most countries. A 7:1 option was listed for the export territories where petrol was still poor, and the distributor advance and retard curve was modified to suit the new characteristics. Officially, the new engine gave only 100 bhp as before—but it was 100 more honest horses because the readings were taken with vital ancillaries, such as the generator, in place. This was the equivalent to 105 bhp stripped, or 115 bhp by the exaggerated SAE readings favoured by American manufacturers. The reason for officially downgrading the power output was that it lowered a car's insurance ratings . . .

 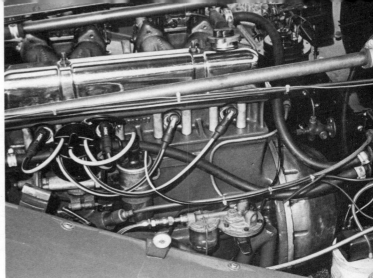

*Above:* The Plus Four Super Sports was fitted with twin Weber carburettors and a four-branch exhaust system for maximum power output.

*Above right:* The 'other' side of the Plus Four Super Sports engine was almost as impressive.

The Morgan Plus Four then became available with either the 1,991-cc engine or the 2,138-cc, depending on whether the owner wanted to compete in the two-litre competition class. Most owners, naturally, opted for the larger standard engine, the smaller units—in reality—only being fitted to the odd competition car.

Meanwhile Chris Lawrence, of the LawrenceTune competition preparation firm—who first raced a Morgan Super Sports threewheeler in 1952—had been enjoying a lot of success with a Plus Four, winning the most important British racing series for production sports cars in 1959. He had managed to extract as much as 131 bhp from the TR engine while his firm acted in the capacity of an unofficial competitions department of the factory in Malvern.

For road-going applications, however, around 115 bhp was more suitable in the 1,991-cc capacity and up to 125 bhp from 2,138 cc. To raise the power of a Triumph TR unit to this level it was necessary to gas flow the cylinder head with a 9:1 compression ratio, fit a higher-lift camshaft, and balance the crankshaft, connecting rods and pistons. Two double-choke

But the Weber carburettors needed a considerable bulge in the side of the bonnet.

Weber 42DCOE carburettors were then fitted on a special inlet manifold—which needed a large box-section fairing on the left-hand side of the bonnet when viewed from the front—with a four-branch dual pipe exhaust system.

There was a ready market for a model with such a specification—particularly in America—so Triumph engines were supplied to Lawrence-Tune for modification to the 115 bhp specification, before being returned to Malvern for installation in a Plus Four chassis. Obviously they were likely to be used in competition, and expected to maintain high revs for long periods, so these cars were fitted with an oil cooler in front of the normal radiator but behind the grille, and a water radiator with extra capacity achieved by fitting a larger, remote, header tank. The rest of the competition options, such as alloy panels (although the steel scuttle was retained), wire wheels and disc brakes, were then specified for what was to be the Plus Four Super Sports, introduced in September 1961. Weight was critical on such a car—being kept down to around 1,800 lb—so it was made at first only in two-seater form, and then generally with competition bucket seats rather than Morgan's normal bench. These seats not only saved weight, but were generally reckoned to be worth a second a lap because they gave a driver so much better location.

Bucket seats were standard equipment in the high-performance Plus Four Super Sports.

The more normal cars, which made up the bulk of production, were not neglected. First access to the coupé was improved with lower door sills from October 1961 with a 1.75-inch deeper windscreen making the interior much lighter when the hood was up. This change was not carried over to the other models in the sacred name of wind resistance—and because it was still expected that their occupants would spend most of their time in the cars with the hood down.

Supplies of ready-made 1,991-cc engines had begun to run out in June 1962, so the 2,138-cc unit was made a standard fitting on the Super Sports, although the 1,991-cc engine could still be fitted to special order. It was still listed for the TR4, but only to enable cars of that capacity to qualify for international competition. A small advantage in wind resistance was also gained at this point by lowering the body slightly on the chassis mountings, with LawrenceTune offering a neat bolt-on glassfibre hardtop which weighed only 22 lb and, with vastly superior aerodynamics, made a great improvement to a car's high-speed performance.

The frontal aspect of the Plus Four Plus took its inspiration from the recently-departed Jaguar XK150 coupé.

The dashboard of the Plus Four Plus represented an amalgam of traditional Morgan practise and the leather-grained specialities of other marques.

It needed only an inquiry from a Greek customer to trigger off what had been on the Morgan car firm's collective mind for several years since Clarkson had the 'Ferrari' body built on a Plus Four chassis: would a change of body shape be a commercial success? A firm called EB Plastics was one of several building glass fibre bodyshells to fit on existing chassis, and had—in fact—taken inspiration from the Clarkson Morgan with their Debonair GT.

Morgan asked them if they could produce a similar body for the Greek customer on a Plus Four Super Sports chassis as a prototype for a future production model. EB Plastics were only too happy to oblige, basing the design on the Debonair, but incorporating a Morgan-style radiator grille and front bumper so that the car would not lose the old-established identity, despite having—for the first time—a curved, rather than a flat, windscreen. The Greek customer seems to have faded from the scene by the time the first of these cars was completed at EB's works in Tunstall, Staffs, in April 1963. But Morgan, faced with a sales crisis of what was now considered to be a very old-fashioned car, were ready to take the plunge with a radically-different shape. They reasoned that it would do no harm because the Plus Four Plus as it was called would merely be an addition to the range, offering a far less cramped and more aerodynamic fixed-head coupé body which needed little investment—because it did not need the complex tooling of more conventional mass-produced steel panels.

The construction of the body followed conventional lines for glass fibre at the time, with local reinforcements of wood and metal, to ensure rigidity.

*Above left:* But, when viewed from the side, the Plus Four Plus was pure Morgan.

*Above:* By Morgan's previous standards, the luggage boot of the Plus Four Plus was positively generous in its capacity.

*Below left:* But it still had a boot rack to supplement the carrying capacity.

*Below:* The rear light cluster of the Plus Four Plus was distinctly modern.

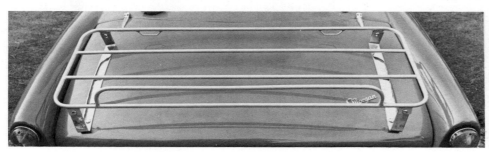

The doors of the Plus Four Plus were extra wide for easy access and exit to what was meant to be a grand tourer.

In the event, the front of the new body was so rigid that it gave a very hard ride to the Plus Four Plus because the chassis could not flex as much as before. The entire front hinged back like that of an early Austin-Healey Sprite (rather than forward like Jaguar's E type) to give unparalled access to everything forward of the scuttle, and the interior was as big an advance with wide lockable doors and 52.5 ins of elbow room against the 45 ins of the normal Plus Four. The overall height was similar to that of the open models (hood erect) at 51 ins, but the overall width far greater—a 5-inch increase giving 61 ins—in keeping with contemporary trends. The integral luggage boot offered a competitive amount of space despite the intrusion of the spare wheel, partly because the capacity of the underfloor fuel tank was reduced to 10 gallons in view of the superior economy expected of a more aerodynamic car. The Plus Four Plus was a pure two-seater despite its name, but offered more luggage space behind the seats as a result. The first car, registered 869KAB, had a bench-style seatback, but the 25 which followed were given more sporting bucket seats. Recesses in the door trim provided useful pockets with a deep cubby hole in the instrument panel. Despite the care taken to ensure that these bodies were really rigid, the overall weight remained at only 1,850 lb.

Production of the Plus Four Plus continued spasmodically until January

Last of the Super Sports . . . a 1967 model.

1967 with a competition model of the normal lightweight Plus Four built for a year from October 1965 with Armstrong adjustable rear shock absorbers and a body line lowered 2.5 ins to that of the companion 4/4 produced at the same time. After the last Plus Four competition model had been built in November 1966, and one four-seater Super Sports to special order in the same month, these body dimensions were made standard on the two-seater tourers.

Part of Morgan's final fling with the Super Sports was to produce a four-seater in 1967 now opened by Allan Cameron.

When Triumph switched to longer six-cylinder engines in the TR, Morgan had to seek an alternative power unit—with dramatic results in the Plus Eight—but while supplies of the four-cylinder TR engine were still available it was possible to continue production of the Plus Four Super Sports until January 1968, the four-seater tourer until November 1968, the two-seater until the following month and the drop-head until January 1969. The name Plus Four was revived from 1984, however, in a two-litre Fiat twin-cam-powered version of the 1,600-cc 4/4 described in the next chapter.

# IV
# The Later 4/4s

The success of kit cars like the Lotus Mark 6 demonstrated that there was still a healthy market for cheaper models than the Plus Four even if they did not perform so well. Many of these machines used the side valve Ford Ten unit that Morgan had been toying with for years because it was so cheap and reliable. There was also an extensive range of tuning equipment available for this engine as a result, which proved an added attraction to Morgan because it meant that potential customers could tailor the performance of a new car to what they could afford. But even more important, Ford had just redesigned this unit to make it stronger and more powerful than the earlier unit. This put it on a par, even in basic form, with the Standard engine used until 1950. The name for new Ford-powered Morgan launched in October 1955 as Standard engine supplies were cut from eight per week to five was obvious: 4/4, the more modern designation, with a stroke in place of a hyphen, having been used occasionally with the earlier 4-4s. In retrospect, the new models were then called the series 11 4/4.

The prototype series 11 4/4 was a delightfully simple car registered RNP 504. This car did have optional outside doorhandles, however.

The 1,172-cc engine, which had been introduced for Ford's new range of 100E small cars at the London Motor Show in 1953, could still accept the established tuning gear because the existing 63.5-mm bore and 92.5-mm

*Left:* In its earlier form, the series II 4/4 featured overriders without a bumper bar to protect the rear end of the coachwork.

*Above:* The cockpit layout and material was equally inauspicious, with two main instruments, the strange gearlever protruding from under the centre of the dashboard, and leatherette forming the basis for the upholstery.

stroke—with the same cylinder centre spacing—had been retained to cut production costs. One of the chief improvements was a new cylinder block incorporating bigger inlet ports and main bearings, a water pump and cooling water ducts in the exhaust valve seatings. Apart from having three 2-inch diameter main bearings, rather than 1.625, the cast crankshaft had been stiffened for smoother running at a higher speed on a higher, 7:1, compression ratio. This meant that 30 bhp could be liberated at 4,400 rpm—20 per cent more than the earlier unit. This engine also produced a healthy 4 lb/ft of torque at a reasonable 4,000 rpm. There were other advantages, too, such as adjustable tappets for the side-by-side valves.

The cast-iron cylinder block included the top half of the flywheel casing and had full-length water jackets providing circulation around each pair of cylinders, with an integral water tube to cool the valves—which were of 1.15 inch diameter for the inlets and 1.05 for the exhaust. A cast-iron head containing the vertical sparking plugs and a cooling water thermostat was bolted on top of the block, with a pressed-steel sump incorporating the bottom of the flywheel casing, beneath it. Aluminium alloy pistons were used with connecting rods which still featured the typically pre-war cast-in white metal bearings, which could now be machined out to accept the later replaceable shells during a rebuild.

The camshaft under the valves was supported by three bearings and driven by a chain from the front of the crankshaft. It also drove a vertical shaft to the distributor on top of the engine and an oil pump in the 5.5-pint sump. The water pump, cooling fan and dynamo were driven by a belt from the front of the crankshaft with an hydraulically-operated 7.25-inch diameter Ford single dry plate clutch at the back.

The fuel was supplied by an AC mechanical pump to a downdraught Solex carburettor—in standard form—on an inlet manifold incorporating an ingenious hot-spotting for enriched cold starting. Exhaust ducts surrounded the carburettor intake riser with a valve worked by a bi-metallic spiral allowing a circulation of heated gas. As the spiral heated up, it closed the valve for normal running. Morgan also listed, from the introduction of the 4/4, an optional twin carburettor kit by the Aquaplane company which was based on the Norfolk Broads. This consisted of a finned alloy inlet manifold to take the existing Solex carburettor and another one, the entire set up costing only an extra £13, with a better-breathing twin SU kit available for an additional £5, plus a four-branch exhaust manifold from the same source for another £5.

Morgan were anxious to market the new 4/4 as cheaply as possible, so the Plus Four's heavy and rugged Moss gearbox was replaced by the standard Ford unit. Unfortunately this had only three forward ratios, although it did have synchromesh on the top two gears. The ratios (with a 4.4:1 Salisbury rear axle) of 1, 1.875, 3.425—and a 4.48 reverse—were hardly sporting either, the second gear having been made low enough to use down to a crawl, virtually eliminating the need to engage the crash first gear on the move. This was all very well for the drivers of the heavier Anglia and Prefect saloons which normally used this power train, but sadly limited second gear's use as an overtaking ratio in the lighter Morgan.

But it all saved money and Morgan were anxious not to use any more than necessary on the new 4/4. So they dispensed with the earlier idea of having a remote gearbox mounting, which was not so necessary now, in any case, that reliability trials were losing popularity. This meant that the Ford power train—with its gearbox bolted onto the flywheel casing in the conventional manner—could be dropped unaltered on its normal mountings into Morgan chassis. The leading U-section crossmember had to be moved forward, of course, but otherwise the chassis was the same as that of the new non-trunnion Plus Four with the Cam Gears steering box and three-spoke steering wheel. The gearchange featured an extraordinary remote control, however, with a rod rising vertically out of normal position in the box to link up with another rod running straight back over a pivot on the scuttle into the cockpit. This rod then followed a U-shaped path to emerge under the

*Below left and right:* The Ford side-valve engine occupied only a small space under the series 11 bonnet, with the gearlever mechanism visible, straddling the main bulkhead.

dashboard. The gear lever was then slid backwards and forwards and rocked about to engage the gears in a pattern in 'back-to-front' pattern with first and reverse on the right rather than, as normal, on the left. There was one advantage in using this system: in company with the forward-mounted gearbox and an 'umbrella handle' horizontal handbrake lever under the dashboard, it meant that the 4/4 had far more foot-room than the Plus Four. And Morgan's careful attention to costing meant that it could be introduced at £200—or 25 per cent—less than the Plus Four, which was quite amazing considering how cheap the larger-engined car was in any case.

Although it had less than half the power of the recently-introduced TR2-engined Plus Four, the 4/4—available only in two-seater form—still had a reasonable performance because it was 15 per cent lighter at 1,600 lb, partly through detail savings such as a 12-pint radiator in place of the 16-pint capacity item. In view of the lower weight, the spring rates were reduced by increasing the length of the front coils to 14.375 ins and using only five leaves

*Top, left and right:* By late 1957 the series 11 4/4 was being fitted with neat indicator lights on the front wings and rear valence. This car, registered KHL 606, was first seen at the London Motor Show in 1957 and was sold to Donald and Cecily Jellyman, who have maintained it in original condition since.

*Bottom left and right:* Cockpit of the series 11 4/4, the first car having been fitted with aeroscreens and bucket seats and the second with a period piece radio and a four-spoke steering wheel.

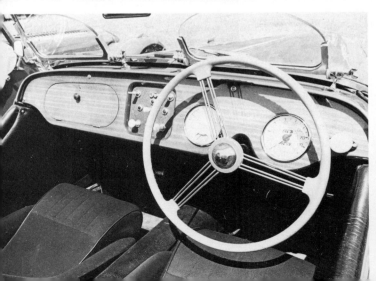

*Above left and right:* Entry to the series 11 4/4 when the weather protection equipment was in place could be gained by putting a hand through a flap at the bottom of the sidescreens, and operating the catch inside the door.

The series 11 was fitted with 5.00-16-inch drilled steel wheels which were lighter than those of the more powerful and heavier Plus Four.

in the rear half-elliptics. It was also possible to fit lighter, 5.00-16 section, drilled-steel disc wheels and tyres. The bodywork was basically the same as that of the Plus Four except that the smaller engine allowed the bonnet line to be lowered by 2.5 ins and a reshaped tail panel, covering an 8-gallon fuel tank, extended the overall length to 147 ins, including the bumper and overriders.

As more customers began to order the 4/4 with twin carburettors, or to fit proprietary tuning equipment after delivery, Morgan decided to offer their own Competition Model in September 1957. This was a normal 4/4—which could now be bought with wire wheels and wider tyres, like the Plus Four—except that it was now fitted with an Aquaplane aluminium alloy cylinder head, inlet and four-branch exhaust manifold, and twin SU carburettors. When used in conjunction with a special thin copper/asbestos gasket, the compression ratio was raised to 8:1. Stronger 'racing' valve springs were part of the deal which provided 40 bhp at 5,100 rpm with only about 5 per cent higher fuel consumption. A high-lift camshaft could also be specified for an additional £18, but made the engine much less flexible. At the same time, Peter Morgan drove a 4/4 in trials with a Willment overhead inlet valve conversion which he recalls as a 'very effective little car, and fast'. Special-bodied variants of the series 11 4/4 were almost unknown, although one drop-head coupé was built for a relative of H.F.S. Morgan in February 1960.

Otherwise the specification followed that of the Plus Four, disc front brakes being made optional equipment from 1959 with the improved steering gear and the other detail changes from October 1960. The disc brakes were not to become a standard fitting on the 4/4 series 11, however, which normally retained the older 16-inch drilled-steel disc wheels for fear of over-revving the 100E engine on the 4.4:1 rear axle.

Meanwhile Morgan—and particularly the 4/4—was about to benefit from three years' intensive development of Ford's small car range, resulting in the introduction of a completely new overhead valve four-speed Anglia 105E in October 1959. Morgan had to wait a year for the new power train—continuing to receive supplies of the old side-valve and three-speed units (which continued in production for two or three years in baseline

Fords)—but the wait was worthwhile. The new 105E power train transformed the series III 4/4 introduced in October 1960.

The new engine—which weighed only 212 lb with accessories—was an absolute gem, having been designed around a 80.96-mm bore for production in a variety of capacities. This meant that the smallest variant, with a stroke of 48.41 mm to give a capacity of 997 cc, was substantially 'over square' by contemporary one-litre standards. In turn, this made it a marvellously smooth revving unit that had even more sporting potential because—despite the large bores—each cylinder was surrounded by a water jacket which ensured freedom from the thermal distortion and head gasket problems sometimes encountered with siamesed bores. The cast-iron cylinder block was rather long as a result, but still fitted well into a space meant for the Plus Four's larger two-litre unit and had an unusually compact overall height of only 7.25 ins because of the short stroke. Again this was marginally advantageous to Morgan because it lowered the 4/4's centre of gravity. The potential of this 'Kent' engine, as it was called, for a sports car was enhanced by another unusual feature, a very robust crankshaft. It was of hollow construction like that used in Ford of Britain's 1956 Consul and Zephyr range, with a lot of overlap for the bearing journals (of 2.125 ins diameter for the three main bearings and 1.937 ins for the big ends), which ensured extreme rigidity and rendered unnecessary the counterweights used on the 100E unit. The steel-backed bearing shells were lined with white metal for the

Competition versions of the series II 4/4 were fitted with a variety of tuning equipment, including this ultimate conversion with alloy cylinder head, special manifolds and twin carburettors by the Aquaplane company which took its name from similar lines in power boat parts.

mains with copper-lead in the big ends within a sump which had a miserly capacity of only four pints.

A 9:1 compression ratio could be used with the cast-iron eight-port cylinder head because, by the late 1950s, top quality petrol was the norm rather than the exception. Bathtub-shaped combustion chambers were exceptionally accurately machined with the sparking plugs set in the side and overhead valves vertically in line for a far more efficient lay out than the old 100E engine. The chain-driven camshaft still ran in the side of the engine, but now operated a pushrod and rocker system for the valves through the by-now familiar mushroom tappets. The distributor and oil pump drive gear was cut directly into the camshaft—along with a mechanical fuel pump drive—the distributor emerging beneath the sparking plugs at an angle from the left-hand side of the block (when viewed from the front), which helped keep down the overall height of the engine. The cooling fan and water pump were driven by an external belt from the front of the engine as before, but the oil pump was now mounted outside as well, in unit with the oil filter. It was laid out like this to allow sump pans of differing shapes to be used in subsequent variants of the basic Kent engine. A single Solex 30ZIC2 carburettor was used again on a cast four-branch inlet manifold to give 39 bhp at 5,000 rpm with 53 lb/ft of torque at only 2,700 rpm.

The single dry-plate clutch was retained in conjunction with what was Ford of Britain's first four-speed gearbox. This had synchromesh on the top three ratios only, but an unusually sweet gearchange and much closer ratios than the old three-speed box. These gave 1:1, 1.41, 2.39 and 4.1 with a 5.23 reverse and used the same 4.4:1 rear axle. The new 15-inch wheels and tyres could now replace the 16-inch running gear with the faster-revving engine exploiting for the reduced rolling radius (similar adjustments to those on the Plus Four having been made to restore the ground clearance), although drum brakes all round were still the normal fitting.

The new gearbox was a little wider than the old one and had to be sited slightly further back in the chassis because of the longer engine, which meant that Morgan had to re-position the forward crossmember and mountings—but somehow they managed to improve the foot-room in the cockpit by a small margin! The scuttle also had to be made wider, but they were able to do this without widening the bonnet. The unique remote control gearchange had to be modified slightly, but still followed the same tortuous path.

As it happened, the 4/4 series III—sometimes known as the 50th anniversary model because it coincided with Morgan's Golden Jubilee— would become one of the rarer variants because Ford soon brought out a larger capacity version of the Kent engine, which was promptly fitted from December 1961. This Series IV was basically the same except that it now had the largest-capacity version of the original 7.25-inch high Kent-blocked engine, the 1,340-cc, 65-mm stroke unit from Ford's 109E saloon, called the Classic 315 (introduced in May 1961), and the Plus Four's 11-inch diameter disc brakes at the front as standard in view of a dramatically-improved performance.

The 109E cylinder block was identical to that of the 105E, but the cast-iron head was new, with deeper combustion chambers. The valve gear was the same, the extra depth being taken up by longer pushrods. The pistons were also interchangeable, but the crankshaft was different, with longer throws accommodated by shortening the connecting rod centres. On the 109E these were 4.284 ins against 4.612 ins for the 105E.

The port and valve sizes were the same, but there were slight changes in the exhaust and inlet manifolds to accommodate a Zenith 32VN downdraught carburettor, which found its way into the 4/4 series IV as the new model would be called, and the lower, 8.5:1, compression ratio needed to retain the smoothness of the shorter-stroke engine. The Zenith carburettor was not only slightly larger at 32 mm, against the 30-mm Solex, but it incorporated an accelerator pump.

Maximum power, 54 bhp at 4,900 rpm, was 40 per cent more than that of the 105E engine, with 74 lb/ft of torque at 2,500 rpm. The same 7.25-inch clutch was retained, but it now had stronger springs and a modified cushioned centre. The gearbox was almost exactly the same as that used with the 105E engine except that it now had provision for a steering column gearchange in the Classic 315. Morgan were not tempted in this direction, but redesigned their push-pull remote control gearchange in a much more direct manner to give a conventional gate.

The 109E engine might have had a longer stroke than the old 105E, but it was still willing to rev hard and Morgan celebrated by fitting a slightly lower, 4.56:1, rear axle ratio which vastly improved the acceleration and flexibility of the series IV. The overall weight was still only about 1,550 lb, with a slightly larger, 8.5-gallon fuel tank, because the new engine was hardly any heavier than the old at 225 lb with ancilliaries.

Later 4/4s were fitted with overhead valve four-cylinder Ford engines, this example being a 1,340-cc unit used in the series IV.

Production of the 4/4 series IV lasted no longer than the series III, as Ford uprated their 116E engine with a longer, 72.74 mm, stroke to give the Classic—and the Capri coupé—a more relaxed performance from the end of August 1962. This was the 1,498-cc unit which also powered variants of their brilliant new Cortina saloon a month later. Naturally this engine was in considerable demand and it was not until the end of the year that supplies were available to Morgan. But when it was fitted to the first 4/4 series V cars from December 1962 it gave them comfortably more performance than the rival Austin-Healey Sprites, MG Midgets and Triumph Spitfires, which had smaller engines but weighed more although their aerodynamics were better.

The new power train was also a notable step forward in that the engine was even smoother, running on five main bearings, and the gearbox had synchromesh on all four gears with selection so light and precise that it set standards for years to come. The new gearbox had to be made fractionally longer than the old one to accommodate the additional baulk ring synchromesh, but not enough to affect the Morgan chassis. It also had a higher bottom gear now that the engine had more torque, with ratios of 1, 1.41, 2.39 and 3.71 with a 3.96 reverse, but Morgan retained the new 4.56:1 rear axle.

The new engine, code-named 116E, looked the same as the smaller units, but its cylinder block was 0.66 ins taller. This was necessary to maintain a common piston assembly and keep the connecting rods long enough to avoid problems with excessive wear caused by rough running. Introducing five main bearings to make a larger engine smoother had always been a consideration for Ford's engineers, so the cylinders were far enough apart at the same spacing used in the smaller Kent engines. But it had been realised after three years' experience with this power unit that the benefits of a hollow crankshaft were more theoretical than real. The extra coring cost a lot but resulted in a shaft that in three-bearing form was no stiffer than one with flying webs—so the new engine got a solid webbed crank which was stiffer in any case because the main bearings were now closer. Extensive testing detected no measurable increase in overall friction from the extra bearings.

No other changes were made to the cylinder block but cylinder heads were not interchangeable because the combustion chambers machined into them differed in volume, an 8.3:1 compression ratio being used in the 1,498-cc engine, a 7.3:1 version being available for export. It also had larger, 1.43-inch diameter inlet valves than the 1.27-inch valves used earlier. Other changes included a slightly larger 33VN downdraught Zenith carburettor and a larger, 5.6-pint sump, with a weight that was now up to 275 lb less clutch, but including flywheel.

Overall power and torque figures of 59.5 bhp at 4,600 rpm (56 bhp with the low compression) and 81.5 lb/ft at 2,300 rpm gave the new 4/4 series V a much improved performance with the option of even greater grip from 155-15-inch tyres now that radial ply rubber was becoming more popular.

Only three months later the series V could be ordered in Competition form with a 78-bhp variant of the 116E engine, introduced for the Classic GT and then the Cortina GT. The extra power gave the 4/4 a truly formidable performance well on the way to that of the Plus Four. There were no delays in supplying this engine; it was basically the same as the normal 116E except that it had a new downdraught twin-choke compound Weber carburettor, higher lift camshaft, higher compression cylinder head, larger exhaust valves and a freer-flowing tubular exhaust manifold. The extra power was achieved at high revs—5,200—however, at the expense of low-speed torque, the higher maximum figure of 91 lb/ft being achieved further up the range at 3,600 rpm. Ford decided, therefore, to retain the same gearbox, which highlighted a relatively low second gear ratio. But Morgan's new Competition Model—using the early Plus Four's 4.1:1 rear axle ratio—still showed a great improvement on the performance of the previous 4/4s.

It was the first time this type of carburettor—in which the primary choke progressively opened first, as the throttle was depressed, and the secondary choke came in as the pedal was pressed harder—had been used on any British engine. Advantages included superb economy at part-throttle and easy tuning. Flat spots could be a problem with this type of carburettor, however, so the main chamber of the induction system was water-heated. The inlet manifold itself was a light alloy casting consisting of two pairs of separate curved pipes, one to each port, joining in a communal chamber directly under the carburettor. The two outer joints with the inlet ports each had a spigotted ring for accurate mating with the manifold.

Exhaust valves 0.125 ins larger in diameter were used with the high-lift camshaft which had been developed by Cosworth Engineering, already famous for their work on the 105E and 109E engines. The compression ratio was returned to the 9:1 used on the 105E, and a four-into-one exhaust fitted. New pistons were needed, with the copper-lead bearings used in the 109E engine replacing the 105E-style white metal bearings of the 59-bhp engine. Stronger clutch springs were fitted to cope with the extra torque and the propellor shaft diameter increased from 2.75 ins to 3 ins.

The 4/4s continued to use these engines until January 1968, virtually unaltered except for the availability from mid-1964 of the 'uprated second gear' kit developed for Ford's Lotus Cortina competition saloons. This involved fitting a new layshaft cluster and second gear to give ratios of 1, 1.41, 2.04 and a slightly-higher 3.54 first gear (and a 3.96 reverse) that represented a great improvement on the earliest gearsets. A diaphragm spring clutch with a lighter action was also fitted to all 4/4s—in company with Cortinas—from September 1966.

Then, from January 1967, the Competition Model was fitted with the Ford 2000E gearbox, which had ratios even better than the earlier Lotus Cortina box, and could be fitted to the standard model. These ratios made such a dramatic improvement at 1, 1.4, 2.01 and 2.97, with a 3.32 reverse, that Ford kept quiet about the change on the Cortina GT!

The Cortina had been reskinned as a mark II version in August 1966, with a new 1,599-cc version of the Kent engine a year later that found its way into the smaller Morgan—now called the 4/4 1600—in 1968. This was a bowl-in-piston unit in which the combustion chamber was virtually taken out of the cylinder head and cut into the tops of new alloy pistons to improve fuel consumption. The capacity increase—to improve performance—was achieved by lengthening the stroke yet again to 77.6 mm (at which the engine was still oversquare!), which meant increasing the height of the cylinder block by 0.44 ins for what was now known as the 2737E engine. The bottom end of the engine followed the earlier layout except that it now had a longer-throw crankshaft with different balance weights. Bearing sizes remained the same as did the oil pump and distributor, water pump and camshaft, although the bearings were now made of copper lead like those of the earlier GT unit.

When viewed from the outside, the most obvious change was the transposition of the carburettor and inlet manifold from on top of the exhaust manifold to the left-hand side of the engine when viewed from the front—which led to it being called a 'crossflow' unit. The inlet ports now curved in between the pairs of pushrods with the sparking plugs on the right-hand side. The GT version of this unit incorporated the same changes as before—with the exception of a livelier 18.5-lb flywheel rather than the normal 26-lb dreadnought, and lighter, plastic, cooling fan—to give power outputs of 71 bhp at 5,000 rpm for the standard engine and 88 at 5,400 for the GT. The torque figures were increased as well, to 91.5 lb/ft at 2,500 rpm and 96 at 3,600, the 2000E gearbox being adopted as standard now with a slightly larger, 7.5-inch diameter, clutch.

*Below left and right:* The 4/4 1600 was fitted with a crossflow Ford Cortina engine, this one being equipped with an optional pancake air filter.

Morgan celebrated by offering the old Plus Four 5.60-15-inch wheels with 4J rims in pressed steel to a Rostyle spoked pattern and 4.5J in wire, the front and rear tracks now being lined up at 48 ins. Now that the power from the GT engine had raised the performance of the 4/4 sufficiently, Morgan were at last able to reintroduce the four-seater bodywork on the 4/4 chassis from January 1969. It was felt that there would be sufficient demand because only two-seater bodywork was available on the new Plus Eight, which had replaced the Plus Four and was now being produced alongside the remaining four-cylinder cars.

Later that year, during October, in the interests of standardization, Morgan changed the dashboard of the 4/4 to the pattern of the Plus Eight, increasing the cockpit width in this area to 49 ins at the same time. The new dashboard had the rev counter to the right of the steering column on right-hand-drive cars with the other instruments, and rocker-type switches, in a wide central oval panel. It meant that the speedometer was now to the left of the panel so that it was not obscured by the driver's hands on the steering wheel, the right-hand position on the panel being occupied by the ancillary instruments with the switches and warning lights in the middle. These changes were partly in line with those demanded from European manufacturers by American safety campaigners. The rest of the interior was also restyled along the lines of the Plus Eight, with Ambla leathercloth upholstery.

Such was the demand for the Competition Model, (which cost only £80 with tax more than the standard car) that the lower-powered variant was phased out in November 1970, by which time a collapsible column—incorporating a steering lock—had been adapted to the existing steering box, as on the Plus Eight.

When Ford brought in a new overhead camshaft engine for the Cortina range in October 1970, Morgan elected to stay with the Kent engine—which was still available—because it was more compact. Its power had, however, been increased by 5 bhp, without affecting the torque, by a new cylinder head which retained the 9:1 compression ratio, but was now of pure 'Heron' type without the small combustion chambers machined in it. It used slightly larger inlet valves with a higher lift camshaft and, of course, had different pistons. The inlet manifold had a longer tract and carburettor choke and jet sizes were revised. The main bearing caps were also strengthened, and the tappets made harder. The width between the front mounting pads was also increased by 10 mm to make it interchangeable with the new overhead camshaft units. Ford also decided to use a cable-operated clutch, so Morgan had to follow suit, the first such power train being used in a 4/4 1600 in February 1971.

At the same time, Ford changed to a single selector rail gearbox which inherited the wide ratios of the earlier Cortinas for the Kent engine, but luckily the closer ratios were still available for the overhead camshaft version of the 1,600-cc engine, so Morgan did not have to consider changing back.

Later that year, in October, Girling went over to dual circuits for their braking system, so Morgan followed suit, with additional padding around the dashboard to provide extra protection in an accident. The rear lighting was also revised at the same time because the old Morris Minor-style lights and indicators were no longer legal in Europe because they were not mounted vertically on the Morgan's sloping rear panel and wings. They were replaced with more futuristic-looking lights mounted in tubular nacelles.

Further improvements included a better fresh-air heater from May 1973 when falling demand led to Smith's Industries stopping production of their antique unit which simply recirculated the air inside the car. The new heater was mounted on the scuttle with a boxed vent taking in air from the louvres at the back of the bonnet. The system eventually reached maturity when channels were cut in the scuttle at the cockpit side of the windscreen and ducting was fitted to give demisting vents from November 1974.

Items such as the lights, steering wheel and road wheels continued to change in detail from time to time, according to what component manufacturers had to offer. New regulations introduced in 1976 called for slightly larger sidelights, for instance, and Lucas had practically worn out their pressing tools for the existing Morgan units. Happily the tools used for making the longer and deeper series 1 sidelights were still in existence and in good condition because not many such cars had been made. So they promptly replaced the series V's sidelights in 1976, with plastic lenses in place of the obsolete glass! Aluminium bodywork—in which only the cowl and scuttle remained in steel for overall rigidity was also made available on the 4/4 as an option for the first time now that it had an engine which was competitive in production sports car racing.

The new regulations also aimed at reducing the emission of fumes by making it necessary to fit all internal combustion engines on production vehicles with air filters, so Morgan had to follow suit by changing the 4/4's 'brick-stopper' cap to the rarely-ordered optional fine mesh filter.

Further changes dictated by the new laws meant that full-width bumpers had to be introduced on all Morgans in the same year. These were made from aluminium because no suitable ready-made steel ones could be obtained.

The optional aluminium body parts had been so successful that from January 1977 they became standard for the rear and quarter panels in which accidental damage was less likely. This demand was primarily from Plus Eight customers, but it proved more economical to include 4/4 buyers as well.

The following year the braking system of the Plus Eight was revised to use to a new master cylinder which did not need a servo. This was incorporated in the 4/4 during 1978, which meant that larger front calipers had to be fitted, although they were still smaller than those on the higher-performance Plus Eight.

Demand from other manufacturers for the standard steel Dunlop disc wheels used on the 4/4 since the series 11 model eventually ran out in 1979 and Morgan had to switch to a German-made version for customers who did not want the frequently-ordered optional wire wheels. These new wheels had the advantage of having a 1.5-inch wider rim at 5.5 ins, which put far more rubber on the road.

At that point Morgan were still able to use the tried-and-trusted Kent engine in the 4/4, but its future seemed bleak as it became known that Ford were planning a new engine and transmission for transverse installation its main slot in the Escort range. Ford reassured its customers that the Kent engine would be kept in production—partly for commercial adaptations, but primarily for their highly-successful Formula Ford 1600 racing—although another problem was looming; by April 1982 it could no longer be sold on the West German market, where even stricter new exhaust emission laws were being introduced. And West Germany was, by the early 1980s, Morgan's chief export market after similar laws had ended normal sales in America.

Once more, Morgan looked for an alternative power train, with Fiat's old-established twin cam emerging as the front runner. In essence, the Fiat engine was similar to Lotus's twin cam adaptation of the original Cortina unit in 1962. It had first appeared in a similar 1,600-cc form as early as 1966 in the Fiat 124 Sport, which had a more efficient alloy head fitted to the cylinder block from an existing 80-mm bore in-line four-cylinder pushrod engine. One of the reasons why twin cam heads were rarely used at the time was that the camshaft drive—usually by chain—was long and expensive. Fiat were one of the first firms to get over this problem with a toothed rubber belt. The cylinder head was a straightforward aluminium casting with inserts for the valve seats. The cost of production was kept down by making each cam box a single, box-shaped casting, in which the bottom face formed the tappet block and partitions carried the camshaft bearings. The cast-iron camshafts ran directly in the cam box. Very thick shims, sitting in recesses in the top faces of the tappets, were used for adjustment.

The valves were opposed symmetrically at an included angle of 65 degrees to operate in pentroof combustion chambers which followed an oval pattern to give a desirable degree of squish. The sparking plugs were set in the rear side of the chamber on the engine centreline. The inlet valves measured 1.36 mm, with 1.26-mm exhaust valves. Each camshaft was driven from a cog at the front by a belt which also ran round a tensioner above the crankshaft drive. The cover concealed this timing gear and belt with a second external belt being driven off the front of the crankshaft. This operated a centrifugal filter—to supplement a normal oil filter—and an alternator, with a cooling fan pulley above working the water pump. A jackshaft half the length of the engine worked an oil pump in the eight-pint sump and the distributor through skew gears, in addition to the petrol pump mounted beneath a Weber carburettor on a water-heated inlet manifold on the right-hand side of the engine when viewed from the front. The crankshaft, which was the only part shared with the pushrod Fiat 124 engine, ran in five two-inch main bearings with conventional pistons and connecting rods.

This engine subsequently formed the basis of that used in many Fiat cars, including the 132 introduced in 1972. The capacity was stretched to 1,755 cc in this case by increasing the bores to 84 mm, which meant moving out their centres to a 91 mm spacing, with the engine then linked to a five-speed gearbox, with an overdrive top, from Fiat's 125 Special.

Subsequent Fiat twin-cam engines retained the 84-mm stroke, a 1,585-cc capacity being achieved by reducing the stroke to 71.5 mm. It was in this form that the engine was fitted to the 4/4 late in 1981 to improve the performance further with 97 bhp at 6,000 rpm. The 94 lb/ft maximum torque delivered at 3,800 rpm looked rather high up the range until it was realised that this engine had an unusually flat torque curve from as low as 2,000 rpm. In its Morgan adaptation, either a Weber 32ADF52/250 or Solex C32TEE/10 downdraught twin choke carburettor could be fitted. The gear ratios on the five-speed box worked out at 0.83:1, 1, 1.36, 2.05, and 3.61 with a 3.2 reverse to run with the 4.1 axle ratio.

Morgan were still developing this version of the 4/4 when a Ford executive, who had a 4/4 on order, realised that he might have to accept it with a Fiat engine. He immediately got Morgan involved with plans to adapt a new four-cylinder transverse engine for an old-style in-line installation in new Sierra saloons, with the result that this unit was introduced only nine months later for the 4/4 at the same time as the Fiat option!

Ford had spent six years developing this engine to meet ever more stringent exhaust emission regulations and the problems associated with squeezing the rather long Kent engine into a transverse installation. Fortunately for Morgan, Ford were keen to retain elements of two of the best aspects of the Kent engine—the water passages which completely surrounded the cylinders, and the short-stroke configuration. So far as ultimate performance in competition was concerned, there had to be a compromise over the valve gear: it now became hydraulically operated to save maintenance and noise at the expense of an ability to withstand high revs (which is the main reason the old Kent engine had been kept in limited production for Formula Ford racing).

Otherwise the new CVH (compound valve-angle hemispherical chamber engine), introduced in the Ford Escort Mark III late in 1980, was in many

In 1982, the Ford CVH engine was adopted for the 4/4.

ways superior to the Kent. It had a new aluminium alloy cylinder head with what could be loosely described as hemispherical combustion chambers that was, like the Fiat unit, more efficient than Ford's earlier head. But it avoided the expense of twin overhead camshafts by angling steel tappets so that they could be worked by a single overhead cam, driven—like the Fiat's—by a cogged belt. The ports were quite generous culminating in a 1.457-inch diameter exhaust valve on the 1,597-cc engine which Morgan would be using, with 1.496 ins for the inlet. The five-bearing camshaft ran directly in the head casting with the belt drive at the front and a distributor with contact breakerless ignition directly off the back. The cast-iron cylinder block had quite generous bore centres of 91.8 mm, for a transverse engine, to avoid siamesing the bores, and extended down only as far as the centreline of the five-bearing crankshaft to improve beam stiffness. This feature also allowed easier access to the bearings. A 79.96-mm stroke with the familiar 80-mm bore allowed the engine to remain just square in its dimensions and the latest American technology in producing the hydraulic tappets allowed a maximum of 7,000 rpm against the rather slow 5,000 that had been norm with such units. The rest of the engine followed established practice with a very efficient new crescent gear oil pump developed from those used in automatic transmissions and an electric cooling fan which did not absorb engine power. With a twin-choke Weber DFT carburettor and 9.5:1 compression ratio as used in Ford's new 'hot hatchback,' the XR3, this engine developed 96 bhp at 6,000 rpm with a less-pronounced, but still welcome, 98 lb/ft of torque at 4,000 rpm.

In the Morgan installation, the XR3 engine's sump was replaced with a more tapered Cortina equivalent, and mated to the bell housing of a Capri (the Cortina-based type built from 1969), so that it could be used with the existing four-speed Cortina gearbox via a Morgan-designed flywheel. Morgan also developed new engine mountings and reshaped the 4/4 bulkhead to provide a recess to clear the distributor.

In this way, Morgan were able to offer the 4/4 with the choice of the Ford engine and four-speed gearbox, or the Fiat twin cam with similar power, but a five-speed gearbox, at extra cost, for 1982. But this was only a stopgap on the way to a better Ford-powered car.

*Below left:* The XR3 engine was topped off with a Morgan air cleaner.

*Below right:* Some enthusiastic 4/4 owners even equipped their cars with turbochargers.

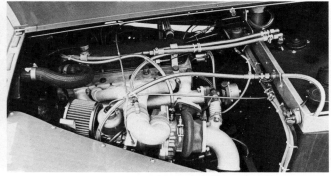

*Above:* Rostyle steel wheels were fitted to many Morgans in the 1970s.

*Above centre:* Later 4/4s were fitted with sliding sidescreens rather than the earlier type with opening flaps at the bottom. This car is a 1973 model.

*Above right:* Tonneau covers have become popular equipment with Morgan owners.

*Right and right above:* Luggage racks are vital for carrying bulky items such as suitcases or picnic hampers.

Aluminium bumpers are used on late-model 4/4s, such as this 1982 London Motor Show model.

*Far left:* The neat interior of the late-model 4/4. This car is a 1980 model.

*Left:* Wire wheels have become popular optional equipment on 4/4s.

*The three photos below:* The four-seater 4/4 was introduced once the engine had enough pulling power. This is a 1982 model.

Triple windscreen wipers are fitted to late-model 4/4s for better visibility in bad weather.

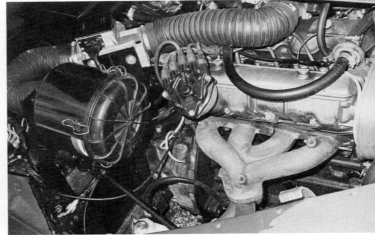

*Above left and right:* The Fiat twin-cam engine as fitted to the late-model Plus Four.

The following year Ford introduced a five-speed gearbox for the Sierra and Capri which was promptly made available for the Ford-powered 4/4, offering similar ratios to the Rover SD1 gearbox in the Plus Eight and a very economical 25.55 mph per 1,000 rpm top gear.

It looked as though considerable problems might develop soon after as Cam Gears were about to stop production of the 4/4's steering box, so Morgan tooled up for a special rack-and-pinion which, although it improved the steering, would add £250 to the cost of a car. At the last moment, however, a French firm called Gemmer produced a suitable recirculating ball box, which became a popular fitting on the 4/4 as an option to the rack.

By 1984, it was still evident that there was a demand for a more powerful four-cylinder car, so the 1,995-cc version of the Fiat twin-cam engine was installed in a 4/4 for a new Plus Four. In this form, the twin-cam engine produced 130 bhp at 5,900 rpm on twin Weber 40DCOE carburettors (harping back to the Super Sports) and a 9.4:1 compression ratio, the 90 mm bore contributing to 130 lb/ft of torque at only 3,600-rpm. In this case, wider, 6-inch rim, wire wheels were fitted as standard running with a unique combination of low-profile Avon tyres (and wider wings, of course).

Sadly this became one of the shortest-lived models when problems involving the gearbox supplies forced its abandonment at the end of 1986. Morgan then switched their attention to a new Plus Four powered by the British Rover M16 engine.

# V
# The Plus Eight

The Plus Eight was born of the necessity to find a new engine to replace the Plus Four's four-cylinder unit—already a year out of regular production by the time the new Morgan made its debut in September 1968. The six--cylinder engine which replaced the four in Triumph's TR was too long and Ford's equivalent engines far from attractive: their V4 was inferior to the in-line engine used in the 4/4 and the larger V6 too tall and too heavy—an important consideration in a light car like the Morgan. Happily, Rover were willing to supply their new low-line all-alloy V8, which weighed little more than the cast-iron TR unit. It was also hardly any longer, and had vital parts—such as exhaust manifolds—in places convenient for the Morgan chassis.

The Plus Eight was introduced in fairly spartan form without outside doorhandles and with contemporary 80-section tyres.

This engine was to form the basis for much of the Rover—and, subsequently British Leyland, then Austin-Rover—range for at least 20 years, so it had the benefit of extensive initial development. At present it is expected to stay in production until 1995. Casting methods represented an improvement over those used by General Motors and the webs for the 2.29-inch diameter main bearings were stiffened at the same time in case a larger capacity was needed later. These were two features the American

Later cars, such as this 1977 model, were more fully equipped.

creators would have liked to have put into production had they been aware of their value when the unit was designed 10 years earlier.

Like the 4/4's engine, it was oversquare, the bore and stroke of 88.9 mm by 71.1 giving a capacity of 3,528 cc. It used a five-bearing central camshaft—driven by chain from the crankshaft below—to operate short, small-diameter, pushrods and rockers through self-adjusting hydraulic tappets. These typically American devices were considered essential to provide a reasonably quiet valve gear as the aluminium alloy used for the cylinder block did not have the sound-deadening qualities of cast iron.

In the British engine, the cylinder liners were pressed into place and located by stops at the bottom of their housings rather than by flanges on the tops of the cylinders—shades of the old TR! A two-plane cast-iron crankshaft ran in five main bearings with a torsional vibration damper combined with pulleys for ancillary drives and an externally-mounted AC mechanical fuel pump at the front. The big ends of opposing connecting rods

The Morgan Plus Eight bonnet badge.

shared a single journal in the normal way and the gudgeon pins were a press fit into the little ends.

The distributor was mounted at the front of the engine in the centre of the 90-degree vee, with its drive inclined to the left (when viewed from the front of the engine). The centre of this shaft was driven from the camshaft with the lower end operating a Hobourn-Eaton oil pump. This had a short-circuit oil relief valve set at the typically-low American maximum pressure of 40 psi, and also featured a filter casing mounted on its lower cover to form a neat little unit. Because of the low pressure, the sump was also relatively small, holding only eight pints of oil, contributing to the engine's compact dimensions and low weight.

An alternator on the left-hand side of the engine shared its belt drive with an impeller which pumped 15 pints of water from the front to the back of the cylinder blocks and then through transfer passages into the heads. The water was biased towards the exhaust ports inside the heads before passing into the inlet manifold and on to the cooling system's thermostat and radiator. The belt also drove a cooling fan on the standard Rover unit—which would have fouled the Morgan's front subframe, so it was replaced with a Wood-Jeffreys electric fan with 10 blades, controlled by a thermostat, between the suspension and the radiator.

No change had been made in the design of the combustion chambers in the British engine's crossflow cylinder heads. The shape of the chamber was, in effect, a segment of a sphere deformed in the valve area to take the seats of two parallel valves, inclined at 20 degrees to the cylinder axle, with a single central sparking plug. Separate rectangular-section inlet ports were used for the 1.495-inch diameter inlet and 1.308-inch exhaust valves, operating with double springs. Square-section four-branch cast-iron manifolds routed the exhaust gases directly down the outside of each bank of cylinders into a single-pipe Rover-style exhaust system.

The fuel mixture was supplied by two 1.75-inch diameter SU HS6 carburettors mounted high on a one-piece manifold between the cylinder blocks—which did not matter too much as the actual height of the vee was relatively low compared to that of an in-line engine's cylinder face. The steel manifold's joint was extended to form a cover which spanned the vee and enclosed the camshaft and tappet blocks. Initially, this engine had a relatively high compression ratio of 10.5:1 to take advantage of the 100-octane fuel which was readily available in the 1960s. In its Morgan form, it produced 163 bhp at its red line of 5,200 rpm with a massive 210 lb/ft of torque at only 2,600 rpm by 1968 ratings which were subsequently recalibrated to 152.5 bhp and 210 lb/ft. But whichever way you measured it, the new unit gave at least 50 per cent more power than the Plus Four's TR engine and 60 per cent extra torque.

Obviously the running gear had to be altered to accommodate such a dramatic change, but by surprisingly little, so that the overall weight of the Plus Eight went up by only 3 per cent to 1,950 lb. Even more important was the fact that the weight distribution was virtually unaltered because the engine was so light and could be squeezed into the same position in the chassis.

This was exactly what was done with the first Buick-powered prototype, registered OUY 200E, which meant that the bonnet had to be relieved with two prominent bulges to clear the SU carburettors' dashpots. Rover had considered the possibility of using a single four-barrel fixed-jet carburettor, like the Americans—which would have allowed a lower overall height for the unit—but had rejected the idea because the SUs were such a well-known quantity in Britain and were cheap if you had a good relationship with their manufacturers (at that time the British Motor Corporation). A single Weber installation was also available, but it would have cost a lot more.

Morgan were happy to go along with anything which reduced the overall cost of a new car and decided to invest £1,500 in tooling up for a revised chassis frame which made V8 installation easier and got rid of the unsightly bonnet bulges.

In essence, two inches was let into the front of a reinforced chassis ahead of the scuttle and another two inches into the width, giving a wheelbase of 98 ins and track of 49 ins at the front and 51 at the back. This had the advantage of allowing the body to be made a couple of inches wider, too. Its lines

*Below left and right:* The famous dent in the air cleaner distinguished the early Rover V8 engine installation in the Plus Eight.

followed those of the Plus Four, giving an overall length of 152 ins, width of 57 ins and height of 50 ins, although subtle reshaping of the panels meant that hardly any were exactly the same. The engine was still a tight fit—needing a dent in the top of the air cleaner to squeeze it under the bonnet rail.

Attempts were made to stiffen the chassis by plating the footwells between the crossmembers at the front and rear of the gearbox with steel plates, instead of the normal wooden floorboards. The notch under the rear

axle was also made deeper to allow more movement. Handling was further improved by dropping the front anchorages of the rear springs (still with six 0.25-inch thick leaves) by 2.5 ins to give them a 7-degree tilt forward. All told, there was now 4.5 ins more room for axle movement, although it was found that the springs were still stiff enough, and benefited sufficiently from the re-angling, to render unnecessary anti-tramp devices, such as radius arms. The traditional Armstrong lever arm shock absorbers were also retained.

But it was considered prudent to fit a limited-slip differential with so much extra torque available. This Powr-Lok unit was made by Salisbury, the rest of the 7HA axle being the same as that of the Plus Four except that it now had a higher, 3.58:1, final drive ratio.

The extra track at the back was made up by new 5.5-inch wide 15-inch alloy five-stud wheels specially cast for Morgan by the Midlands firm of J.H. Robinson. These were fitted with the latest 185VR Dunlop SP Sport radial tyres of the 80-section typical of the times! The wheels, in particular, had been selected because they were stronger (and lighter) than the equivalent Dunlop wire wheels, which were not offered as an option, but one of the drawbacks of having wider rims was that the turning circle was increased to 39 ft 6 ins left, 40 ft 6 ins right.

*Above left and right:* Early Plus Eights—this is a 1969 model— were fitted with simple dashboards carrying a rev counter on the right-hand side, and ventilated plastic upholstery.

*Below left:* By 1974, the Plus Eight had advanced to the sophistication of a pancake air filter . . .

*Below:* The original pattern Plus Eight alloy wheels.

The old Moss gearbox proved sufficiently strong for the job, so it was retained. But Morgan had to design a new flywheel and starter ring and torque tube to link the new engine to the existing gearbox through a 9.5-inch Borg and Beck single dry-plate clutch because the Rover engine was made only in automatic transmission form at the time. Clutch operation also went over to hydraulics at the same time in keeping with the normal Rover practice.

Even if the gearbox was strong enough, the brakes were not, so they were uprated by fitting Girling 16P (instead of 14P) calipers at the front. The new calipers used only slightly larger pads on the existing 11-inch discs but were far more fade resistant. The Plus Four's 9 x 75-inch rear drum brakes remained unaltered although there was now a scuttle-mounted servo to boost pedal pressure.

The column to the 2.4 turns lock-to-lock Cam Gears steering box had to be re-routed with two universal joints to clear the cylinder bank. Although these joints gave a good measure of impact protection, the opportunity was still taken to incorporate an AC-Delco system with collapsible extruded mesh along with a combined lock and ignition switch to a trendy new 14.5-inch diameter leather-rimmed three-spoke alloy wheel.

A new negative-earth electrical system with a single 12-volt battery mounted behind the passenger seat was linked in with the alternator. Accessory manufacturers were moving over to rocker switches en masse to meet American-inspired safety demands, so the Morgan's dashboard was modernised as well. It now had the speedometer with main beam tell-tale light, and ignition warning light on the left-hand side, with screenwash, two-speed windscreen wiper, foglamp and spotlamp and two-speed heater fan rockers mounted across the top of the central panel, with headlamp, hazard warning lights and side-lamp switches lined up below. The ammeter, water temperature gauge, oil pressure and fuel gauges were contained in a matching circular instrument on the right-hand side of the central display with a rev counter to the right of the steering column. Indicators, dipswitch, headlamp flasher and horn were operated by a single column stalk (from a Ford Cortina) to the right below the rev counter. But the glorious old fly-off handbrake remained beside the torque tube on the passenger side. A further modern touch—doubtless inspired by the Jaguar E type—could be seen in three smaller, and more rigid, windscreen wipers needed to clear the screen better at high speeds.

The Plus Eight had been developed by former racing mechanic Maurice Owen, who appreciated the value of a good, secure, location for the occupants of a car—it often being said that a proper seat can be worth a second in lap times! So Owen took the opportunity to redesign the Morgan's seats in a conventional bucket pattern, with fore and aft adjustment, to be made by the specialist firm of Restall. These seats were trimmed in Ambla leathercloth, like the rest of the interior, traditional leather having become very expensive in Britain by the 1960s.

*Above left:* This 1974 model Plus Eight is equipped with leather upholstery and outside door handles.

*Above right:* Large plastic windows in the 1974-model Plus Eight made the interior far brighter was the hood up, besides improving outward vision. The twin exhaust outlets are also visible beneath the rear bumper bar of this car owned by Ray Springthorpe.

An early decision was taken to make the new Morgan only in two-seater sports form, partly because the construction four-seater bodies took so long that they cut back on the number of cars which could be completed partly, because a much larger 13.5-gallon fuel tank was needed to give the Plus Eight a decent range of more than 200 miles. It was still possible to build a four-seater (and Morgan did for one dealer's personal use) but it now meant that a great deal of weight would be concentrated at the back with a full complement of passengers and a full tank, which could lead to difficult handling for what was a very fast car. The presence of the large oblong tank, which was mounted as low as possible directly behind the rear axle, was marked by twin snap-action filler caps either side of the spare wheel—so that one could be used for filling the tank while the other to let out displaced air and fumes.

The Plus Eight not only became the fastest Morgan made so far but, needless to say, the most expensive, at around 40 per cent more than the Plus Four it replaced. Naturally, Morgan were worried about this and initially items such as a back bumper were listed as extras. Early production was confined to right-hand-drive cars, with the first left-hand drive example being made in March 1969.

At the same time an 'all-alloy' body was introduced to save 100 lb in weight for competition-minded customers who were willing to sacrifice durability. The radiator cowl and scuttle continued to be made from steel on all cars, however, in the interests of rigidity.

In company with the 4/4, the rear lights were revised to the new tubular-mounted pattern, this change being phased in on the Plus Eight late in 1970. Some other changes to the 4/4's specification were also shared by the Plus Eight, of course, such as the dual circuit braking and dashboard padding changes in October 1971.

It was also obvious that the rather-primitive exhaust system could be improved, so during 1971 some cars were fitted with a freer-flowing dual system with a balance pipe at the front like that used on Jaguar's Daimler V8 saloons. This proved very resonant, however, acting rather like a tuning fork, so the solid balance pipe was replaced by a flexible one during 1972 and the exhaust pipes routed out through the wing valences rather than the chassis. Owen estimated that this system liberated an extra 5 per cent power.

Throughout the period of the Plus Eight's production, it had been becoming increasingly obvious that the old-fashioned Moss gearbox—abandoned by its last major customer, Jaguar, in 1966—would have to be replaced because, although it was a good strong unit, it was simply too cumbersome. Its slow and awkward gearchange, without synchromesh on first, was never better highlighted than by the quick and efficient Ford unit used in the contemporary 4/4 . . .

But Morgan, who could not afford to finance a new gearbox, were happy to note that Rover had at last built a manual gearbox capable of taking the V8's torque for their new 3500S sporting saloon introduced in October 1971. It would only be a matter of time then before they could lay hands on limited supplies of the new gearbox. It was an altogether more attractive proposition than the Moss box because it came in unit with the V8 engine with a remote control change ready fitted, which would allow them to dispense with the complication of the torque tube. Its ratios, being intended for the heavier saloon, were wider and not quite so sporting at 1, 1.391, 2.133 and 3.625 with a 3.43:1 reverse, but the improved quality of the synchromesh—which extended to first gear—and the speed of the gearchange more than made up for this.

Changes were needed to the crossmember positions to accommodate the new unit, but were easily made, with the engine being moved back slightly to bring the gear lever into a convenient position. The steel plating which had been welded in to stiffen the chassis was found to be more trouble than it was worth as it rusted easily, so it was replaced by the old floorboards. The chassis and power train changes made the Plus Eight fractionally more tail heavy at 47.4 per cent front/52.6 rear against 48.1/51.9, but Morgan felt that it was still within acceptable bounds—particularly as there was no four-seater. Overall weight was slightly down because the Rover gearbox weighed around 15 lb less than the old one. The first of the new Plus Eights was built in April 1972 with the last Moss-boxed car finished the following month.

Detail improvements, such as the fresh-air heater from March 1973, continued to be shared with the 4/4 before the overall width of the Plus Eight was increased again in August that year by spacing out the Z-section chassis members by another 2 ins, giving a front track of 51 ins and rear of 52. The cockpit was unchanged so body panels, such as the wings, had to be reshaped to cover the extra width.

This change had been forced by the introduction of a new rear axle from Salisbury which was 1.5 ins wider than the earlier example. The advantage of this new axle was that it incorporated a 3.31:1 final drive which would raise

*Left and below:* The early model Plus Eights, such as the first car, had a narrower track than their successors, illustrated by the second car.

the Morgan's speed at 1,000 rpm in top gear from 19.7 mph to 21.85, thus giving it a far more relaxed cruising ability, with lower fuel consumption, particularly on motorways. The ratio change was, however, a mixed blessing, because the lower ratio used before—which was no longer available—gave slightly superior acceleration which was more desirable in competition applications where top speed was not of paramount importance.

During the height of the worldwide energy crisis in 1974, the Rover V8 engine was detuned to 143 bhp. This was partly achieved by the use of 9.25:1 compression ratio cylinder heads, and partly by retarding the timing. These changes found their way into the Plus Eight, of course—happily without making a massive difference to the performance of such a light car although the rival MGB GT V8 suffered more by having to use an even lower-powered version of the engine, normally fitted to Range-Rovers! This was because it was visualised that the engine would be needed in much larger quantities for the mass-produced MG. There was also an advantage to Morgan in that the new engines they received now met revised European exhaust emission regulations, which were particularly keenly upheld in what had become their biggest export market, Germany. (The Plus Eight had been sold in America during 1971 and 1972 but had to be withdrawn when expensive 50,000-mile tests were demanded of minor manufacturers.) But a further advantage to the people who could buy a Morgan Plus Eight was that their engine would now run without trouble on lower-octane fuel—which was to become the norm by the end of the decade.

The works car registered MMC 11 continued to be used for development, in this form into Sports Lightweight trim with 14-inch wheels for Prodsports racing.

Minor improvements during 1974 included the windscreen demisting vents as fitted to the 4/4 from November before a special run of cars with aluminium body panels was built from October 1975. These were dubbed Sports Lightweight models and fitted with 14-inch diameter wheels to lower the ride height and give them access to a wider range of tyres as well as to provide the car with even livelier acceleration. The wings were stretched outwards at the same time to cover the 6-inch rims needed for the new tyres, which increased the track to 52 ins at the front and 53 at the back. The wheels, made by Millrace, were basically the same as the 15-inch ones but of slightly different pattern, incorporating large squared-off cooling ducts in place of the former multiple drillings. The purpose of building this limited-edition model was two-fold: to restore some of the performance lost

by the reduction in engine power and to counter objections by some scrutineers in production sports car racing that aluminium-bodied Morgans were illegal because they cost more than standard cars, as did 14-inch wheels.

Meanwhile Isis Imports, in San Francisco, which had been involved with Morgan parts sales and repairs since 1969, began to convert new cars to run on propane gas so that they could avoid the crippling American exhaust emission regulations, the 50,000-mile tests having reverted to the previous stipulation of 4,000 miles from 1976. The cars were shipped to Isis at the rate of about 25 a year without the fuel tank but in otherwise standard form. With the Plus Eight, this meant that they also needed further modifications to meet new safety regulations which had been updated as recently as 1974.

Strengthening members were fitted behind the bumper bars, which were then mounted on Fiat gas-filled shock absorbers to meet head-on and tail-end impact laws. Aluminium bars were let into the doors and tied in with a front hoop that ran under the scuttle, and a rear roll-over bar, to cope with further regulations dealing with side impacts and turning over. Then a number of other modifications were made, including fitting intertia-reel seatbelts, padded sun visors, headrests and a seat belt warning buzzer. The interior of the car also got a dose of flameproof fluid.

The conversion to propane power started with the installation of an 18-gallon fuel tank with the filler valve neatly hidden beneath the spare wheel's mounting lug, sealed fuel lines, a vapourizer and lock-off to stop the flow of fuel when the engine is shut off. The normal inlet manifold was replaced with an Offenhauser unit and the SU carburettors with an Impco propane carburettor. Surprisingly a power increase of 10-12 per cent was claimed—and attributed to the better gas flow of the Offenhauser manifold—although further claims of slightly smoother running because propane had a higher octane rating than normal petrol, and 16-18 mpg were more convincing.

Later on an additional option became available from Isis: turbocharging. In this case a Rajay turbocharger running up to 6 psi boost was fitted to increase the claimed power output to around 200 bhp at the rear wheels. The

*Left and right:* A five-speed gearbox and modified body was fitted to the Plus Eight in 1977. This car, owned by Donald and Cecily Jellyman, is the first road car to be built to this specification.

*Below:* The Plus Eight's doors continued to be fitted with massive inside catches after they adopted outside door handles.

*Above:* Rear light configurations had to be modified from year to year to meet ever-changing regulations. This is the late 1970s set-up.

*Right:* The air cleaner was changed on the Rover SD1 engine, allowing it to fit neatly, without a dent, beneath the Morgan's bonnet.

105-octane rating of the propane gas made this a viable proposition on their Lucas electronic injection engines, which had the 9.25:1 compression ratio. In this case the ignition needed minor resetting to restore more of the initial advance and reduce it slightly overall. By 1980, also, the more readily available impact bumper struts from the Volkswagen Rabbit (Golf in Europe) had replaced the earlier Fiat items on the special bumpers.

But the next big change in British cars—minor styling changes, such as the sidelights shared with the 4/4, were made in 1976—had been introduced in January 1977 when Morgan were able to fit the new five-speed manual gearbox that Rover introduced for their SDI saloon six months earlier (a prototype five-speed Plus Eight having been built in October 1976). The new unit was bulkier than the earlier four-speed box, but had the advantage of an 'overdrive' fifth gear, giving a 0.833:1 ratio which further improved high-speed cruising and saved fuel in the economy-conscious mid to late-1970s. The lower four ratios were also closer at 1, 1.396, 2.087 and 3.321 (with a 3.428:1 reverse) which gave a more sporting effect.

Morgan would have preferred to have reverted to the earlier 3.58:1 final

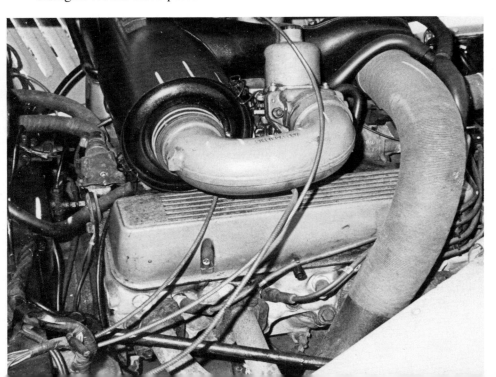

drive with this higher-geared box, but it could not be resurrected at a reasonable cost. So they compromised by fitting the 14-inch wheels as standard, with more modern—but still inner-tubed—Michelin XWX 195VR70-section radial ply tyres, the 6-inch ground clearance necessary for road use being maintained by suspension adjustments. These tyres still gave a higher overall gearing than before, running out at 26.2 mph per 1,000 in top gear rather than 21.84, but the engine could cope, particularly as the fourth ratio was similar to the old top. It meant, however, that maximum speed was achieved in the direct drive rather than the overdrive fifth gear, thus steering the Plus Eight more towards a relaxed gait than outright, searing, performance. The wider track that came with these wheels further improved ultimate handling, the wing section changing at the same time, of course.

One of the other side effects of fitting the five-speed gearbox was a change in the chassis from a bow-shaped crossmember under the bellhousing to a straight channel-section. The new gearbox's bellhousing also caused problems with the clutch withdrawal mechanism. Already restricted footroom in the cockpit (which meant that the driver of a right-hand-steering car had to rest the left foot on the clutch pedal) meant that the normal Rover throw fork operating on the right-hand side of the bellhousing had to be moved to the top.

Rover revised the engine extensively in detail for the SD1 to restore the power lost to emission controls with the result that the new unit gave 155 bhp at a slightly-higher 5,250 rpm with 198 lb/ft of torque at the same 2,500 rpm when installed in an SD1 saloon. As such, it could now easily cope with the rise in gearing. The chief problem had been to take the engine beyond the 5,200-rpm limit imposed by its hydraulic tappets in basic form. The first step was to alter the valving in the tappets to delay the point at which they 'pumped up,' a development which had been carried out on the LawrenceTune racing Plus Eight as early as 1971. Once the valving had been changed, the breathing had to be comprehensively improved. This was done chiefly with changes to the inlet and exhaust manifolds. But bigger valves were used in the cylinder heads—with a 0.07-inch increase for the inlets and 0.04 ins for the exhaust—which could be readily identified by their single valve springs. Lucas electronic ignition was also fitted along with new piston rings capable of dealing with the higher revs, modifications to the oil pump ensuring adequate lubrication with a noticeably higher output at low speeds. There was also a new slim-line air cleaner that did not need a dent in the top to squeeze it under the bonnet rail . . .

This was all done by Rover, but the most dramatic change which resulted in a total increase in the power output of around 10 per cent was achieved by Morgan. Two four-branch exhaust manifolds, fabricated from steel tubing, were designed so that the balance pipe could be eliminated and give a better extractor effect to the twin tail pipes. The increase in power and torque which resulted was made all the more desirable by the fact than an extra resonator had to be fitted to the back of each pipe to reduced noise for markets in which the exhaust note had become critical—notably Germany.

The Sport Lightweight model was discontinued at this point, now that the lightest version of the Plus Eight had been qualified without question for production sports car racing and the overall performance had been restored. The aluminium body which typically suffered from damage through stones being thrown up inside the wings was offered simply as an option on the new 14-inch wheel chassis with the full width bumper being made standard on all models.

The instrument panel was also made far neater in a style which had been pioneered by Jaguar, and adopted by the SD1's makers, British Leyland, with the speedometer, rev counter and warning lights directly ahead of the driver and visible through the top segment of the three-spoke steering wheel. The other main instruments, the ammeter, and gauges for oil pressure, water temperature and fuel were grouped in line across the top of a central panel with rocker switches below.

The 1977-model Plus Eight had a Jaguar-style dashboard with matching speedometer and rev counter.

The next significant change to the Plus Eight followed in 1978 when Girling started supplying larger front calipers to major manufacturers such as Jaguar for their series III version of the XJ6 and XJ12 saloons. The discs were machined to a new profile at the same time with the result that the heat generated by heavy use was better dispersed. A new master cylinder was also introduced in conjunction with the larger brakes, which meant that a servo was no longer necessary, and that the front brakes now received 55 per cent of its effort against 60 before. Minor changes included higher-backed seats.

Cooling—which had been an occasional problem in hot climates when air locks developed—was then improved from March 1979 by increasing the capacity of the radiator. The use of a more efficient water pump in the Rover engine had also led to problems with the top hose bulging on the more restricted early radiator. This was now additionally countered by eliminating the swirl pot leading to the radiator and running the top hose straight into it, moving the filler cap that had been on top of the swirl pot to the header tank at the same time. A small tap for bleeding the system was also incorporated in the manifold.

The Plus Eight then led a relatively settled life for three years before moving over to Stromberg carburettors with automatic chokes to accompany a higher-lift camshaft from February 1982. This change was dictated by new European emission regulations which required all new road cars to have automatic chokes as it was thought that drivers were leaving their conventional manual chokes out too long. Mixture richness and tickover speed had to be set and sealed by the factory at the same time.

Further improvements in tyre technology then allowed the use of lower-profile, 60-series, tubeless Pirelli P6 rubberware of 205-section which had roughly the same rolling radius on a 15-inch diameter, 6.5-inch wide

*Above:* Later model Plus Eights reverted to 15-inch wheels of a similar pattern to the originals.

Stromberg carburettors as fitted to the Plus Eight.

John Allen ordered several extras on his new Morgan in 1985— including leather upholstery, two-tone paint and a wings-off respray before it was despatched.

rim—to which Morgan promptly returned in their original pattern. The track was, of course, widened once more, to 53 ins front, 54 ins rear, with slight reshaping of the wings.

Rover, meantime, were revitalising their image in a battle with BMW by introducing the limited-production run Vitesse. This high-performance SD1 used Lucas L-system fuel injection (virtually the same as the well-tried Bosch L-Jetronic) which had been carefully engineered to meet exceptionally tough Australian exhaust emission regulations. It needed only recalibrating to meet similar laws anywhere else—Germany included—before producing no less than 190 bhp at 5,280 rpm with 220 lb/ft of torque. This was obtained far higher up the scale at 4,000 rpm, but still proved highly attractive for a lightweight Morgan, which could liberate around 200 bhp with its throatier exhaust, new cam and air intake on the side of the bonnet.

The actual installation was the by-now traditional 'shoehorn job' with modified bonnet hinges to clear the fuel-injected engine's plenum chamber and the computer which controlled its running eventually located above the passenger's knees after occupying part of the floor on the prototype! Morgan managed to avoid making a totally new wiring loom to operate this electrical wonder by simply linking in a subsidiary harness. The revised induction system also required a new high-pressure electric fuel pump and a swirl pot in the petrol tank to stop the pump sucking in air when the level was low.

The petrol injection engine in the late-model Plus Eight just squeezes under the bonnet when the central hinge is trimmed.

The neat new door handles on the Plus Eight injection.

Rolls bars are frequently-ordered options on Morgan and can provide a good mounting point for seat belts although the laminated-wood wheel arches used normally for this purpose are even stronger—allowing a hoist to pick up the car by its belts!

At the same time, it was realised that Cam Gears would have to stop making the old worm-and-nut box (because nobody else seemed to want it), so Morgan commissioned the steering rack made by the specialist gear firm Jack Knight at Woking, Surrey. When fitted to the prototype Vitesse-powered Plus Eight (intended as an option alongside the standard car) in October 1983, this provided a far lighter action at low road speeds and eliminated the by-now traditional inch or so of free play at the straight-ahead position. The use of such a design enforced an increase, however, of approximately one turn from lock to lock and with different geometry made the steering feel less responsive at high speeds even through it was working more efficiently. But overall, the increase in performance was so dramatic that there was an immediate high demand for the new model. Subsequently the Rover V8-powered Range Rover was introduced in the United States in 1987, leading to Morgan being able to plan to step up production of petrol-powered Plus Eights for America.

# VI
# Contemporary Road Testers' Reports

Road and track tests of Morgans in specialist magazines—which tend to scrutinise a car far more thoroughly than newspapers and publications with wider-ranging interests—have always been a rarity because Morgan have rarely had to try hard to sell their cars. As a result they have seldom felt it necessary to advertise their wares by lending new cars to journals covering a market which had demonstrated that it will take every car that is produced. But, inevitably, some new cars have escaped . . .

In the early days, before the Second World War, road tests of any car tended to be couched in the most respectful terms because the magazines involved were fearful of losing manufacturers' advertising to rivals. They didn't have to worry about this with Morgan because they did not spend much on advertising in any case! Nevertheless *The Autocar* testers were distinctly complimentary in December 1936 about their 4-4 test car. Like so many Morgans to follow, it was a prototype, because that was all they had to spare for demonstrations as customers queued for the production cars. But they said of the 4-4 registered WP7490:

> 'Entirely fresh as this car is to one at the outset, observation of its behaviour on the road is apt to be unusually keen. At once several particularly good things can be said from the point of view of the owner to whom it is intended to appeal. This Morgan is outstandingly steady and corners exceptionally well, has light, accurate steering, extremely effective braking and a lively, willing performance.'

Many of these comments hold good today, of course, but it is interesting to note that the cable brakes were well up to the standards of the day. *The Autocar* then went on to comment on a favourite Morgan party trick:

> 'Straight away one is struck, of course, by the exceedingly low build, it being possible to touch the road surface from the driving or passenger seat . . .
>
> 'This construction no doubt has a good deal to do with the remarkable feeling of safety that is speedily induced in the driver, though it does result in seating positions which, from the point of view

The Morgan 4-4 prototype that endeared itself to *The Autocar* and its 'fraternity'.

of entry and exit, are best suited to the younger and more agile members of the fraternity.'

The use of the word 'fraternity' clearly describes how *The Autocar* viewed their readership—so closely comparable with Morgan's clientele—in 1936. They then went on to explain enthusiastically:

'Once seated, however, driver and passenger find themselves to be comfortable, and vision is very satisfactory, the bonnet line not being unduly high even in relation to the low seating position.'

So much for the first impressions of leaping into the definitive Morgan four-wheeler, confirming that nothing much has changed in the half century or more since. The mechanical side of the 4-4 might have been dated even as it first appeared, but that didn't worry *The Autocar,* using words such as 'on',

*Below left:* The engine of WP7 490 that kept it 'swinging along happily . . .'

*Below:* 'Once seated, the driver and passenger find themselves comfortable . . .'

rendolent of horse-drawn days, rather than 'in', which has become universal today:

> 'As to the performance, the four cylinder engine is a unit that pulls particularly well at low speeds on top gear . . . or will keep the car swinging along happily at 50 to 60 mph, besides lending itself to use of the gears, third being valuable for extra acceleration and fast hill-climbing.'

They were also quite happy to accept the fact that the early 4-4 was a noisy little machine, in the true tradition of sports cars, pointing out:

> 'There is a noticeable exhaust note, though this is not of a nature to annoy either those in the car or others outside it, while the engine is quiet mechanically at ordinary speeds and smooth as well. The gears are inclined to make more sound than is usual today, especially second and first.'

The *Autocar* then went on to emphasise some qualities that may have been forgotten about the early 4-4s:

> 'An outstanding feature is the sure and accurate way in which it can be put round either a fast open bend or, for instance, a sharp turn of the modern arterial road roundabout type, with no tendency whatsoever to heel or sway, and only a mild "scream" from the low-pressure tyres under such extreme use to show that anything out of the ordinary is being done.
> 'This ability is contributed to not only by the special type of front springing, the underslung rear springs, and the low build, but also by a steering gear which is finger-light, though quick and high-geared, at the same time free from road shocks and possessing enough castor action . . . at speed or slowly, it can be one-handed steering, so well does the car control, besides which it feels solid.'

Perhaps a hint of caution could be perceived in this comment on the brakes:

> 'The Girling brakes are light to apply, smooth and progressive, even in an emergency stop, and exceedingly good as regards ordinary slowing down.'

But overall impressions of the 4-4 on the road were excellent:

> 'The driving position has a big influence upon one's general opinion on a car, of course, and the fact that the steering column of the Morgan is well raked, that vision is good, and that both wings are in sight of the driver have much to do with the feeling experienced right from the commencement of being able to do anything one chooses with it.
> 'It is a most handy size of machine in town streets or on a busy

main road, and, steering as it does to the proverbial inch, can get through safely where many another car would be held back. It feels very safe on wet roads, also.'

Comprehensive instructions on how to change gear strangely avoided describing the 'back-to-front' gate, in which the first-second and third-fourth planes were transposed. The road testers also cleverly skirted round a controversy of the day as to whether synchromesh was 'cissy' or not. They simply played along with the conviction that most readers had been brought up on cars without synchromesh, in which double-declutching was a normal way of life, while continuing to welcome newcomers who preferred such responsibilities to be delegated to synchromesh. *The Autocar* said:

'The gear lever is admirably placed . . . and handles very well indeed; first is reasonably low and really needs not to be used for starting on the level. The clutch gives a quite smooth start and is light to operate. The change from first to second is a deliberate one in the ordinary way, or, alternatively, for a quick getaway, a very rapid pull-through change can be made from first to second, with a single clutch depression. From second to third a quick movement is possible, synchromesh on the latter gear assisting, as also between third and top or the downward change.'

The trials-bred handbrake also came in for praise:

'In a convenient position to the left of the gear lever is the handbrake lever, this being of fly-off type, engaging its ratchet only when the knob is pressed down; it will hold with absolute certainty on a 1-in-4 gradient, on which, too, a very easy restart can be made.'

Morgan motoring at its best.

But even in 1936, the Morgan's suspension was considered to be rather severe, although, evidently, the roads left a lot to be desired as well. *The Autocar* said:

'The car's suspension is admirable on ordinary surfaces, on the firm side over certain types of less good surface at low speed, and inclined to be hard over a really severe potholed section.'

The 4-4's real purpose in life was not overlooked by *The Autocar,* which pointed out:

'During the course of a test of some 300 miles the Morgan was taken up several well-known gradients of the kind used until quite recently in trials. There is plenty of power for this sort of thing, the engine revving freely . . .' and: 'As was specially noticeable from driving the car along muddy byways, the mudguarding is very effective.'

Motorists in the 1930s were far more inclined to make adjustments to their cars and to make allowances for them than many today. Nevertheless, the journalists felt that they had to mention:

'Though fixed in by screws, and in one section, the seat back rest can, of course, be set at the commencement to suit any individual driver's ideas. Actually, with the seat as arranged on this particular car both an average-height man and a tall one were comfortable. Some people prefer more support in the lower part of the back than this seat achieves.

'The body sides are fairly high; if protection were not thereby sacrificed it would probably be an advantage as regards the driver's right arm if his door could be cut away partially. The windscreen can be folded flat on the scuttle, and it was with this down that the best timed speed (of 77.59 mph) was taken, the speedometer then showing a reading of 82. With the windscreen up normally, the best timed speed was 74.38 mph, the speedometer then not going above 78.'

Other performance figures included a 0–30mph time of 6.1 secs, 0–50 of 15.9 and 0–60 of 28.4, with an approximate fuel consumption of 35 mpg.

*The Autocar* also managed another Morgan test—of a 4-4 four-seater registered CNP 507 used by the works teams in trials—in August 1938. This car proved no less economical although it weighed in at 60 lb more than the two-seater. It also managed a slightly higher top speed of 78.26 mph with a similar 0–60mph time of 28.3 secs, although the 0–30 time (7 secs) and 0–50 (17.3 secs) were, as expected, a little slower. The speedometer, however, was commended for its accuracy! In this case, however, the full Brooklands circuit was available for gaining speed, which had not been the case with the two-seater, so it could be concluded that there was a penalty to be paid for the extra weight of the back seats.

The works four-seater registered CNP 507 proved a little slower than the two-seater because it weighed more.

Nevertheless, the four-seater was not found wanting for performance. *The Autocar* reported:

'Useful power is produced by the engine, which is capable of revving freely. Thus the indirect gears can be used to advantage, and they are needed fairly frequently if the best is to be obtained from the car. On the other hand, top is a 5:1 ratio, and the flexibility and climbing power afforded is good—indeed, somewhat surprising at times.

'Not often in average country is second gear wanted, third being a good gear for the kind of hill which is too much for top, or allowing faster climbing than would be possible on top gear, again, for a spurt of acceleration. Second gear is on the low side, and a rough-surfaced 1-in-4½ to 1-in-5 gradient of trials calibre with sharp corners can be

The generous rear compartment of the four-seater.

The free-revving engine of CNP 507.

taken on it, leaving first as an emergency ratio for the worst sort of gradient, or for restarting on a steep section.'

Such descriptions of the advantages of changing gear may seem odd today, but in the late 1930s there were still many potential owners who tried to make a car do everything in top gear—rather like a horse, which has no gearbox, of course. And the advice on which gear to use in trials is still perfectly valid. . . *The Autocar* added:

'As to general running, it is not a car that suggests a best speed to hold; it keeps up 50 mph or so readily and the engine is not much more noticeable at 60, whilst on clear stretches of road the speedometer needle will go round to the 70 region readily.'

It must be born in mind that smooth-surfaced dual carriageways were virtually unknown in those days, which must have made a Morgan quite exciting at such speeds on the average bumpy, twisting, British main road. *The Autocar* made no mention of bump-steer, for instance, when describing the 4-4's steering, ride and handling:

'Outstanding features are the steering and the stability. The steering is finger light, easy even at low speed and when turning round, yet properly firm and accurate, giving the driver the all-important feeling of having direct, responsive control. There is definite castor return, and no more reaction is felt from the front wheels than a slight shake over some road surfaces . . .

'Regarding stability, a steadier, safer small car would be practically impossible to find. It goes round corners fast without the least sign of lurching or heeling over, following an accurate course close to the near side. At speed on the straight it is firm and shows almost no trace of pitching motion.'

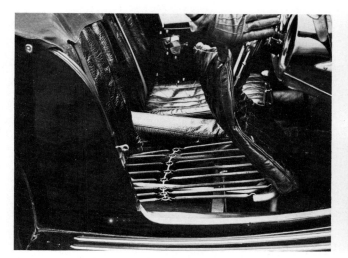

A clue to the different standards by which cars were judged long ago can be found in this sentence:

'The insulation against shock over poor surfaces is striking in this size and type of car, in the back seats as well as the front, even though the springing tends towards firmness rather than softness.'

There are some things, however, which never change . . . *The Autocar* adding:

'The steadiness of the machine contributes much to its good averaging capabilities, besides which it is a size of car overall, with the necessary degree of acceleration, for ready overtaking. Again, it does not occupy much room in narrow lanes, and the driver is placed so that he can see what he is doing.'

*The Autocar* then went on to praise the brakes—'capital in an emergency'—and emphasise that only 'ordinary double-clutching' was necessary to change down into second gear providing you revved the engine hard enough.

So far as the seating was concerned, the testers commented:

'The front seats give just the right position and support. Also, there is plenty of leg room, with freedom for the driver's left foot when off the clutch pedal . . . although the seats are not specially soft, they do not prove tiring on a long run. At the back, there are foot wells, and, again, leg room is generous. It is a proper back seat for two people, not an occasional one, and the occupants sit well down in the car.'

Such comments may be extraordinary today, when motorists are used to far more space-efficient cars, but judged by the standards of its day—when an Austin Seven was considered to offer perfectly adequate accommodation for four people—the Morgan was quite roomy.

*Above right:* Fully-grown people could be accommodated in the back of the four-seater.

*Above left:* The sprung supports for the front seat squabs.

Three-quarters rear view of the four-seater.

*The Autocar* was not above criticism, however, pointing out that because no exterior door handles were fitted 'it is not the easiest matter to open a door with the sidescreen up,' before adding, after lowering and raising the hood: 'There are a good many turn buttons to deal with and it would be better if all the fasteners were of the quick-action type.'

A final indication of pre-war attitudes is indicated by the deadpan

*Photographs left and below:* The drop-head coupé that was a contemporary of the two and four-seater 4-4s.

reporting of an oil consumption of approximately 3,000 miles per gallon. Presumably many cars got through such a quantity of oil in a much shorter distance.

No magazine managed to test a Le Mans Replica Morgan before the war or immediately after, but Michael Bowler, editor of the British monthly *Thoroughbred and Classic Cars,* was lucky enough to be able to drive one much later, reporting in February 1975:

'This car is absolutely immaculate and a credit to its owner, Ken Hill, who is a frequent concours winner, and it was certainly a pleasure to drive; it isn't very quick in modern terms—not much faster to 60 mph than an 850-cc Mini—but has a nice willing engine which can be taken through 5,000 rpm to give reasonable speeds in the gears and enough acceleration out of the corners to affect the attitude. As ever it uses a Moss gearbox with rather lazy synchromesh and you are more certain of a graunch-free change, double-declutching up and down the box; there isn't a lot of useful torque until you get beyond 2,500 rpm so you use the box fairly frequently which the ratios and its precision of movement encourage.'

'The steering is remarkably heavy and high-geared and the front suspension seems to lack castor action, so it is difficult at first to keep the car in a straight line until you stop trying to countersteer every deviation. Given its head it seems quite stable and in the corners it is easier to place it accurately. The overall grip is not high but the almost complete lack of roll encourages the familiar to throw the car around as long as you remember that there isn't the power to help you out. With

*Below left and right:* Ken Hill's Le Mans replica Morgan 4-4 as tested by Michael Bowler.

the basic suspension layout identical to that of the later years (Bowler
was also testing the historic Plus Four Super Sports registered TOK258)
the ride, too, is similar, rather jerky and pitchy but no rattles on a
well-maintained car . . . I didn't drive the car with the hood up but you
sit so deep down in the car that the weather really can pass over the top
as long as you are still moving.'

Eleven years later Mike McCarthy had the opportunity to compare
John Orton's Le Mans Replica with a new Plus Four for *Classic and
Sportscar* in February 1986. He reported:

'The steering of the Le Mans car is superb. It's light and direct, but
without slop or play; you neither have to fight it nor use the gentlest of
finger movements. John has worked on it, and it shows. That of the Plus
Four, by contrast, is not one of its better features; it feels heavy and
dead by comparison, and the first impression you get is that the Plus
Four is an enormous understeerer, but it soon becomes clear that the
effort of turning those fat 195/60HR15 tyres effectively disguises the
handling. Strange, that, having to put more muscle into the Plus Four
than the Le Mans car . . .

'Obviously the Plus Four is much, much quicker . . . which makes it
all the more amazing when you discover that the Le Mans car is actually
no slouch! John reckons top speed to be about 90mph, and,
subjectively, it feels about as quick as something like a current Metro
(up to 50mph anyway) . . .'

McCarthy found the action of both gearchanges unexpectedly similar in
that they offered short, precise, movements, although the Le Mans car had a
lighter, yet smoother and more progressive, clutch. He added:

'Yet another area where the older car shines compared to the Plus
Four is in the handling stakes. On skinny 4.50x17in tyres, cornering

*Below left and right:* The skinny
4.50-17-inch tyres that gave John
Orton's Le Mans replica so much
character.

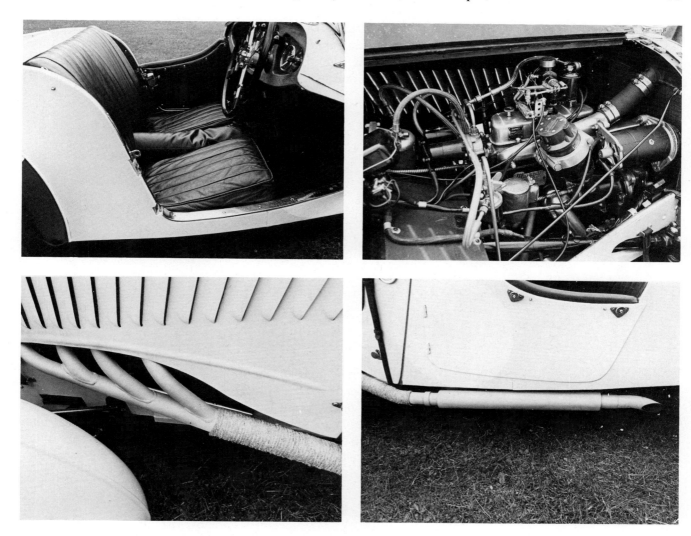

*All photographs above:* Interior, engine and exhaust system of the Orton Le Mans replica.

powers cannot be compared, but the Le Mans car is eminently more chuckable, and much, much more fun.'

Back in 1941, *The Autocar* were lucky enough to be able to give the supercharged 1,021-cc 4-4 a brief test near H.F.S. Morgan's home, despite war-time petrol restrictions. Their representative reported:

'I was pressed for time, and, letting restraint go briefly, I "wound it up" for the first and only time. It took gradients on the Maidenhead–Oxford route at a cracking pace, with the speedometer indicating 80 mph on a level stretch. This was surprising—not, for the moment, in the sense of suspecting its veracity, but because I had not appreciated that much more than an easily-seen 60 or so was being indicated at that point. An aircraftman whom I was able to pick up enjoyed his ride, apparently, saying that he had never travelled so fast in his life!'

The early post-war Standard-
engined Morgan 4-4 differed little
outwardly from the pre-war
version.

## The Standard-engined 4-4

The British monthly magazine *Motor Sport* was one of the few publications
to report what it was like to drive a new Standard-engined 4-4, editor
William Boddy using one as a staff car during the early part of 1951. He

reported in the July issue that the handling was excellent, the suspension
seemed softer than that of the pre-war Morgans, and the brakes were good,
although they needed fairly frequent adjustment. He found the high-geared
steering pleasant, the headlamps very good and the central pass lamp
'sensible.' Other credit points included the 'good' clutch, effective quick-
action fuel filler and well-padded seats. But he did not like the plywood floor,
which was 'smitten far too frequently' by the back axle.

Bill Boddy found the early Morgan's hood rather claustrophobic.

Despite being a fan of open-air motoring, Britain's spring weather had forced Boddy to keep the hood up for most of the time. He noted that protection was good on the move, except when the 'rather oddly-contrived sidescreens part company with the hood.' Rain also collected on the seats while the car was parked and visibility, hood up, was 'akin to that from the driving slot of a tank.'

A fuel consumption of 34.4 mpg was adjudged excellent although the engine protested at the enforced use of low-grade Pool petrol, despite its 7:1 compression ratio. Performance was similar to that of the rival MG TD up to the maximum of around 70 mph, with between 50 and 60 as the comfortable cruising speed.

Even by the standards of the immediate post-war years, Boddy considered that the Morgan needed a lot of maintenance, commenting that the factory 'more or less advised carrying a grease gun in the cubby hole and attending to the two nipples on the front suspension slides at every red traffic light if wear was to be avoided.' He yearned for the new Plus Four's one-shot lubrication in this respect and added that the back spring trunnions called for similar attention and did not retain the grease very well. The wisest precaution seemed to be to oil just about every moving part once a month . . .

But he did not complain about three equipment failures in the first four months, during which 6,200 miles were covered. The first, a short circuit in the distributor, was cured by a new rotor arm, the second, the loss of a jet in the Solex carburettor, was expensive, and the third, stripped teeth in the Moss gearbox's constant-mesh pinions, was considered unlucky. The shortages of supply which caused car manufacturers so much trouble at the time was illustrated by a complete absence of spares at Malvern and only secondhand cogs at the makers! Boddy was happy to note, however, that the Dunlop tyres had suffered not a single puncture so far although there was a suggestion of 'independent front suspension scrub' at the front.

## The early Plus Four

Further indications of the maintenance levels expected in the early post-war could be gleaned from Boddy's experiences when the 4/4 was replaced with a new Plus Four, registered KAB 303, midway through 1951. He reported in the October issue of *Motor Sport* that Morgan recommended that the Vanguard engine's head should be removed after 5,000 miles for a decoke and 'light valve grind'. Although officially this engine did not need to be run in, Boddy drove gently over the early miles and liberally laced the Pool petrol with Redex or Carburol upper cylinder lubricant.

He was most impressed with the new hydraulic brakes, especially as they needed no attention 'of any sort' in the first 4,000 miles. The one-shot front suspension lubrication was a boon, the drop in oil pressure from 75 psi to 25 psi showing that it was going in, with the front tyres confirming it visually!

Boddy expected a few 'bugs' with a new model and got them: a bent

*All photographs above:* The Boddy Plus Four registered KAB 303 survives as an immaculate concours car.

clutch operating lever had to be replaced with a stronger one, and both front suspension dampers broke within the first 2,000 miles, followed by a rebound spring, rendering the car undriveable above 40 mph and attracting frequent attention from the police as Boddy wobbled on for another 2,000 miles while awaiting replacements.

Evidence of the Morgan's hard ride—made worse by using tyre pressures of 20–22psi to improve handling over the recommended 16–18psi—could be seen in the way the scuttle floated over rough surfaces and the frequent need to tighten the sidescreen securing knobs and the spare wheel's retaining clip. A bonnet bracket also broke, a wing stay came adrift and the silencer joints blew—to emit 'lovely noises'.

Nevertheless, Boddy found the Plus Four a joy to drive, with its acceleration as the most impressive feature. He became 'king of the traffic hold-ups' by hitting 40 mph in second gear, and 60 in third on the way to an easy cruising speed of 65–70mph, with so much flexibility that he could pull away in top gear from 20 mph. The gearchange itself was also highly commended . . .

It is significant that by 1951 an absence of roll when cornering fast was regarded as a 'vintage' feature, rival sports cars already being fitted with far softer suspension. Boddy added, however, that 'no car is perfect' and the Plus Four's hard suspension was really a weakness, requiring a good constitution if you were to hurry over rough roads. The upholstery absorbed a lot of the bumps, but the chassis still seemed hard put to cope with bad surfaces.

The quick steering contributed to the Plus Four's ability to average 45 mph in the wet on poor secondary roads, but Boddy was disappointed that more than 2 ins of lost motion had already developed in the steering box.

Nevertheless, his conclusions were in favour of the Morgan, which proved economical to run at 23–26 mpg in regard to a performance which made it 'very good fun to drive, remarkably handy in traffic, and possessed of very good acceleration, cornering stability and brakes. These are qualities which melt the miles.'

By the time Boddy got his Plus Four, *The Autocar* had also managed a test of a coupé version, the works demonstrator and Land's End Trial car registered JNP 239. They found its specification an 'almost startling recipe' with a power-to-weight ratio that was 'right out of the ordinary'. They added, in April 1951:

'Its ability to cover ground rapidly, even over roads such as those in England, with their many deterrents to high-speed travel, is equalled by very few cars, though this is not the whole picture of this car . . .

'The suspension is firm to the point of harshness over some kinds of surfaces, there is a good deal of mechanical noise when the car is driven hard, and it is relatively stark as regards one or two items of equipment which have come to be regarded as normal in these times. Above all, however, *it goes,* in the full sense of that phrase. It gets up very quickly indeed to about 65 mph and does not want much road to see 70–75, around which figure it can be kept apparently indefinitely, with no sign of heat or falling oil pressure.'

*The Autocar* then became the first magazine to record scientifically-accurate performance figures on a Morgan by using a fifth-wheel electronic speedometer. From rest to 30 mph took 4.6 secs, 50 mph 11.3, 60 mph 17.9 and 70 mph 28 secs with a maximum speed of 85.5 mph and fuel consumption of between 22 and 26 mpg. Such figures are modest by today's standards, but were outstandingly good in 1951 as *The Autocar* pointed out:

'The Plus Four's extreme handiness makes it ideal for narrow roads and town traffic. Journeys can be made in outstandingly good time owing to the vivid acceleration and high natural speed and the way in which it can utilize every legitimate traffic opening with safety'.

The *Autocar* found that it was possible to drive the Plus Four coupé 'really hard with impunity' in such a way that 'there is much amusement

100

104

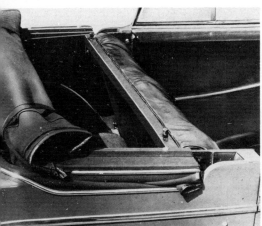

*All photographs above: The Autocar's* 1951 road test Plus Four, JNP 239, started life as a works entry in the 1950 Exeter Trial, and continued as Peter Morgan's car in the 1953 MCC Rally before returning to the Exeter with Peter Garnier in 1954.

value from an enthusiastic driver's viewpoint to be had from free use of the gearbox . . .

'Rock-firm stability enables remarkable liberties to be taken in fast cornering, though with enterprising handling methods tyre squeal can be produced even with pressures recommended for fast driving. The front suspension . . . has none of the roll characteristics associated with most present day coil spring independent systems . . .

'There is noticeable understeer and the car has to be pulled through the faster and more acute bends. The steering has strong self-centring action out of a right-angle bend and a light wheel hold is found best on the straight. At speed there is an unusual feel of slight lateral movement, probably arising in the driver's mind from movement of the scuttle structure. Slight lost motion in the steering may have influenced the impression. The fact that to obtain the best from it, the car has to be "driven" to some extent is no detriment to enthusiastic eyes.'

'The hydraulic brakes achieved all that was asked of them during a great deal of fast motoring; they needed fairly heavy pedal pressure for maximum results, but proved dependable.'

Although *The Autocar* testers like the coupé, they felt that it was beginning to feel rather old-fashioned, with an absence of back rest adjustment 'somewhat surprising,' the handbrake placed too far forward 'for maximum convenience,' and a seating position which hardly allowed a driver of average height to see the left wing. Visibility in general came in for unfavourable comment, despite the evident goodwill of the testers. *The Autocar* pointed out that with the hood erect, leftward vision was seriously restricted at road junctions and 'rearward visibility, through a small rear window, cannot be described as good, especially in view of the fact that with the type of side windows used the driver cannot put his head out to see astern. Nor is the mirror view comprehensive. It would be a distinct advantage if the doors were lockable, but it is not easy to contrive effective locking in conjunction with sliding windows.' The answer was simple: you either drove a Morgan with the hood down, or forgot about the rest of the world when it was up . . .

The lack of a rev counter and foot space to the left of the clutch pedal came in for similar criticism, as did the length of beam with the headlights dipped, although the dashboard-operated horn and manually-returned trafficators were merely considered quaint. However, *The Autocar* concluded:

'The Morgan Plus Four has many of the advantages of the often-lamented older types of sports car, and certainly offers all the benefits that are so frequently argued for by motoring enthusiasts as deriving from a very favourable power-to-weight ratio. It feels rugged and suggests that it can take rough going staunchly, even though not so comfortably as a more softly-sprung car; and clearly it has a real value for trials and sports car competitions of the kind open to private owners.

'It has faults of both omission and commission as seen through eyes accustomed to the entirely modern plan of car; but none of them is of a character to prevent it being great fun to drive, and to some large extent they can be forgiven. It is not difficult to believe that the keen minority of owners whom such a car interests would become very fond of it because of its fundamentally honest outlook and achievements . . . Few machines, irrespective of price, could run away from it on a journey, and such performance is not easily bought today at the basic price of the latest Morgan; some accompanying sacrifices are perhaps inevitable.'

*The Autocar's* rival weekly, *The Motor,* were largely in agreement when they tested a Plus Four roadster, registered HUY 982, in September 1951. They pointed out:

'It has for many years past been the proud claim of the Morgan Motor Company that their cars were faster than anything else obtainable at the same price. Costing rather more than preceding models, but also performing very much better, the latest Plus Four proves that the "fastest at the price" claim of its manufacturers is very fully justified . . .

'Emphasis on performance at a moderate price means that, inevitably, touring car luxury and carrying capacity are sacrificed to a greater or lesser extent. But, given acceptance of this bartering of spaciousness for speed, the open two-seater Morgan is a car which can give immense pleasure to the right sort of owner.'

*The Motor* also went far further than *The Autocar* in recording performance figures, revealing that the two-seater sports Plus Four was a good deal quicker than the coupé although the two magazines' weight figures were not comparable. *The Motor* recorded a 0–30 mph time of 4 secs, 0–40 of 6.5, 0–50 of 9.9, 0–60 of 14.1, 0–70 of 19.7, 0–80 of 33.2 and standing quarter mile of 19.5 secs with a mean average top speed of 84.7 mph. A lot of extra data was compiled, including acceleration times in the top two gears indicating that the Plus Four took only 8.2 secs in the 40–60 mph zone which was of particular significance in the early 1950s. A car's best cruising speed was also frequently bandied about in those days, and *The Motor* said that this—'as far as it can be defined'—would be between 70–75 mph. Amazingly, the Plus Four would also climb a 1-in-10 hill at 62 mph in top gear and could cope with inclines as steep as 1-in-4 in second. But to stop within 30 ft at 30 mph needed more than 100 lb pedal pressure . . . and despite all this testing work, it averaged 25.6 mpg. *The Motor* said:

'The figures for mileage per gallon are creditable in themselves, but certain comparative interest attaches to results obtained on a 500-mile circuit of the Welsh mountains at fractionally over 30 mph running average speed: with a ten-minute change-over of jets and choke tube made before the start, at some very slight sacrifice of maximum speed but not seemingly 'of acceleration, and with a considerable amount of coasting indulged in, 38.6 mpg was recorded.' It was amazing what a Morgan Plus Four could do on an economy run!

*The Motor's* comments on what it was like to drive a new Plus Four were an absolute delight. They said:

'Essentially the Morgan has the "alive" character on the road which in an era of soft suspension and slow-to-respond steering is called "old-fashioned." Considerably more flexibly sprung than its predecessors, and giving its passengers ample insulation against shock on any but the very worst surfaces, the chassis nevertheless does follow the contours of the road more precisely than do many of its contemporaries. In relation to the character of the car, of which reasonably firm springing is a natural part, our main criticisms of the suspension would be that the rear shock absorbers did not match the telescopic units fitted to the front suspension in ability to resist bouncing on awkward surfaces negotiated at high speed, and that at just 58mph there was a perceptible front-end shake on the test car.

'The same "alive" character which distinguishes the car's riding is to be noted in the steering. There is no marked oversteering or understeering characteristic to attract comment, but rather a measure of balance, of prompt, but not exaggerated response to steering wheel movements, which takes most of the conscious effort out of fast driving. There are imperfections; in the form of a rather unexpected springiness of the steering linkage which, feeling like slight lost motion, allows gusty side winds to induce wander of the car on straight roads; and in the form of castor action so progressive that considerable effort is needed to get full lock on a hairpin corner. But, overall, the standard of easy controllability provided by the quick and reasonably reaction-free steering is very good.'

*The Motor* considered the body 'just the right size and shape for two people' and the driving position 'strictly sporting and, for alert driving, very comfortable also.' Entry 'is not as easy as it might be,' and 'a stranger is at first apt to find rather a lot of knobs and corners against which to bruise himself.' Obviously you expected to be both agile and durable to drive a sports car in those days!

The Plus Four's cockpit design did have its good points, though, *The Motor* adding:

'For weather protection, two sidescreens which are easily mounted on the doors combine with the raked fold-flat windscreen to make the car very reasonably draught free—there is no trace of the common open car trouble of exhaust fumes sucked forwards into the cockpit . . .

*The Motor* considered the Plus Four's body to be 'just the right size and shape for two people' with a driving position which encouraged alertness.

Experience showed that a quite surprising amount of hood-down
motoring was possible even in showery weather, since with the car in
motion rain is thrown over the heads of the driver and passenger.
Further, the presence of wide running boards as part of the car's
effective mudguarding layout means that an elbow projecting through
the flaps provided in the sidescreens does not become wet as it does in so
many low-built sporting cars . . .

'Our overall impression is that the Morgan has shortcomings, but
they are of the kind which do not seem terribly important when one is
driving an open car, the vivacious character of which makes the use of it
a potent rejuvenating tonic.'

Part of *The Autocar's* test data had included comparisons between their
new electric speedometer and that fitted to the Plus Four, revealing that the
car's instrument was fairly optimistic, recording 90 mph at a true speed of 83
and 95 flat out at 85 mph. So John Bolster's claims that the Plus Four
registered HUY 982 used by *The Motor* was a 'genuine 90 mph car' when he

The Plus Four registered HUY 982
appeared in varying forms, latterly
with cowled-radiator bodywork.

tested it for Britain's new sporting weekly, *Autosport,* in July 1952 have to be
treated with reserve, as do his acceleration figures of 12.8 seconds for the
0–60 despite a proven ability as a sprint driver. Nevertheless, Bolster's
comments on the car's handling were valuable as he tested it at Boreham and
Brands Hatch race circuits. He said:

'The handling has no vices whatsoever, and the authentic
four-wheel drift technique is within the Morgan's compass. It sticks to
bumpy roads like a leech and no bouncing or wheel lifting is ever
apparent. The exceptionally high-geared steering gives a feeling of
mastery, and it would be a poor driver indeed who did not find himself
quickly at home behind the wheel.

'Less travel is allowed on the suspension than is usual these days, and consequently the ride is a good deal harder than is fashionable. If rock steadiness and controllability are your first consideration, you will fall in love with the Morgan, but if you like a boulevard ride, it is not the car for you . . . At today's prices, it represents quite remarkable value, and for those who prefer to take their motoring neat, without air-conditioning, radio, or built-in cocktail cabinet, it is quite a proposition.'

## The TR2-engined Plus Four

*The Autocar* was again first to test a new Morgan—another works rally car, the TR2-engined Plus Four registered KUY 387—in May 1954. At first, they seriously doubted the accuracy of the speedometer, but then checked it and found that the car really was capable of a mean average of 96.3 mph and a

best one-way run of 102 mph. Acceleration was similarly impressive, with a 13.3 secs 0–60 and standing quarter mile covered in 18.5 secs. The fact that the TR2 engine was a far more efficient unit was confirmed by fuel consumption figures of 30 mpg overall.

*The Autocar* pointed out that the new Plus Four—with its cowled radiator grille—had progressed from a lively sporting car to a definitely potent machine, adding:

*Above left and right:* HUY 982's sister car, KUY 387, is pictured, first, with a flat radiator body, then, with cowled-radiator bodywork and Peter Morgan at the wheel, before being converted to left-hand-drive American specification.

'The likeable robust character of the car is still there, however. Minor styling changes have been made around the front—concessions, only, to the modern trend—but the car remains a survival of the off-the-peg competition car of the 'Thirties and what, to many people, is the best type of sports car. There are slight crudities, possibly, and certain refinements to which the somewhat spoilt modern motorist is accustomed are lacking. Fundamentally, however, this recipe of an excellent power-weight ratio and a simple chassis gives reliability without high stress. The extraordinary performance is proof that the ingredients are right . . .

'One of the outstanding features is the sheer joy an enthusiastic driver gets from the handling . . . the ride is still stiff and firm, and despite this, the car does not tire the crew; on two 300-mile journeys undertaken during the test period very much the reverse was found.

'The chassis and bodywork give the impression of being sturdy and on rough surfaces there is no tell-tale sideways movement of the scuttle. The cam and sector steering which has replaced the type used on the previous models is light, sensitive and accurate. There is none of the feeling of having to "steer" the car along fast, straight, stretches; one needs only to hold the thin, notched, wheel rim lightly in the fingers and the car does the rest. The steering is sensitive to road "feel", yet transmits very little shock.

'On fast, open, bends it is necessary only to bear on the wheel towards the corner, rather than to steer the car round; there is a slight understeer, a good point with a car of this type . . . On sharper corners the Morgan holds the road beautifully and one finds oneself looking forward to the twisting bends of a familiar route, for the pleasure of dealing with them without a reduction in speed and free from the slightest signs of roll.'

*The Autocar* then went on to criticise the brakes, which had a peculiarly 'dead' feel and needed a lot of pressure, plus the usual points—with the exception of the lack of a rev counter, because this car had one—before summing-up:

'The Morgan with the engine now fitted is a specialist car with a wonderful performance. It does not pander to the creature comforts and, in exchange for a slightly Spartan outlook on the part of the driver,

*Below, left and right:* KUY 387, hood up and down, with left-hand steering in the second picture.

it will give him real pleasure. Its ability to cover the ground is outstanding and it is a joy to drive no matter how long the journey. Though one or two criticisms may be directed at the car tested, it must be remembered that the Morgan is not a quantity-produced car in the true sense; it can hardly be said that any particular example is "standard". The points criticized are there, but one forgets most of them in enthusiasm for the performance. It should be born in mind that though by successive increases in engine output for a given total weight a brilliant straight road performance must inevitably result, the steering and chassis development—with the possible exception of the brakes—have kept pace with the performance.'

John Bolster then had another chance to test a Plus Four for *Autosport,* this time equipped with a TR2 engine. It was an interesting car, bearing the same registration number, HUY 982, as the flat radiator Vanguard-engined car he tested two years earlier. But this car had cowled-radiator bodywork, full depth front wings and a front bumper besides being to left-hand-drive American specification with new-fangled flashing indicators, a special grade of upholstery and a spot lamp. Bolster also referred to the previous car, but did not give the impression that the new one was a rebuild, leading to the assumption that it was only temporarily bearing the works number plate. He was also conscious of criticism that the way in which he obtained his performance figures with the flat radiator car was far from scientific, explaining:

'To put all doubts at rest, let me say, straight away, that against the stopwatch, timed in both directions, the car does achieve 100 mph. It needs a long run to get the last 2 or 3 mph, but the Morgan is now definitely in the exclusive 100 mph class. Incidentally, the speedometer reads 5 mph slow at maximum speed.'

Bolster then went on to list better performance figures than those of *The Autocar* with a 100 mph top speed, 10.8 secs, 0–60 and 17.9 secs standing quarter mile that could be attributed to a superior driving ability—although his fuel consumption did not suffer at 31.6 mpg 'driven hard'.

He also made an interesting point about the new bodywork, which married up with *The Autocar's* comments on their cowled-radiator Plus Four. Bolster said:

'There may be a fractional reduction in wind resistance, but the greatest gain is in rigidity. The new front end stiffens up the chassis and suspension assembly to the benefit of roadholding . . . The car is firm and steady and travels smoothly on reasonable surfaces, but the more severe bumps are definitely felt. Nevertheless, it rides more comfortably than any previous Morgan, principally due to the improved bracing of the front end.'

His other comments tended to back up those of *The Autocar,* including an assessment of the brakes, now robbed of the direct cooling from the air stream they had enjoyed on the flat radiator cars. Bolster said:

'They are powerful in normal use and are smooth and responsive in action. Really hard driving, however, including frequent heavy braking from near the century mark, may cause some lack of progressiveness to be noticeable. Serious fading does not occur, but a slight tendency to pull or grab gives a gentle hint that things are warming up. The brakes quickly return to normal . . .'

In addition, he found the Plus Four a good deal more enjoyable to drive in open form, commenting:

'With the sidescreens in place, the driver and passenger are well protected, and the slight burble of the exhaust is carried away on the wind, so one covers the ground with effortless ease. The hood is effective, and easy to erect, but, like most of its kind, it does magnify engine noises somewhat. I do not say that the car is then unusually noisy, but the delightful silence of the open vehicle is lost. I have no doubt that a little extra padding, or the use of carburettor intake silencers, would overcome this slight criticism.'

Bolster's performance figures were substantiated in February 1955 by the American monthly *Road & Track,* which had grown rapidly in stature by specialising in reports on imported cars. They wound a privately-owned Plus Four up to 98 mph with a 10.8-second 0–60 and 18.3-second standing quarter mile despite the nearly-new engine feeling a little tight, before saying:

'Short on comfort, long on performance, this agile two-seater . . . is strongly reminiscent of the old M.G. TD—but with lots of muscle. The chassis is now extremely rigid and the suspension gives a ride which can only be described with kindness as "firm". However, as a result, the car handles with astounding precision and accuracy, and the driver is never without a feeling of complete control.
'Not many concessions have been made to comfort . . . and you have to fit the car instead of the other way round. Quietness is not one of the car's virtues, but engine and exhaust noise does not reach an objectionable degree, and the most noticeable sound at speed is a carburettor whistle that makes the car resemble a boiling tea-kettle.
'Inevitably, the Morgan will be compared with the Triumph TR2 since the engines are identical. The TR2 we tested in March 1954 had a test weight 150lb greater than the Morgan; it also had a four-speed gearbox with overdrive. Although the TR2's top speed was about 3mph faster, the Morgan's 0–60 time was less by $1^1/_2$ sec, and the standing quarter times were virtually the same, as was gas consumption. The Triumph costs about $100 less and offers a little more in the way of

comfort, but the Morgan looks and feels a little more like the classic conception of the old-time sports car.'

## The 4/4 series II

The series II came in for a surprising amount of praise from *The Motor* in the first road test of the prototype, registered RNP 504—in the first road test, published in August 1956, the obvious deficiencies of its three-speed gearbox, strange-looking gearchange, and performance that could be described only at the best as modest. *The Motor* road testers went to a lot of trouble to emphasise the car's good points. They pointed out that although it would do only 74 mph, with a 0–60 mph time of 26.9 secs (and standing quarter mile in 23 secs) it was possible to attain 60 mpg by keeping the speed down to a constant 30 mph. Overall fuel consumption was 35 mpg, however, although it has to be said that this was good for a 1950s car which could do 75 mph. *The Motor* added:

> 'The car will cruise happily at a true 65mph, regaining that speed fairly readily after a check. Right up to the maximum—as, indeed, at any other part of the range—the unit is free from vibration periods, but acceleration tails off appreciably over the last 10 mph of the speed range.
>
> 'In second gear, 52mph is possible before valve bounce sets in and 45 mph may be regarded as the easy maximum for normal use, with 50mph available when maximum acceleration is required. Undoubtedly a four-speed gearbox would be an advantage for opportunist overtaking on winding or busy roads, but the cost of departing from the complete Ford engine-gearbox unit would have entailed a disproportionate increase in the cost of the car.'

With the benefit of, perhaps, a slide rule (for the series II had no rev counter), *The Motor* was able to point out:

> 'There is the fact, too, that the Anglia engine had good low-speed torque and the Morgan will trickle along very happily at 1,000 rpm (approximately 17mph) and accelerate away quite readily . . .'

Hardly the stuff of which sports cars are made, but *The Motor* refused to be deflected from its path, emphasising:

> 'The clutch is one after the enthusiast's heart, taking up the drive without need for any undue finesse in engagement. In conjunction with an unusual, but effective, gearchange mechanism, it assisted in providing the sort of quick concise gearchanges which delight the keen driver . . . the arrangement being such that movements across the gate are achieved simply by moving the knob to the appropriate side, actual engagement being by a push-pull motion. Once one obtains the knack

of using the gearlever in this manner (and resisting any temptation to impart a twisting action as called for by some Continental designs) the Morgan arrangement is entirely straightforward and positive. The only snag of the arrangement is that the normal gearlever positions are reversed laterally . . .'

Apart from having a back-to-front gearchange that wouldn't work with a natural twisting motion, *The Motor* said 'the other controls are nicely disposed for easy operation and a strange driver rapidly feels at home . . .'

The usual Morgan roll-free handling came in for fullsome praise, and the reduction in spring rates which made the series II much softer than earlier models was appreciated, even if the ride was still firm by contemporary standards with the springs bottoming out on potholes, and the rear axle making contact with the chassis at the extremes of suspension movement.

*The Motor* road testers also found that although the scuttle and bonnet

*All photographs below:* The first series 11 4/4, registered RNP 504, came in for a lot of praise from *The Motor.*

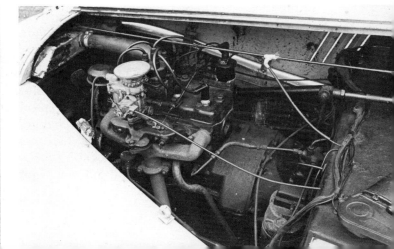

line had been lowered $2^{1}/2$ ins the occupants sat so low that even a tall driver
still peered through the centre of the windscreen. And just to show that their
critical abilities had not been impaired, they took rooted objection to the
position of the speedometer, saying sternly:

> 'The manufacturers have fallen into the all-too-common fault of
> placing the speedometer on the extreme edge of the board where only
> the driver can see it, the passenger being given a good view of the
> ammeter, fuel and oil gauges which do not interest him or her at all.'

*The Autocar* was much more objective in its test of RNP504 the
following month, saying:

> 'At 14 cwt, this Ford-engined car is 3cwt lighter than its more
> powerful counterparts (the Plus Fours) and $1^{1}/2$cwt lighter than either
> the Ford Prefect or Anglia, from which the power unit is derived. The
> engine and gearbox are fitted in standard form as supplied by Ford, and
> thus the acceleration is superior to that of the Ford saloon only in
> proportion to the reduction in weight and frontal area. However, the
> extra performance is worth having—50 mph is reached in 18 secs
> compared with 21.8 for the Prefect, and the 4/4 is 9.5 secs quicker to 60
> mph than the Ford. Top speed is approximately the same for both cars,
> the Morgan (which achieved 70.5 mph when driven by *The Autocar)*
> being slightly faster when the hood is up. The overall top gear ratio of
> both cars is almost the same, but the substantially larger wheels of the

Morgan step up the gearing, so that at maximum speed the 4/4 is not over-revving.

'The acceleration figures are not exciting, but the company has probably been wise in its decision to keep down the initial cost in this type of car, in part by installing the engine in production form. There are several tuning kits available . . . which owners can buy and fit themselves according to the dictates of their pockets. Thus the relatively high overall gearing in top, resulting from the larger rolling radius, is an advantage for owners can enjoy the fruits of extra power without engine speed being excessively high at 70 mph or more.'

*The Autocar* then went on to point out that the first and second gear ratios in the Ford box had recently been lowered, with the result that the series II Morgan had a second gear ratio of 8.9:1 instead of the earlier 8.2 which might have been fitted. The magazine commented:

'Even with the larger road wheels, the Morgan would have been better with the former higher ratio, for maximum speed (in second) is under 50 mph and few owners would regularly exceed 40 mph in that gear. As a result, when one wishes to accelerate after being held up behind other traffic in the 30s, a shortcoming of the intermediate ratio is revealed.'

*The Autocar* also carried a far better analysis of the essential character of the series II:

'Top speed and acceleration are comparable with those of the small family saloons when studied on the impersonal data recorded by the stopwatch, but the difference in handling characteristics between the two types of car ensures an improvement in journey times. On smooth roads, the roadholding of the 4/4 is particularly good. Quite sharp corners can be taken at speeds that are astonishingly high even for a sports car. On bumpy surfaces, the car tends to hop at the rear, disturbing the predetermined line through the corner . . . but on British main roads the taut character of the suspension can be enjoyed to the full. Again on bumps, there is a noticeable tendency for the rear to "bottom" on its axle stops, but the construction of the car as a whole is so obviously strong that this is of little account . . . the scuttle also shakes perceptibly, primarily because of the firm suspension.'

The average person in the 1950s was accustomed to a much higher degree of maintenance for domestic items than is common today—especially with pieces of machinery like motor cars. This meant that even new cars in the lower price brackets were far more likely to be maintained by their owners than modern ones. As a result, *The Autocar* testers took a long, hard, look at the series II Morgan from the point of view of the by-now traditional 'impecunious enthusiast'. They noted that the centre-hinged bonnet offered excellent mechanical accessibility, even if it was rather awkward in that the Ford engine—normally housed under a one-piece bonnet—had the oil filler cap on one side and the dipstick on the other; this meant series II owners would have to lift one side of the bonnet to check the oil, close it and then open the other to replenish the supply, and then, perhaps return to the other side to check that they had done it properly . . . such were the foibles of Morgan ownership.

*The Autocar* considered the lack of luggage space more important, parcels that could not be squeezed into the 'slit trench' behind the seats having to be stuffed into the confined, and probably hot and smelly, space under the bonnet. It was the first time they had encountered a car which could not carry two road testers and their equipment without resorting to extremes. They also found the driving position, with its lack of room for the right elbow and left foot, and insufficient space to stretch the arms, somewhat dated. But, like *The Motor,* they found the 'unusual' gearlever 'quite delightful for snappy changes.' Lowering and raising the hood was, by now, a laborious task, and entry and exit difficult—particularly for tall people when the hood was up.

In conclusion, *The Autocar* said:

'The 4/4 is a creature of compromise. Main items on the debit side are performance which is not exciting in standard form, difficulty in getting in and out, the laborious hood mechanism and the lack of accommodation for luggage. On the credit side are low price, fuel economy, handling of a high order, the ease with which engine power could be increased, and the accessibility of those parts subject to routine attention. In recent years there has been little to satisfy the motorist who wants an economical sporting car at a relatively low initial cost, and the . . . series II fills just that gap.'

By the time John Bolster tested RNP 504 for *Autosport* in April 1957 it had been converted into a Competition model with an Aquaplane head and twin SU carburettors to increase the power output to 40 bhp at 5,000 rpm. In this form, the series II cost 10 per cent more at £518 before purchase tax, or £531 with a rev counter. Bolster was pleased with a top speed increased to 80 mph with no penalty to the 35 mpg fuel consumption (and a 0-60 mph time of 20.2 secs,) but commented of the unchanged gearbox:

'Second is really too low and one constantly bemoans the lack of a gear for overtaking. Proprietary gearsets are available which would overcome this trouble, and it is understood that a new heavy duty version is just out. With second gear raised to give an easy 60, instead of a doubtful 50, the car would be transformed . . . and with a radical conversion, such as the Elva overhead inlet valve arrangement, the machine would certainly exceed 90 mph.'

And he wound up by saying:

'The series II is a highly individual type of sports car that is peculiarly British. Though its attraction would be incomprehensible to

By the time John Bolster tested
RNP 504, it had been fitted with
an Aquaplane conversion to the
engine.

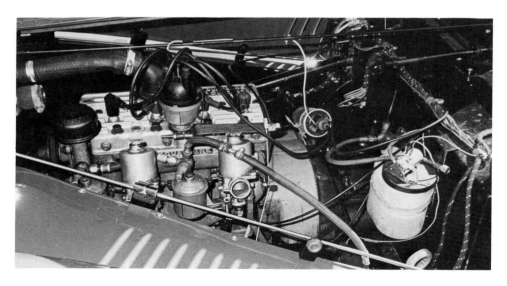

a Continental, it has its passionate devotees in this country and,
curiously enough, in America.'

American testers had mixed feelings over the series II, however. It was
relatively expensive in the United States at £2420 when that sort of money
would have bought a perfectly good 'full-sized' sedan offering similar
performance and economy of operation was hardly important with a gallon
of petrol priced at only a few cents. The monthly magazine *Road & Track,*
which specialised in coverage of imported cars, returned substantially the
same performance figures as *Autosport* with a Competition model, but felt
that it had to explain to its readers in June 1957:

> 'What is a British company thinking of, to export to America a
> classic, fierce-looking sports car, complete even to running boards, but
> with an 1172-cc engine? Does it expect big sales, or perhaps a movement
> to do away with the envelope body, as suggested in this months's Letters
> to the Editor?
> 'To understand, it helps to know that Morgan is a company so
> small as to be almost unbelievable by our standards, and that has a long
> history of having built strange vehicles for a limited, but apparently
> ever-loving clientele . . . there is a certain smug satisfaction in getting a
> lot out of a little; most Americans might find it more enjoyable than
> they suspect.'

*Road & Track's* rival, *Sports Cars Illustrated,* devoted a lot more space
to their coverage of the series II in November 1957. Not surprisingly, they
took a nostalgic line, comparing it to the by-now obsolete MGs which had
started the sports car craze in America 10 years earlier:

> 'If you are one of those small multitude of automotive reactiona-
> ries who feels with passion that all post-MG TC design is decadent and

that the performance and appearance of that vanished breed added up to supremely happy answer to basic sports car requirements, then take heart. Morgan, staunchest guardian of the vintage look, ride and feel, has brought forth what can be called a latter-day successor to the immortal Midget—albeit at a rather stiff price.'

*SCI* applauded the way in which the Morgan's appearance had been revised as 'thoroughly successful and a delight to Morganeers everywhere' and expressed surprise at the quality of the paintwork. Otherwise, their praise and criticism was much the same as those of the other testers, with an additional plea for a water temperature gauge because the high-compression head had a tendency to make the engine run hot. They said of the gearbox:

'There are remedies if you care to pay for them. This Ford transmission is used a lot by the specials set in England and close ratio gears made specifically for it are inexpensive and easily available. The car's owner, Hollywood art director Walter Herndon, has ordered a set which will permit him to wind out to 70 mph in second, which will greatly improve performance. A better move is swapping the Ford box for a four-speed unit. This can be done at little cost and with a minimum of adapting problems if you use the transmission from a side-valve Morris Minor.'

## The TR3-engined Plus Four

By the mid-1950s the Plus Four was enjoying a great deal of success in British national competition, so it was appropriate that the British Racing and Sports Car Club's monthly magazine, *Motor Racing,* should publish the first road test of a TR3-engined Morgan in a section devoted to rallying—where the Plus Four was most extensively used. The opinions of the tester—Ian Walker—were also to be respected as he was not only one of the leading tuners at the time, but a highly-successful driver on road and track. Walker reported:

'There are very few sports cars that I have driven that are capable of cornering with such a feeling of safety, and if the car is provoked to such an extent that the back does break away, it is quickly checked by a slight movement of the steering wheel. The steering is extremely sensitive and accurate, and on fast open stretches of road one gains the impression that the car steers itself. On fast winding roads, only a gentle pressure is needed on the wheel to change the direction of the car without any reduction in speed whatsoever. There is a slight tendency to understeer, and the car can be drifted under power. I had the opportunity of driving the car in torrential rain, and I found myself going through corners at speeds much higher than I would have driven certain contemporary sports cars. The windscreen wipers under such circumstances proved quite adequate, and though they look ridiculously small, clear an adequate area of the low windscreen.

'When I collected the car, I had never before driven a Morgan, but it was not long before I had put 50 miles into the hour. This car soon makes friends, and I found myself at home in it after only a few miles of motoring. By most standards, it is not a really comfortable motor car, but the thrill of driving a car so well mannered is worth the slight discomfort of a harsh ride. The seating, however, is particularly good, and gives support to the driver and passenger in an upright position . . .

'I had the feeling that the car was overgeared (3.73:1) and I feel a much better acceleration and top speed would have been gained by using the alternative ratio of 4.1:1.'

Nevertheless, Walker's performance figures were good: a maximum speed of 105 mph, with a 10-second 0-60, 17.1-second standing quarter mile and overall fuel consumption of 21 mpg, driven hard, which he suggested could drop to 28 mpg with more normal useage.

*The Motor's* figures for a TR3-engined Plus Four, registered TUY 875, were especially interesting, not only in that they used electronic timing gear to record 100 mph flat out in good conditions on the same final drive ratio, but because it was fitted with the optional wire wheels which lowered the mph per 1,000 rpm by about 3 per cent. In this trim, *The Motor's* test, published in January 1958, revealed that the Plus Four was capable of a 9.7-second 0-60 mph time with a standing quarter mile in 17.5 secs, fuel consumption averaging not less than 27 mpg.

After praising the vintage handling and steering, *The Motor* noted from its files:

'The 6.8 secs recorded by the Morgan to accelerate from standstill to 50 mph has been beaten only by two sports racing cars, of $3^1/2$ litres and $5^1/2$ litres respectively. The vital fact is that this test involved three violent operations of the clutch and two of the gearbox, neither of which (nor the rear axle) showed any sign of protest against decidedly abnormal treatment. The clutch, let in suddenly at 2,500 rpm, took up without slip (momentary wheelspin sufficing for take-off) and without judder, yet was reasonably light to disengage. The gearbox, although the synchromesh is barely effective even for leisurely gearchanging, could be snatched from first to second with open throttle, and from second to third below 5,000 rpm with only a slight lift of the right foot. Movement of the lever is light and positive, with a rather ineffectual spring-loading to guard the reverse position.

'In contrast to the transmission arrangements, braking is adequate but no more. In terms of friction lining area per ton of car, it is certainly better than adequate, and the brakes showed no fading tendency, but they are prone to occasional grabbing and the high proportion of effort

The Plus Four TUY 875 led a hard life, combining rallies—such as the 1961 RAC Rally—with road tests.

on the front wheels could cause them to lock at low speeds on a very slippery surface.'

*The Motor* said it was obvious that the Plus Four lacked modern refinement, but still appealed to a relatively small number of enthusiasts prepared to exchange central-heated luxury for driving that is fun 'and, incidentally, fast.'

Such people would have to get used to the hissing of the carburettors at every throttle opening, the engine noises undulled by the bulkhead, the whining of the gearbox intermediate ratios, and the sound of the wind buffeting the hood and sidescreens . . .

None of this worried John Bolster when he tested the wire-wheeled TUY 875 for *Autosport* in August 1958, particularly as he commented:

'The Morgan has one of the best hoods I have used. The frame opens up out of the luggage boot in one quick movement, and the actual hood, of best quality heavy material, then buttons down with no difficulty at all. Why it should be so easy to fit, I do not know, but even at 100 mph there is not the slightest sign of flapping.'

Further comments by Bolster spoke volumes about English weather and typical motoring habits of the 1950s:

'On one journey, I had been enjoying the sensation of driving an open car on a summer evening. Then, as night fell, it began to grow cold. Instead of putting on my overcoat, I stopped for a few moments to raise the hood. So, in saloon-like comfort, I sat behind the powerful beams of the headlamps, and continued to put the miles astern.'

Those were the days when sports car drivers hardly ever raised their hoods and were never caught without their overcoats, even in mid-summer . . .

There were days when sports car drivers hardly ever used their hoods, said Bolster.

Even Bolster could not extract more than 100 mph from TUY 875—although he said he might have managed it by pumping up the new wide-section tyres harder—but he was most impressed with the acceleration up 80 mph, which took 18.4 secs (with a 0-60 of 10.6 secs, a 17.6-second standing quarter mile, and 28 mpg).

The American edition of *Sports Cars Illustrated* (a British version had just been launched) managed to extract 98 mph from 1 TR3-engined coupé in September 1958 but found that it paid a penalty for its extra weight in the initial acceleration—11.8 secs for the 0-60—although it could be wound up to a 17.8-second standing quarter mile. The testers commented of its more luxurious body when exposed to the West Coast climate:

'The car does demand the sort of care that it will get only from the affectionately appreciative enthusiast. One of its mixed blessings is the instrument panel of mahogany—varnished smooth as glass—and, in the case of the convertible, door mouldings of the same. The wood is beautiful . . . as long as it's properly maintained. In a closed car, such maintenance is inconsequential, but in an open car constant attention is required. A tonneau cover or top and windows should be used to protect the woodwork from exposure to the weather. And, depending on the success of this care, the wood should still be refinished periodically . . .

'The Morgan body contains a good deal of wooden framing and keeping the wood, the frame and the sheet metal as united as they were when delivered calls for strict discipline. Says one owner: "Just let the body go and in a year you have something like a tin can full of marbles. But if you go over the car with a wrench and screwdriver once a month and keep all the joints tight, the structure stays like new. It's like the MG TC in this respect . . ."'

Historic gathering of works and ex-works Plus Fours, including TOK 258 in its original form, HUY 982 and TUY 875 in their eventual forms, at the 750 Motor Club's Silverstone Six-Hour Relay in 1959, in which Chris Lawrence and Bill Belcher teamed up with Peter Morgan, Bill Meredith, Jim Goodall and A.J. Blair to form the winning team.

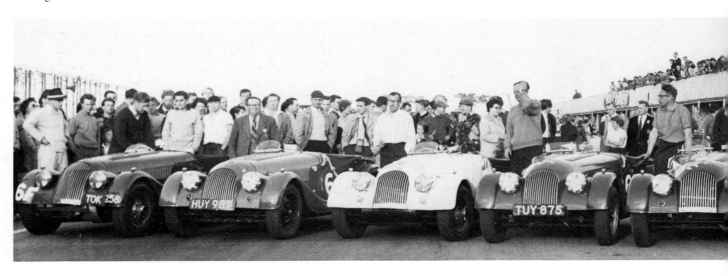

*Sports Cars Illustrated* made familiar comments about the lack of visibility when the hood was up and commented of US coupes, fitted with a Smith's heater as standard:

'It can drive you out of the car if both vents are opened and the rheostat twisted all the way. Demisting ducts are not standard, but they can be ordered and, in damp weather, they most definitely are needed . . .

'Other criticisms of the Morgan? Well, the top starts drumming loudly above 40 mph, but the owner says that all it takes to stop this is stuffing a pair of driving gloves between the forward top bow and the fabric. The factory might take note of this. A couple of cents' worth of padding could eliminate this annoyance . . .'

*Road & Track's* testers resolutely kept the hood down on their TR3-engined Competition roadster, but still managed to squeeze 102 mph out of it on a 4.09:1 final drive in September 1959. Surprisingly, however, they could manage only a 9.9-second 0–60, 20-second 0–80 and 17.5-second standing quarter mile.

They devoted most of the road test to explaining, in an era when American cars were updated every year in the most garish manner, just why the Plus Four was such a magnificent anachronism:

'The long-prevailing philosophy in the small English factory where Morgan automobiles are made is one of lofty disdain toward the fluctuating fashions that less conservative companies call progress . . . every alteration in standard practice has been met with a truly massive indifference (call it fidelity to tradition if you wish), and change, when there is change at all, has been so slow as to be almost undetectable. The Morgan of today is the Morgan of the past, and, in all likelihood, the Morgan of the future.'

*Road & Track's* Plus Four, which basically cost only $400 more than 'the ill-fated series II', had an aluminium body and wings, competition exhaust, wire wheels, Dunlop racing tyres, finned alloy sump, electric fuel pump and disc front brakes, which raised the cost from $2,850 to $3,600—still several hundred dollars less than a similar Chevrolet Corvette. Such options met the thorough approval of *Road & Track*, but one $40 extra did not:

'We did not understand at all what was described as "strengthened front frame and gearbox mounts." To us, this seems perfectly ridiculous. We can understand many extras offered for competition work only, such as a higher-than-standard compression ratio or stiffer dampers. But we cannot agree with a policy that obviously says: "Our cars are strong enough for the streets and if you intend to race you should expect to add bracing or they will break." In our opinion, when a manufacturer sells a sporting-type machine to a customer, he has an obligation to make that machine strong enough to take any normal use—and normal, applied to sports cars, includes racing. Obviously, the marketing of Morgans was naive compared to, say, Porsche, which made its profit from loading baseline models with 'compulsory' extras but never admitted any lack of integrity in the unobtainable standard item.'

*Road & Track* went on:

'The first principle of modern chassis design dictates that a car should have a rigid frame and a supple suspension. This condition is the exact opposite of that in the Morgan. The frame of the car is so limp that, when it is parked with one wheel up on a bump, its doors can be very difficult to open. The suspension is not quite unyielding—but it doesn't miss it by much. However, the end result is great sport: the Morgan will corner quite rapidly and probably exhibits less lean than anything else in the world . . .'

Then, in a summing-up which could have been written decades later, *Road & Track* said:

'By statistical standards, one can prove that the Morgan is out of

*Right and photographs below: Road & Track said the Plus Four was well on the way to becoming a legend . . .*

date. Other cars of the same engine displacement sell for less money, are faster and more comfortable, yet handle just as well. However, these other cars do not, and probably never can, inspire the kind of loyalty and affection that devoted Morgan owners give to their truculent beasties . . . the Morgan is well on its way to becoming a legend as the very last of the "hang the comfort, let's have sport" automobiles.'

*Road & Track* made no special comment on the brakes, but John Bolster did when he had the opportunity to test a disc-braked Plus Four for *Autosport* in July 1960. He also commented on wave of nostalgia for old cars that was building up in Britain now that everybody except Morgan was producing modern machinery:

*Above, left and right:* The competition Plus Four roadster as tested by *Road & Track.*

'The vintage car is all the rage and more and more people like to read about them, tell lies about them in pubs and clubs, and even drive them. The reasons are not far to seek, for the modern sports car, with its all-enveloping body and soft suspension, is simply not so much "fun" as were its forbears, nor does it look like a powerful piece of machinery, ready to be unleashed . . .

'However, the Morgan that I have recently been using had one big advantage over the vintage type of sports car. It had disc brakes, and these render the very considerable performance an even greater asset, because one can use "the lot" all the time without ever sparing a thought for the anchors. Let me say, straight away, that the knowledge of this immense braking power lying dormant adds immeasurably to the pleasure of hard driving. In the past, I have found that drum-braked Morgans tended to pull to one side or grab when the brakes were applied repeatedly at high speeds. With discs, one can rely on as many straight-line stops as one wants, and there is never a sign of distress. Truly, the disc brake is the biggest single step forward that has been made for many a year.'

*Above left and right:* John Bolster opined in 1960 that the Plus Four filled a fast-appearing gap in the market for a vintage car—and it had brakes.

Bolster's Plus Four was fitted with Dunlop Duraband tyres, in which the carcass was reinforced with steel wire. These covers were highly popular with contemporary rally drivers and Bolster found that they made the steering agreeably lighter although they helped induce the rear end to break away when accelerating hard on a greasy surface. Skid correction called for more wheel movement than normal, but he considered it by no means excessive. He also managed 104.6 mph in this nearly-new car, with a 9.6-second 0-60, 17.4-second standing quarter mile and 25 mpg (driven hard) before concluding:

> 'In the hands of the right kind of driver, the Plus Four is nearly unbeatable, and the roadholding and braking are more than adequate for the very real performance. There are many smoother, quieter and more comfortable cars, but if the object of the exercise is really high average speeds in absolute safety, there is nothing to compare with the Morgan at less than twice the price.'

## The Kieft-Morgan Plus Four

During the early 1950s, steel company magnate Cyril Kieft constructed a small number of specialist racing cars which were successful chiefly in the 500cc Formula Three—before quitting when the de-nationalisation of Britain's steel companies in 1954 placed more demands on his time. By 1959, the Kieft Sports Car Company had passed through various hands to be taken over by Birmingham-based motor sports enthusiast Lionel Mayman, who began marketing tuning kits for Triumph cars alongside an ambitious project to contest the Formula Three's successor, Formula Junior, before entering the new $1^{1}/_{2}$-litre Formula One. Publicity for his tuning kits was provided by his exploits in races and rallies during 1960 with a TR3-engined Plus Four, registered VON 777. This car featured a fully-balanced engine with high-compression gas-flowed cylinder head, oil cooler, twin SU carburettors with ram pipes, and a special exhaust system emitting from under the driver's door; a 4.1:1 final drive was fitted, revised steering with a three-piece track rod, Dunlop R5 racing tyres, lowered suspension, adjustable Woodhead-Monroe shock absorbers and a Panhard rod to help locate the rear axle. In this form, Mayman was capable of lapping Silverstone's Club circuit with VON 777 in slightly less than 1 min 17 secs—which was considered fast in 1960.

When Martyn Watkins tried this state-of-the-art Morgan competition car on the road for *Autosport* at the end of the season in November 1960, he found the car so noisy he was twice stopped by police! He then added:

'This point apart, however, the machine is a perfectly practicable means of transport, and the enormously increased power means that journeys can be accomplished in a remarkably short space of time. The shortest stretches of straight road allow speeds of 100 mph to be indicated on the speedometer . . .

'Careless use of the clutch will result in wheelspin on wet surfaces . . . in almost any gear at almost any speed, and a brief encounter with another sports car, which was passed very suitably in third gear, saw the Morgan snaking in a manner which caused passers-by to stare in horror . . .'

*Motor Sport* behaved themselves better when they tested VON 777 in December 1960, but noted:

'On the open road, the Kieft-Morgan is exhilarating to drive. The ride only becomes objectionable on really bad surfaces, when the car does its best to knock the breath from the occupants' bodies and the steering wheel has to be gripped hard if the driver wishes to avoid having it snatched from his hands.'

Nevertheless, *Motor Sport* considered it an ideal beginner's racing car, although perhaps it is just as well for other road users that nothing more was heard of the Kieft Sports Car Company after 1961 . . .


## The LawrenceTune Plus Four

There was obviously a market for a higher-performance version of the Plus Four, but, after the publicity received by the Kieft version, it was hardly surprising that Morgan—who could not justify the expense of a full-scale factory competitions department—became interested in a far more controllable rival produced by West London tuner Chris Lawrence.

When tested by John Bolster for *Autosport,* in December 1960, Lawrence's Plus Four, the well-known car registered TOK 258 that became the prototype for the Plus Four Super Sports, had a full race TR2 engine producing around 120 bhp on twin 45DCOE Weber carburettors. Other modifications to this alloy-bodied wire-wheeled, disc-braked, 1956 car, running on a 3.7:1 rear axle ratio, were confined to an oil cooler, bucket seats and an undershield.

In this form, Bolster managed 121.6 mph with a 7.5-second 0–60 and 16-second standing quarter mile, with 15-18 mpg, in damp conditions before commenting:

> 'There was a good deal of wheelspin at the getaway, which is difficult to prevent on any fast car with a rigid axle. Nevertheless, the sheer performance is something which puts this Morgan in a class far beyond any normal sports car . . . the test car car was still fully controllable when all its great power is exploited.'

When editor Michael Bowler tested TOK 258 for *Thoroughbred and Classic Cars* issue of February 1975 the specification was similar: it was fitted with a low-line 4/4 body and a twin 42DCOE Weber-carburettored engine that gave 128 bhp and 'understandably-quick' acceleration on a 4.1:1 rear axle ratio. As he compared it with Ken Hill's 1939 Le Mans car, Bowler said of the LawrenceTune Morgan, which had been competing in the Spreckley series for Thoroughbred sports cars:

> 'Despite its hard racing season it still seemed very solid and rattlefree with a less pitchy ride than the earlier car—a function of

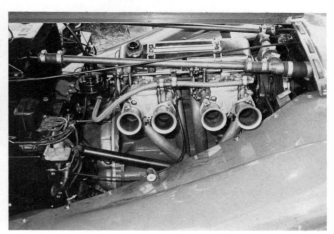

newer damping. The steering response was excellent and with plenty of torque despite a hottish cam the car was very nimble in traffic. Cornering was much as expected with roll-free suspension and racing tyres; it went round very rapidly but side-stepped on bumps in a fashion

*Opposite page and above:* In its early form with Lawrence, the Plus Four registered TOK 258, had an aluminium hard top, full-width undertray, and Weber-carburettored full-race Triumph TR2 engine.

TOK 258 acquired a glass fibre hard top later.

By the time TOK 258 was tested by Michael Bowler (seen peering under the bonnet) it had open bodywork with a roll cage and large front oil cooler.

similar to that of a current Plus Eight which is also well-shod. It feels as though the tyres grip and the chassis gives until the grip is lost as the tyres momentarily leave the deck, then the car side-steps and the axle regains its normal place so that the re-grip is fairly sudden.

'All controls, switches and instruments were very much as the car was originally built with the lubrication pressure switch almost inaccessible above the transmission tunnel. It looks a well-used car without being tatty and still features its Le Mans class colours and fastening holes for the plombeur reservoir seals. It must have been quite a noisy exercise to drive for 24 hours with the hard-top and 13th overall reflects a fair amount of credit on both drivers and preparation. Driving it now 12 years later, it still feels as if it might go on forever.'

## Modified Super Sports

Meanwhile *Road & Track* had tested a Super Sports modified for Sports Car Club of America production racing by West coast distributor Lew Spencer, for which around 150 bhp was claimed although it is difficult to see, from the twin Weber-carburettored TR4 engine specification, how it could have had much more than 125 bhp. Nevertheless *Road & Track's* comments of the test, in conjunction with a standard 4/4, were interesting:

'Pulling a 4.4:1 final-drive ratio, Spencer's Super Sports was a most impressive performer. We used a 6,000 rpm limit, which held the top

The North American-specification
Super Sports as tested by *Road &
Track*.

speed to 106 mph, but gave us a standing start quarter mile in 16.2 secs,
with a terminal speed of 88 mph.

'When we began to press the car a bit, we discovered something
very interesting: that limp-chassis, antique-suspensioned Morgan is one
of the best-handling, most forgiving automobiles in the world. It does
not have exceptionally good adhesion, especially on a bumpy surface,
but it behaves in exactly the same manner every time, and with little
experience on the part of the driver, it can be drifted, slid, skidded and
just generally flung about in a fashion that would be suicidal in many a
more modern sports car. There are two turns in the rather tricky Willow
Springs course over which we tried the cars that tighten as they end and
one is taken at about 40 mph; the other at just short of 100 mph. Both of
those could be taken in exactly the same way, easing on the throttle
halfway around to skid away some speed, then exiting at full blast in a
great long drift. Virtually all other cars require that the driver take into
account his absolute speed.

'Actually, we must confess that only the Super Sports was driven
this way; the 4/4 would not go fast enough to require any technique at
all on the faster bends. On lower-speed turns, however, it behaved just
like its more powerful brother.'

## Farewell from America to the Plus Four

*Car and Driver* were feeling distinctly emotional when they realised that their
staff might never drive a new Plus Four again. They reported in December
1967:

'When word got out that the classic Morgan would very likely be
off the market, there was a run on the cars, and all that was available to
use was a tacky four-seater . . . with a proper mood carefully cultivated,
we set off. The four-seater wouldn't start. Nothing could persuade it to.

*All photographs above: Car and Driver waxed lyrical over their Plus Four.*

Nothing in the world. Typical. We went back to the office to call the distributors and found a call waiting for us. A salesman had been sent out to our garage with a customer, the car had been sold, and would we mind taking another? Of course not, but didn't the man know the car wouldn't start? Of course he did, and it didn't make a bit of difference in the world. The customer was a Morgan buyer, said the salesman, as if that would explain it all. In fact, it explained it perfectly well. Antiques are not meant to run on time. Antiques are meant to be looked after, tended, coaxed. It is a reaffirmation and a joy when an antique won't start. How else can you be sure it's an antique?

'Park a Morgan in a country lane in the autumn sun near a tree so that the dapple sunlight can reflect from its long louvred hood, hinged at the top. Park it so its wire wheels glisten, so its leathery seats invite you to tour winding back roads. Park a Morgan in the city on a Sunday morning and watch a father, trailing a troop of daughters, look at the car with wistfulness and envy. Park a Morgan in the rainy night with the tonneau zipped and see the drops bead on its taught surface. And when you come to drive it, stand back a moment and look at its stance: long in the engine, short-coupled rear. Only one spare tyre these days . . . sitting vertically at the back; high wheels, forthright fenders—genuine fenders, fenders as they were meant to be. And as you get in the Morgan—opening the door from the inside—listen to the pneumatic cushion sigh as you settle down in the cockpit and stretch to reach the pedals; your right leg, knee and thigh pressed against the transmission tunnel. Of course everything is close: the wheel and the wooden dashboard with its big, round, simple instruments; shouldn't they be? Where did this arms-out stuff come from anyway? Surely not Morgan, not MG, not Bugatti. Why did the great Tazio forever have his elbows crooked out when he was sawing away at the wheel of his Alfa?

'The Morgan starts—when it starts—on a familiar key. The 2.2-litre TR4 engine fires with a well-known sound (somehow changed by its surroundings). Depress the clutch (God, it's hard), crunch the old Jaguar non-synchro low gear, and you're off. That's the very first thing you notice about the Morgan. Everything's so damn direct. You feel

every pebble on the road through the steering wheel, and your foot
(time and marshmallow cars have made it clumsy) seems to operate
directly on the engine. You can't get the Morgan operating smoothly
for miles. Ah, but when you do—and when you find a relatively smooth
surface—you understand what was exciting about sports carring in the
Thirties . . . You understand *laissez faire* motoring at its best. Twitch the
wheel, and out goes the tail of the Morgan. Just as far as you want, for
just as long as you want, for just the result you want. Fangio used to set
up a slide for each corner. Be Fangio; the Morgan makes it easy. And
you can see what you're doing. Everything you're doing. You can see
the front fenders pounding from the sliding pillar front suspension
(welds will break in exactly the same places on those fenders in time;
they always have, they always will). You can look out over the side and
see the bump that put the Morgan five feet in the air; a bump a Porsche

Some of the Plus Fours had painted wheels for fear that chroming
the spokes would make them
brittle.

*Above and left:* One late model of
the Plus Fours was given a four-
seater body.

would have brushed aside. And later—straining to turn round in front of a full-length mirror at home—you will see the beginnings of the bruises on your backside. The steering, like the rest of the car, is direct, almost too direct. You have to give a great wrench on the wheel to go anywhere, and any subtlety is absolutely lost on the Morgan. The result is a dramatic change in direction, with a suddenness that is startling. And should you be imprudent enough to set forth upon a bad road, you will live to regret it. A tar divider strip will launch the Morgan on a flight that would put a Hell Driver to shame—a genuine bump will qualify you for flight pay. Still, it's not the take-off that gets you; it's the landing. About three landings a week should be tops. Anatomically. If you're contemplating a Morgan, see your doctor first.

'With all this, however, there's a generous portion of performance. The Morgan—lighter than the TR4—performs smartly in the quarter mile, turning 81.2 mph in 16.9 sec. Add the smooth-track handling, and things begin to make sense. Top speed is about 110 mph; our test car was taken up to 95 mph and was still pulling when our technical editor backed off. The trouble with our technical editor was that he actually tried to understand the Morgan, what it was, what it did, where it managed to fit into the community of nations. What the Morgan meant in the greater scheme of things. Futility. You either accept a Morgan as you accept the Himalayas, or you go on to more splendid things. Butterfly classification, phrenology, alchemy. A Morgan merely is. That should be enough.'

## The Fiat-engined Plus Four

*Autosport* were the only magazine to manage a road test in the brief

The Fiat twin-cam-engined Plus Four as tested by Mike McCarthy.

production run of the 2-litre Fiat-engined Plus Four, which delighted Technical Editor Mike McCarthy in December 1985. He did not have the benefit of the latest high technology timing equipment, but with the time-honoured hand-held stopwatch he estimated the 0–60 mph figure at 9.5 secs, which put it well on a par with its predecessors bearing the same name. McCarthy's estimated top speed was also similar at 112 mph. He commented:

'One of the best things about this Plus Four is the engine/gearbox combination. Previous experience with it (in Fiat saloons) has not been too happy, as we've found it in the past to be harsh and strained and clattery at the top end of its range. But in this application it sounds and behaves just right . . . The gearchange is especially delightful, with very small throws and a narrow gate . . . The clutch, on the other hand, felt very heavy.'

## The 4/4 series III

*Car and Driver* had always liked Morgans, particularly the two-seater series III they tested in November 1961, although they suffered in the process, reporting:

'Despite the snug appearance of the top, rain poured in over the windshield, around the edges of the side curtains and dripped steadily on the driver's right ankle from under the cowl. Being a true enthusiast's car, it had no heater or defroster. If you want ventilation, you're supposed to leave the top at home . . . if the Mog had a top arrangement like that on the Austin-Healey Sprite, leaks at the leading edge would probably be minimized.

'Once at Thompson raceway, we abandoned the top altogether to take some laps. Despite the persistent rain and the squishing every time we moved in the seats, the 4/4 proved a real ball to drive. The handling of the car is one of its strongest virtues and skids could be provoked only with deliberate wheel movements. The billiard table flatness and the light, quick steering kept things in hand at all times. The Dunlop Gold Seal tyres gave a good bite with predictable breakaway and good recovery characteristics.'

Second gear proved too low for some corners, however, and third too high, to the detriment of lap times, whereas at Lime Rock race track there was no corner that needed second gear—and like Thompson, it was impossible to reach peak revs in top. In retrospect, *Car and Driver* decided that the series III needed more power, and thought it might be a good idea to modify the engine to the specification of the new 1,340-cc Ford Classic unit. For the record, their performance figures were 25.8-secs for 0–60 mph, 23 for the standing quarter mile and 80 mph maximum, with between 26 and 29 mpg. The gearchange worked well and 'was not so screwy as it sounds,' but they bitterly bemoaned the lack of a water temperature gauge with an engine which overheated in traffic under a bonnet lacking top louvres. They did, however, praise the leather interior as being one of the nicest they had seen regardless of price and loved the instruction book which recommended 'the necessity of keeping nuts, bolts and screws tight . . .'

## The 4/4 series IV

*The Motor* were the first magazine to test the 1,340-cc-engined 4/4 series IV, a two-seater registered 296 FNP, in April 1962, reminding readers of the marque's changing status:

> 'It would be difficult to judge the Morgan 4/4 on the strength of an ordinary trial run. Drivers who are thoroughly conditioned to modern cars find it difficult initially to accept a vehicle that departs so far in so many ways from the current trend. But a real acclimatization, such as we obtained by driving our Morgan nearly 2,000 miles in the first week of its test, reveals some fascinating traits and strongly recalls the almost forgotten virtues of the traditional type of sports car of which this is almost the only surviving representative.'

*The Motor* then noted that the 4/4 had an unexpectedly good top gear performance, with a 0–60 mph time of 18.6 secs and standing quarter mile of 20.9 secs, but added:

> 'For road use, however, some of this acceleration might with advantage be sacrificed in favour of higher gearing which would give easier high-speed cruising, better fuel consumption, a more useful second gear and probably a higher top speed.'

*The Motor's* two-way timed top speed was only 80.3 mph. with a touring fuel consumption of 32 mpg, leading to the comment:

> 'The Ford engine proved both smooth and mechanically quiet, but a fairly prominent exhaust note and an unsilenced air intake produced a high internal noise level with the hood and side screens in place. Thus, on good main roads, any cruising speeds over 65–70 mph felt rather too fussy for use for long periods. In third gear, 55 mph is usefully available and constantly used, but in second peak revs correspond to about 32 mph and although this speed can be exceeded quite easily, second remains essentially a town gear; only the sharpest bends justify its use in country motoring.'

Of the cockpit, they said:

> 'The Morgan feels different as soon as one sits inside it. It is tailored for a driver about 5 ft 10 ins tall and although there is no seat adjustment of the usual sort it is possible for a shorter legged driver to replace the bottom edge of the single-piece softly sprung squab in an

alternative position some 2 ins further forward than normal; this gives a rather more reclining angle which is, in fact, more comfortable than the normal very upright position . . . after sitting for a long period in this car, one wonders why pneumatic seats have gone out of favour since very few if any other forms of upholstery combine such comfort with light weight and freedom from bounce.

'A comfortable feeling of being housed well inside the Morgan is accentuated by the closeness of the windscreen and the facia, an arrangement which certainly has advantages in bad weather when rain and dirt on the glass impair vision less than with most cars . . . the steering wheel, which necessarily comes unfashionably close to the driver's chest, is also close to the facia on which the controls are grouped in such a way that many of them can be used by extending a finger without removing the hands from the rim . . .

'The driver surveys the road ahead over a long low sloping bonnet which is flanked by separate square section wings surmounted by small traditional side lamps; all these "aiming marks" make the Morgan particularly easy to place accurately and it can be driven very close to kerbs and verges with confidence.'

The lack of room for the left foot to rest, other than on the clutch pedal or flat on the floor, came in for criticism, but the brakes—although heavy to

*All photographs above:* The series 1V Morgan 4/4 registered 296 FNP awakened almost-forgotten memories for *The Motor's* testers, performed well with *Autosport* and beat its rivals for *Motor Sport*.

work—were reassuring. So far as handling was concerned, *The Motor* were largely in agreement with *Car and Driver's* findings, although they added:

> 'Rear springing which is softer than that at the front allows considerable pitching on certain surfaces and . . . the back of the body may sometimes touch the road after a bad depression.'

They also had a word of advice for the uninitiated:

> 'It is inadvisable to splash through deep puddles too fast as quite large quantities of water can be forced in through the removable jacking covers under the seats.'

By the time Patrick McNally tested 296 FNP for *Autosport* in January 1963, it had been fitted with the factory's optional competition equipment—incorporating a special camshaft, single 1.5-inch SU carburettor and four-branch exhaust—which made a lot of difference to the performance. Maximum speed rose to 92 mph with an amazing 10.5-second 0–60 mph time and an 18.1-second standing quarter mile. Fuel consumption fell to only 27–30 mpg, driven hard. Higher speeds were now obtainable in second and third gear—as much as 43 mph and 68 mph—but McNally recommended only 40 mph and 62 mph, pointing out that close-ratio gears would be a great improvement. But he noted that weather protection was now much better with a rubber strip stopping water seeping under the hood at the windscreen joint.

When *Motor Sport* tested the same car in May 1963, they managed 90 mph flat out, but could only extract a 0–60 mph time of 13.4 secs, which nevertheless proved 2 secs faster than Triumph Spitfire, and 2.7 secs better than an MG Midget.

## The 4/4 series V

*Road & Track's* dual test in July 1963 with the Super Sports was also the first with a series V 4/4—a two-seater with a standard 1,500-cc engine—which was hardly surprising as 85 per cent of Morgan's production was intended for the United States at the time. It was a very early model and suffered from a carburation defect which meant that it had to be run most of the time with the choke in operation, which is unlikely to have helped the fuel consumption of 28 mpg! Its top speed at 80 mph was also no better than that of *The Motor's* series IV, although a 0–60 mph time of 16.5 secs was a logical improvement. But the real difference, as *Road & Track* saw it, was:

> 'This stock engine has made the Morgan extremely docile and pleasant as a day-in, day-out transportation car. The engine's torque curve is very flat, holding over 90 per cent of maximum from 1,500 rpm all the way up to 4,000 rpm, which covers a fourth-gear speed range from 25 to 65 mph. Reduced to practical terms, this means that the Morgan can be driven briskly without a lot of rowing at the gearlever.'

**Plate One** Morgan's finest hour with Lawrence at Le Mans in 1962.

**Plate Two** The Classic 4-4 roadster.

**Plate Three** The greatest early Morgan, the Le Mans replica.

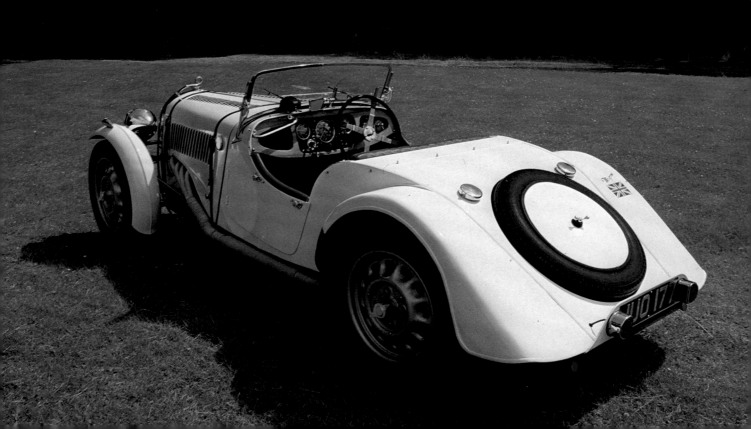

**Plate Four** Ready for anything ... the early 4-4 roadster.

**Plate Five** Rarer than rare ... a Standard-bodied 4-4 coupé.

**Plate Six** Sweet and civilised ... a Vanguard-engined Plus Four coupé.

**Plate Seven** Rhapsody in red ... the flat rad Plus Four roadster.

**Plate Eight** Old campaigner ... a TR-engined flat rad racer.

**Plate Nine** First of the new wave ... the 'interim' four-seater.

**Plate Ten** Impecunious Moggie ... the series two 4/4.

**Plate Eleven** The new world Morgan Plus Four Plus.

**Plate Twelve** Survivor of the Sixties ... a Plus Four roadster.

**Plate Thirteen** Ready to fly ... a Plus Four two-seater.

**Plate Fourteen** Last survivor ... the Morgan SLR.

**Plate Fifteen** Family hot rod ... the Plus Four Super Sports four-seater.

**Plate Sixteen** Long and lithe ... the early Plus Eight.

**Plate Seventeen** Hard charger ... the wide-track Plus Eight.

**Plate Eighteen** Star attraction ... Charles Morgan in his prodsports Plus Eight at Brands Hatch in 1979.

**Plate Nineteen** Instant nostalgia ... the late 4/4 four-seater.

**Plate Twenty** Picnic for two ... with a two-seater 4/4 complete with hamper.

**Plate Twenty-One** Monte Carlo or bust with Phil Young's Plus Eight in 1980.

**Plate Twenty-Two** Hectic night-time pit work for the Morgans in the 1984 Willhire 24-hour race at Snetterton.

**Plate Twenty-Three** Active author ... Chris Harvey crews Barrie Taylor's 4/4, first car home in the 1984 Land's End trial.

**Plate Twenty-Four** Shining example ... a 4-4 coupé on display at Mog 86.

**Plate Twenty-Five** Top performance with a fuel-injected Plus Eight.

**Plate Twenty-Six** Three or four wheels for my first Morgan?

They then commented on the Cortina engine's exceptional smoothness, and added of the transmission:

'Its most outstanding feature is that it has synchromesh on all four ratios, and the synchro is so powerful that even fast, slam-through, shifting produces no crunch.'

But they were not so happy about the gear ratios, commenting that the still low second gear did not work well with the series V Morgan, although the extra torque of the engine helped mask the deficiencies. And of the gearchange, they said: 'After one becomes accustomed to this oddity, it works fine, but it is seriously lacking in aesthetic and sales appeal.'

By 1964, the emergent British monthly magazine, *small car* was starting a revolution in motoring journalism with its outspoken and down-to-earth comments. And at that point it was highly appreciative of a series V Competition model belonging to Morgan works manager Jim Goodall. *small car* reported in August 1964:

'The Morgan's secret, of course, is that it's antique only in looks and feel. In every important basic aspect it offers startling value for money. The 4/4 with Ford's twin-choke GT 1500 engine—which adds another £73 to the bread and butter model's £683—offers really tremendous performance, roadability and finish, for less cash than any open rival.

'Really you can say that with this 1,500-cc version, the 4/4 has finally arrived. Up to now it has always carried (and deserved) a slight taint as the hearty Plus Four's poor relation—a slow slogger for diehards whose nostalgia turned out to be stronger than their sense of proportion. The original 105E Anglia engine gave it less performance than many small saloons, and even the 1,340-cc Classic-powered version which followed left owners wondering what they could do to get over the feeling they were overbraked and underprivileged. Then last year Morgan decided to settle for the then-new five bearing variation on Ford's original theme and at one blow the factory found it had made a killing with far more performance than rival Spridgets and Spitfires for very little money (just £42 more to be exact).

'The Competition model carries the attack still further into enemy territory. Even for dedicated moderns, who may feel that they're having to put up with all those old-fashioned outward survivals just for the sake of a bit of toe, its appeal is undeniable. And for the unashamed traditionalists who make up much of Morgan's market it represents a step forward in an era when they've become all but resigned to marking time.

'Reactions to the Morgan's pre-war styling vary with the individual. We got one or two laughs, and we did find one fellow who congratulated us on a fine restoration job, but by and large we were staggered at the instant, unalloyed affection the little car's rugged outline inspired in the most unlikely quarters. Girls in particular fell for it in a big way.'

*small car* echoed the thoughts of other magazines on the small Morgan and managed to extract 95 mph from the series V Competition model with maximum speeds in the gears of 35, 50 and 75 mph with a 0–60mph time of 11.9 secs and 26.7 mpg before concluding:

'Nowhere can you get such spectacular straight-line performance for so little money. Almost no other cars can have such a big braking reserve. None are safer and few faster in smoothly surfaced bends. And you get the thrill of owning a car so obviously and honestly different it's guaranteed to set every atom of pride aflame in any enthusiast's breast.'

The successor to the British edition of *Sports Cars Illustrated*, called *Cars and Car Conversions*, also tested a series V Competition model in conjunction with a Plus Four Plus in July 1966, and apart from commenting

*All photographs below:* The series V competition model as tested by *Cars and Car Conversions*, proved excellent on and off the road and track.

that it would benefit from the popular conversion to exterior door handles from Ford's old Popular saloon, added that its steering was lighter than the Plus Four Plus and the performance better up to 70 mph. So far as 4/4s were concerned the performance was excellent, with an estimated maximum of 102 mph, a 10.8-second 0–60 mph time and fuel consumption of 32.5 mpg. Speeds through the gears, however, of 30 mph in first, 46 in second and 76 in third highlighted the low second ratio.

For the next few years, magazines wanting to test a Morgan concentrated on the high performance Plus Eight model, until it was suggested to John Bolster of *Autosport,* that the 4/4 might be more appropriate during the world's first energy crisis in the winter of 1973/4. He therefore tried a series V Competition model, registered XUY 836M, and reported in March 1974:

'Morgan motoring is one of those illogical things which cannot be satisfactorily explained. There are people who would never consider owning any other make of car, yet they cannot tell you why. We all know that sports cars are now mid-engined and have soft independent suspension, but whenever I parked the Morgan it collected a much greater crowd than even the [Maserati] Bora or [Ferrari] Dino. To the public, a real sports car still has wire wheels and a long louvred bonnet, for the vintage tradition will never die.'

Bolster found that little had changed about the Morgan in character other than for the new heater—which kept his toes warm even with the hood down, although no tap was evident for turning it off. The biggest change, in reality, was in the gearbox, a Ford 2000E unit which now had an ideal set of ratios to give a maximum speed, with the 1,598-cc Cortina GT engine, of 102 mph (hood up), with 34 mph in first gear, a much-improved 55 in second, and the familiar 75 in third. The extra pulling power of the bigger engine was evident in the 9.8-second 0–60 mph time and 17.2-second standing quarter mile, although the all-important fuel consumption was virtually the same at 28 to 35 mpg.

Rex Greenslade of *Motor* (which had dropped the word *The* from its title for trendy reasons in the early 1960s) then track-tested a series V Competition model, registered RA 444, which Morgan salesman Chris Alford had used to win the British Racing Sports Car Club's Prodsports (or Production Sports Car) Championship in 1975. It was in similar trim to Bolster's car, except that it had an engine which had been 'blueprinted' by Minister Engineering—that is very carefully assembled to the best tolerances specified by the manufacturer—and fitted with a lower 4.5:1 final drive, adjustable Spax front shock absorbers and alloy body panels. Greenslade enthused over the car in May 1976:

'Those are minimal alterations for a championship winner; it shows how good the 4/4 is in the first place. Although Chris says that he did virtually no sorting at all, I'd rate the 4/4 as the best balanced production car of any type that I've driven on a racing circuit—in this case Brands Hatch on a damp muggy winter's morning. Hardly a day for records, yet the 4/4 proved to be very quick indeed.

'Unlike many production cars the brake balance front/rear was near ideal, allowing deep braking into the apex of the corner. As the tail slid gently out of line, a quick application of opposite lock and a simultaneous prod on the throttle were sufficient to send the car rocketing out of the corner in a stable, and most satisfying, manner. Despite the slippery conditions, Graham Hill Bend could be taken flat in top, and given a certain amount of bravery. I reckon that a similar

*Photographs right and below:* Chris Alford's series V prodsports 4/4 was tested by *Motor* in conjunction with John Britten's Plus Eight.

manoeuvre could have been used at Paddock; I just dabbed the brakes once lightly.

'I was impressed by the car's traction out of the corner (no limited slip differential, remember), by the normal slick Ford gearbox (though you need ape-length arms to reach first and third) and especially by the extremely torquey and smooth Minister engine. After 10 flying laps I was circulating in 64 secs (Chris's lap record is 63.6 secs), which is great testimony to the ease with which the car can be driven.'

But David Vivian of *Motor* was disappointed in his 4/4, registered EYV 12V, during a brief drive on the road reported in April 1981. He said:

'Old fashioned it may be, but much of the Morgan's appeal stems from the fact that it looks so right, so exquisitely proportioned. The image isn't everything, of course, but masculinity exudes from it even when you know there's only a 1600 Ford lump under the long, louvred bonnet . . .

'With hindsight, my decision to drive fast in the Morgan was a bad move. Wind in the hair I was expecting, but with its rag top folded and side windows removed the Morgan actually seemed to create a mini whirlwind inside the cabin. Above 50 mph my hair took on a life of its own, alternatively standing on end and covering my eyes . . . I decided to slacken the pace to a more sedate canter.

'Pace is something the 4/4 doesn't have a great deal of—just as well when the hood's down. In contrast to the tarmac-chewing accelerative abilities of the Plus Eight, the 4/4's performance is merely adequate. Its Ford engine is flexible and punchy, which makes the 4/4 feel usefully potent around town, but it is also harsh and breathless at high revs, and on the open road the promise of the Morgan's looks is unfulfilled.'

*Motor* then suggested that Morgans would be better with modern suspension and steering when they tested a 4/4 with the 'virtually extinct' worm and nut steering in September 1982. They compared this early carburettor XR3-engined car, registered JNP 70X, with Ford's donor saloon, commenting:

'The fact that the 2.5 cwt heavier XR3 is both faster and more accelerative is a measure of just how aerodynamically-inefficient the 4/4's shape is. Round the Motor Industry Research Association's banked circuit with the hood up, the Morgan achieved a top speed of 103 mph (XR3 111 mph) and the 0–60 mph time was 10 secs (XR3 8.7 secs). Accelerating in top gear, the Morgan's 30–50 and 50–70 mph times of 9.3 and 11.9 secs show it to have a wide torque spread and respectable mid-range punch, though this must be helped in no small measure by its unfashionably low gearing in top (17.9 mph/1,000 rpm). This combination means that it is seldom necessary to change down for most overtaking manoeuvres, which is no bad thing; Ford's 1.6-litre CVH engine revs well but rather harshly above about 5,500 rpm, though it never gets intolerably noisy and in normal driving it's really quite refined, its muted exhaust note seeming oddly out of character with the car's vintage appearance . . . The low overall gearing isn't mirrored by the intermediate ratios, however, as the first three gears allow maxima of 33, 61 and 88 mph at 6,700 rpm. Nor has it, or the poor aerodynamics, had an adverse effect on economy. Over the test period of over 900 miles, the Morgan returned a commendable overall fuel consumption of 29.3 mpg which is almost 1 mpg better than the XR3 in our hands, albeit a reflection of one's tendency to settle for lower cruising speeds than in more modern machinery.'

## The Plus Four Plus

*Cars and Car Conversions* managed to pull off a scoop when they tested Peter Morgan's prototype Plus Four Plus, registered 869 KAB, for a road test published in July 1966. This 1963 car was basically the same as the production models except that it had Perspex side windows which bowed at speed, contributing to wind noise, and a bench back to the two individual seats. Not only did it look considerably different from the normal Plus Four

The works Plus Four plus, tested by *Cars and Car Conversions*, made its debut at the 1963 London Motor Show.

on which it was based, but it felt different inside. *Cars and Car Conversions*—known as Triple C—reported:

'It looks a big car when one is sitting in it looking out, and there is much more room inside than in one of the open models; in fact 7$^{1}/_{2}$

inches more elbow room. This has been achieved by making use of every inch of the very deep doors, in which there is a very useful sized map pocket. Water did tend to seep down into this, however, resulting in sodden maps!

'Behind the seats there is a very useful space for stowing soft baggage or one suitcase. Though there are two footwells here, I cannot see anyone trying to use it as a two plus two! There is a very good glove pocket, much deeper than usual, so much so one can lose things in it . . .

'The side windows are nearly circular and wind down almost completely into the doors. It was found that a good level of ventilation could be obtained by a permutation of window opening and heater setting. The Smith's recirculatory heater was very efficient indeed. The windscreen seems huge with very slender pillars and the rear window is pleasantly wide, giving first-rate all-round visibility. The doors, too, are very wide, making for easy entrance and exit.

'Some of the initial critics were sure that the glassfibre body mounted on the well-known whippy Morgan chassis would result in the body breaking up very quickly. There was not a sign of a crack on the body . . . If the body has strengthened the chassis it certainly has not affected the superb roadholding.'

*Triple C* found that the superior aerodynamics of the coupé body lowered the fuel consumption to 28.5 mpg, with a top speed estimated at 110 mph, and 0–60 mph time of 13.2 seconds.


## The Plus Eight

Morgan launched the Plus Eight with an uncharacteristic flourish of publicity, Britain's three top weekly magazines simultaneously carrying tests of the company's demonstrator, bearing the registration number MMC 11, in September 1968. *Motor* emerged from this confrontation with the best report, pointing out that the Plus Eight offered tremendous performance— 0–100 mph in 19 secs with an estimated top speed of 125 mph—and handling that was quite good on smooth roads. At the other extreme, the ride was so bad on grade two surfaces that the roadholding suffered even more than the passengers; in addition, weather protection was primitive in an otherwise comfortable cockpit and the Moss gearbox was almost as vintage in its character as the styling. The testers pleaded for a more rigid chassis with extra suspension movement, but added:

'Of course, the Plus Eight would then cost a lot more than £1,500 and would lose most of its vintage individuality which many customers will interpret as charm. So the makers, probably rightly, have chosen to retain the old Morgan flavour with a new ingredient—performance— that at some times enhances the car and at others almost spoils it. For instance, long journeys on bumpy roads in heavy rain reveal the car at

*Photographs above, right and below:* The works Plus Eight, registered MMC 11, made a tremendous impression on the motoring Press in the late 1960s and was later used in prodsports racing by Charles Morgan.

its most Hyde-like —it rattles and bounces and skips and leaks. Yet on a fine day on good roads the car sheds its Hyde clothing and becomes an exhilarating Jekyll and you waft along with the hood down and the sidescreens up (paradoxically, this vintage car is at its best on a motorway). It is perhaps because it is so different from other present-day vehicles that some drivers thoroughly enjoyed the car while others could never quite come to terms with its inherent faults even though conceding that, in the right conditions, its rating as a fun car is very high indeed.'

So far as the contemporary trend for inserting over-sized engines in conventional chassis went, *Motor* said that the Rover installation was unusually good, the lightweight V8 delivering its power in such a smooth and subdued manner that really high speeds became deceptively effortless. The manual adaptation of the engine felt fractionally harsher between 500 rpm and 1,500 than its automatic equivalent, but this was of no importance. Rover advised limiting the revs to 5,000, but 6,000 could be used safely without pumping up the hydraulic tappets.

*Above left and right: Motor* said that the Rover engine installation in the Plus Eight was unusually good. The Girling servo can be seen behind the power unit.

The Plus Eight's acceleration figures were extraordinary, *Motor* reporting:

'It reaches 50 mph in 5.1 secs, 60 in 6.7, 70 in 8.7 and 80 and 12.1 secs, beyond which the drag increases steeply and the E type Jaguar, for example, which the Morgan can hold up to 70 mph, would pull ahead. Even so, there is only a handful of cars, all more expensive, which can reach 100 mph in under 12 secs.'

They noted that, although the makers recommended [the now-unobtainable] 101-octane petrol for this early high-compression engine, it seemed happy on 98 and gave 20.3 mpg, giving a range of around 250 miles.

So far as the transmission was concerned, the ball-and-spring synchromesh system used in the Moss gearbox proved very easy to override. *Motor* said:

'The upper three ratios are very close, so you don't have to wait long to get a smooth snick-free change; but between the unsynchronised first and second, where the gap is greater, waiting too long will let the engine slow down too much and too short a wait will cause a crunch as the gearbox internals haven't slowed enough. It really helps to double declutch upwards on this change; downwards you have to do it anyway on all the changes, though the pedals are so comfortably spaced for heel and toeing that it is an easy task.'

The clutch was one of the heaviest their testers had used, but could be operated comfortably because of the angle of its pedal.

So far as handling was concerned, the whippy chassis gave some scuttle shake with bumpy roads leading to axle hop, although the re-angled rear springs and limited-slip differential prevented tramp. *Motor* said: 'On our standing start tests, the car just rocketed away with about five yards of wheelspin.' Then they added:

'Wider tyres, now 185-15 Dunlop SP Sport, with high self-aligning torque, make the steering heavier than that of earlier models and we found it rather sticky on tighter corners. It frees up at higher speeds though . . . the lock, however, is poor with a 38 ft turning circle. On dry roads understeer is the predominent characteristic if you are trying hard, even when you ease the throttle. On tighter corners, a burst of power can snap the tail round progressively so a skilled driver can steer as much with the throttle as with the wheel. On wet roads, the throttle has to be treated with a lot of respect as the tail can leap out quite sharply, but the tyres grip very well and they come back into line as soon as the throttle is eased. The limited-slip differential lets you put down a surprising amount of power quite early in a corner, without breaking adhesion.

'If you press the car really hard on a track with the standard road tyre pressures of 22 psi, the limit is accompanied by some undamped lurching, as if the chassis were bending under the stressed or cornering power; raising the pressures to 28 psi controlled the lurching and also lightened the steering usefully.'

The brakes were adjudged first class with their bigger Girling calipers and servo, although hard use from high speed could set up a low frequency pitching. As ever, the handbrake, on the left-hand side of the transmission tunnel, was found to be very inconvenient. The ride was as hard as ever, the sidescreens still rattled and the hood still took a long time to erect, *Motor* observing that you had to keep its plastic windows clean as they were harder to see through than glass. They approved of the new bucket seats, however, finding them quite comfortable and supportive.

*Autocar* extracted 124 mph, with a 15.1 secs standing quarter mile, the same 6.7 secs for the 0–60, and 21 mpg from MMC 11, with their best starts done by letting in the clutch with a bang at nearly 4,000 rpm, before commenting:

'In a lazy mood, the car's wonderful flexibility tempts one to think that the stubby little lever on the transmission tunnel is the range selector for an automatic. First gear takes you up to 43 mph, which sends you way out in front of any "drag," second, with a maximum of 72 mph, copes with all awkward traffic situations, though the 105 mph third picks up nearly as well. Top you can use almost exclusively if feeling very lazy indeed. It will take you most effectively from below 10 mph . . . the maximum speed of 124 mph mean was seen with the hood up. With the hood down, this dropped to 118 mph because of the extra drag . . . Maximum speed runs on a bumpy Belgian autoroute were far more exciting at 124 mph in the Morgan than they have been in more modern grand touring cars at over 150. And yet one of the puzzling things about this is that it does not make the Plus Eight anywhere near difficult or dangerous on bumpy roads.'

In general, otherwise, *Autocar* and *Motor's* findings agreed, before *Autocar* concluded: 'There's a lot which could be better, but there's an awful lot right.'

As ever, John Bolster achieved slightly better performance figures for *Autosport,* taking MMC 11 up to 128 mph, with a 6.6-second 0–60 mph time and 14.8 secs for the standing quarter mile, before adding:

> 'It is only the axle ratio of 3.53:1 which limits the speed, and though the car can just about attain 130 mph, the engine is then revving past its peak. If one lived on the Continent, a higher gear might be pulled with advantage and would probably put the maximum up to 135 mph or so.'

*Motor Sport* returned average performance figures when they tested Peter Morgan's Plus Eight, registered AB 16, for their issue in December 1968, and then commented prophetically: 'It is fascinating to think how the Morgan Plus Eight will go when fuel injection or other performance-enhancers are tried.'

Editor Bill Boddy then observed that the very long bonnet—approximately 6 ft 10 ins from his eyes to the front, and 4 ft 2 ins long in itself—masked the road on upward gradients, adding: 'There is the sensation, also associated with long-snouted pre-war cars, of sitting well back and having to steer the bonnet round bends.'

He liked the new seats, but added:

> 'The squabs do not fold, which makes loading and unloading luggage into the carpeted well behind them difficult, hood up—but who wants the hood up, on a Plus Eight? If it is put up, perhaps as a sop to some woman, snags arise . . .'

Apart from his lack of sympathy with the contemporary movement towards women's liberation, his snags included the fact that the hood could jamb the doors shut when the sidescreens were erect. He surmised that this could lead to the occupants being trapped inside the car in an accident. And so far as the new recessed rocker safety switches were concerned, he considered them 'nasty, American-inspired substitutes for flick switches.'

His contemporary, Mike Cotton, reporting on the same car for *Motor Sport's* weekly equivalent, *Motoring News,* had no such trouble with the Plus Eight in October the following year—other than when he erected the hood without its sealing strips in the correct position and got soaked. He winced: 'I pressed on, trousers rolled up to my knees, and cursing freely . . .' He then took a 1,300-mile round trip through Ireland before returning to his Lotus Elan staff car with the comment:

'To return to the modern-day world of creature comfort, I couldn't help thinking we have lost something of the pleasure of motoring along the way.'

*Triple C's* editorial director, Martyn Watkins, tested the long-suffering MMC 11 for their issue in June 1969, commenting:

'Obviously the car is quite quick, it is equally obviously ruddy uncomfortable and as every dent and ripple in the road surface impresses itself on your imagination and the more sensitive parts of your person, you feel that those blow-up seat cushions they used before the war had some point to them. And there's the gearbox. The Moss box was the one which, among other people, Jaguars used to use until they got wise . . . Changing gear is a bit like sloping arms—you do it to a count of "one-two-three". Fortunately, traffic motoring doesn't mean a lot of cog-swopping because the engine is so flexible . . . This is fortunate because it leaves you with both hands free to wrench the steering wheel round . . .

'It's one of those cars which is more controllable at high speed than otherwise: on poor surfaces, 50 mph seems a reasonable gait, but the car marches about all over the road. Go up to, say, 80, and the thing runs as straight as an arrow, and you can enjoy watching the wings flapping up and down, the scuttle shaking rhythmically from side to side, and listen to the creaks and groans from the wood-framed body. On good surfaces you can drive it as hard as you feel brave enough to do . . . but take our word for it, at over the ton you feel as though no one has ever been so fast before.'

*small car* had, meantime, shaken off the ties of covering nothing over 1,500-cc, and emerged as *CAR magazine* to test the Plus Eight registered XAB 998G, owned by Jim Goodall. Editor Doug Blain recounted in September 1970:

'There was a point at which the sleepy little Malvern Link firm of Morgan seemed suddenly to wake up and belatedly try to launch itself into the second half of the 20th century. The reaction of the world at large to the result, a glassfibre-bodied nightmare called the Plus Four Plus, quickly persuaded it to go to sleep again and since then it hasn't looked back.

'The company's present prestige product, the Plus Eight, fits the old image but boasts 1970s performance . . . the new car is an undeniably handsome, rugged looking piece of architecture with a charm that is very different from that of a conscious replica such as the Excalibur SS. It sits four square on its fat tyres, compact, hunched for action and completely lacking in frills. Even a cursory examination shows that it is not a luxurious or even a particularly well-made car, but there is an air of unpretentious honesty about its finish and detail

*Above and left:* Doug Blain found the Plus Eight undeniably handsome.

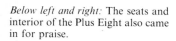

*Below left and right:* The seats and interior of the Plus Eight also came in for praise.

fittings—some of which, such as the spring-loaded bonnet catches and the mounts for the windscreen and side curtains, are period pieces in themselves—that bypasses nostalgia and invites admiration for the way in which its makers have resisted change for its own sake. Obviously the Morgan is an aerodynamicist's nightmare just as it is a chassis engineer's despair, but its appearance suggests good reasons why it should be so and it is in all viable respects a practical car which encourages care and engenders stronger pride of ownership, a more positive urge to keep its fittings polished and tyres pumped up and to juggle hood and tonneau cover in accordance with the weather's vagaries, than any more shapely competitor we can think of . . .

'The business of keeping the car on the road is, predictably, a full-time job. Even on smooth roads (and there are not many of them, as vintagists will know) the Morgan gives a lively ride, its primitive chassis flexing in response to changes of alignment, its heavy and rather imprecise steering juddering and bucking on contact with verges, mended patches, manhole covers and all those other minor impedia that modern, insulated, suspensions have taught us to ignore. Such nostalgic behaviour can be said to add to the fun of driving the car provided it does not become obtrusive. The trouble is that, as soon as one leaves the main roads and takes to the back doubles, the big Morgan becomes positively unpleasant to drive quickly. Its wheels feel as though they are as often in the air as on the road, the ludicrously limited suspension travel means that the bottom bump (ie rebound) stops are in use as often as the top ones, the whole front end bucks continuously at low frequency as in a pre-war beam axle design, the rear end hops bodily as soon as one applies power in a corner and the reaction to humpback bridges and the like is so violent that one feels inclined to wear protective headgear purely as a defence against the relentless head sticks.

'The answer? To go more slowly, of course . . . on minor roads, Bugattistes and Bentley boys travel at a gentlemanly pace. So does the owner of a Morgan V8. His passenger may still complain of a queasy tummy, but he will find himself enjoying the car's responsiveness rather than fighting it all the way and in the end, still good friends, they will reach their destination in very little more time than it would have taken otherwise thanks to the car's spanking acceleration, unobtrusive progress through towns and other restricted areas, and ability to get a move on in the good bits . . . The whole point of a Morgan is that one cannot judge it by modern standards.'

For the record, Blain did drive the Plus Eight as fast as anybody else, recording 126 mph flat out, with a 6.7-second 0-60 time and 19.8 mpg—but he came far closer than any other road tester at the time to describing what Morgan motoring is all about.

Eoin Young opined in *Road & Track* in December 1968—just as a new generation was starting to take interest in vintage sports cars—that MMC 11 must be the newest old car in the world. He added:

'Walking around the factory with the lanky tweed-suited head of the family business, you pass through a joinery shop where all the body frames are made. Fair takes you back, it does. You get the personal pride-in-the-work feeling about the people who make Morgans. If you bought one you wouldn't be just a customer—you'd almost be a friend of the family. They don't want customers who are liable to make a fuss if their car is late or the ride is even more Spartan than they expected. It seems to be an honour just to have your name on the waiting list . . . The Plus Eight is $3,500 worth of rapid instant vintagery, ruddy cheeks and tangled hair. So who needs an Excalibur?'

And Philip Llewellin managed 126 mph and a 6.6-second 0-60 mph time with MMC 11, reporting in the same month for *Road & Track's* rival American monthly magazine, *Sports Car Graphic,* that although the former Buick-Oldsmobile-Pontiac engine met Federal emission standards with its General Motors automatic gearbox, it did not qualify with the Moss manual box.

*Motor* had the first opportunity to comment on a five-speed Morgan Plus Eight in April 1977, after testing a car registered VUY 195R fitted with a 3.31:1 rear axle ratio. Their performance testing was handicapped by a stretched alternator belt that kept flying off, but they managed to obtain 40 mph, 63 and 94 mph in the lower three gears, with a 7.2-second 0-60 mph time. Of the taper roller bearing gearbox, which had relatively high lower ratios, they said:

'In the upper three ratios the lever moves freely and easily, but into first and second it baulked, especially when cold, just as it did in a five-speed Triumph TR7. So our original enthusiasm for this box—so good in the first Rover 3500 we tried—is on the wane.

'In other respects the Morgan is much as before. We like the new instruments and the fingertip stalks, and being able to regulate the heater's temperature from inside the car is an obvious advantage.'

*Autocar* had better fortune with their five-speed Plus Eight, Peter Morgan's personal car, registered YNP 197R, which was fitted with the earlier, but now obsolete, 3.58:1 final drive, as used in 1968. They explained in July 1978:

'Partly because of the extra size and partly because of a succession of small changes, the test car, a standard steel-bodied one (all Morgans have aluminium rear side and back panels), is surprisingly heavier at 19 cwt; this is 1.3 cwt more—an increase of 7.5 per cent. Has this affected the performance?

*Motor* linked the new instruments and fingertip stalks of the 1977 Plus Eight.

'The answer seems to be "Not much". Indeed, remembering that when testing the 1968 car we were blessed with near-ideal conditions—0-5 mph wind—where this time it was 10-22 mph's worth, there seems to be little in it. Looking baldly at the standing start figures (1968 ones in brackets), 30 mph is reached in 2.2 secs (2.3), 50 in 4.6 (5.2), 60 in 6.5 (6.7), 80 in 11.4 (11.8), the quarter mile in an identical 15.1, 100 in 20.2 (18.4) and 110 in 31 (25.7). The wind is seen taking its toll from the quarter mile onwards; the new car did 90 mph there where the old one was 2 mph faster, with proportionate increase beyond. Interestingly, the old car shows up as consistently faster when you compare its top gear acceleration with the new car's near-similarly geared fourth: 10-30 mph in 6.4 (5.8), 50-70 in 5.2 (4.5) and 90-110 in 12.6 (10.9)'

In contrast to *Motor, Autocar* found that the new gearchange was an improvement to use, having 'a light, precise, short-of-excess movement.' Overall fuel consumption was better than before at 20.5 mph against 18.3 But, like *Motor, Autocar* did not comment on the widened body and trunk.

Mel Nichols, editor of *CAR* magazine, then compared the same Plus Eight with its nearest competitor, the Vauxhall Magnum-based Panther Lima, in September 1978. He wrote of the Morgan:

'In bends on a smooth road it is wonderful, but bumps and awkward crests upset the car too much, diluting its performance potential annoyingly. Its awkward doors, its hot footwells, its poor roof-up vision and even its lack of clutch foot space I could live with; but its ride is just too trying and, worse, its steering just too vague at the

*CAR* felt that its Plus Eight had enormous potential.

straight ahead and too heavy when lock is applied. The trade-off for the fun the Morgan offers—and yes, its go—is just too much hard work. Wonderful, charming Peter Morgan says he bases much of his assessment of the Morgan on the race track, where it is undoubtedly very successful. But race tracks have few bumps, and even motorways do. He knows the limitations of his antiquated front suspension and admits that the rear end would be improved if he used better quality springs ("They're cheap because in the past we were building very cheap sports cars," he says). He doesn't want to change the front end because he'd then have to re-engineer the rear to match as, he says, the two work well together. And on the track—or smooth roads—they might. But I think Mr Morgan is being unfair to himself, to his car and to his customers. The thing that is abundantly clear about the Plus Eight is that it has enormous potential to provide great driving pleasure; but its unique styling, its charmingly idiosyncratic construction, its terrific powerplant, transmission and performance are let down appallingly by the suspension and steering. A decent rack and pinion steering system alone would be a great help—and surely the cost is within Morgan's reach? I don't believe that the mass of Morgan buyers expect what they get, nor can I believe that most of them like it. Give them decent steering and suspension, Mr Morgan, and make the Plus Eight truly wonderful.'

*Motor* found that the Plus Eight's performance was virtually the same when they tested a Pirelli P6-shod car, registered **BUY 600M**, in May 1982—but said of the new 15-inch wheels and 60-section tyres:

The Pirelli P6 tyres used on *Motor's* road test Plus Eight.

'To put modern generation tyres at the business end of such an antiquated and unsophisticated system (the front suspension) might seem a bad idea. But according to Peter Morgan, the suspension is ideally suited to the low profile P6s since, even when subjected to high cornering loads, it keeps the wheels perpendicular to the road, which is as it should be if the square-shouldered Pirellis are going to grip to maximum effect.

'This would certainly seem to be the case on smooth sweeping bends. Here the Morgan can generate quite extraordinary cornering forces and feel superbly stable. On more typical roads, however, the Plus Eight remains something of a brute, though not an unlikeable one . . .

'One problem is the car's initial understeer, which gives the effect of reluctance to turn into a bend, especially if the approach is bumpy. Once committed to a line, however, the understeer can be effectively neutralised by feeding in the power while, on tighter bends, the same ploy can be used to kick the tail out—though if the bend is a particularly bumpy one it doesn't need much prompting . . .

'Over big bumps and humps the ride is diabolical and the Morgan can actually take off, but the small bump ride is contrastingly quite good, which may be a side benefit of the P6's low inflation pressures . . .

'Old fashioned it may be, but the Morgan Plus Eight must rank as one of the world's great cars. Elegant yet electrifying, it marries such disparate elements like no other car. Peter Morgan has been careful to preserve that and we think he's right. When the world is full of standardised shoe boxes, it's cars like the Plus Eight we'll miss most.'

Philip Young, editor of the British monthly magazine *Sporting Cars,* had the first test drive in a Vitesse-engine Plus Eight in October 1983. This was the prototype bearing the company registration plate MMC 11 and fitted with rack-and-pinion steering and the 3.58:1 rear axle ratio for maximum performance. Young admitted to having only a hand-held stop-watch—rather than the normal sophisticated electronic timing gear—but reported a stunning 0-60 mph time of 5.3 secs to put the Plus Eight firmly in the supercar class, before commenting:

'We might be out by a few tenths, what the hell, this is an amazing, sensational, Morgan. The take-off is blistering . . . Let it rip, and the Morgan truly blows your mind. You can get a pain in the back of the neck from constantly powering away in second gear.'

*CAR* magazine were the next to test the new MMC 11, in August 1984, commenting:

'As you ease the car out of the factory and into Malvern's surprisingly busy traffic, it isn't the engine that dominates your first impressions, but the steering. This has become a Morgan you can manoeuvre; rack-and-pinion steering has made low speed steering much less of a physical exertion than it used to be in the old cam-and-peg versions. But the prototype shows it's still a demanding car in traffic, especially on the steep Malvern slopes. The clutch is sharp in its take-up and heavy in action, the unassisted brakes always need a firm pressure and a stumpy gear lever makes shifting quicker even if its reduced leverage also highlights the inherent stiffness of the Rover box. "Use two hands to select reverse," was official Morgan advice before we left . . .

'As we leave the Malverns and head for the Welsh border, there's a chance to investigate the performance. It is a process which needs conscious effort; the V8 is a smooth, effortless, engine which almost discourages you from pressing it hard. In the comparatively light Morgan (against a Rover Vitesse) the V8 offers you a surge of acceleration, a change of exhaust note from off-beat throb to mellow rumble at a crack of throttle. Ask it for more: squeeze the long travel, heavy throttle further down and it will give you more. There is a point when many reasonable men cry enough and slot into a higher gear. Yet if you persist: hold the gear and press the pedal flat, the exhaust becomes a howl, your eyes water, your lungs freeze with forced air, and your momentum across a fast-changing road-scape becomes startling. At that point sanity prevails and you ease back, change up a gear—then realise that you still haven't put together a truly flat-out burst of acceleration; all the way through the gears, peak revs in each.

'It's not the speed in itself that brings out your instincts of self-preservation, though a hood-up maximum of over 130 mph is far from cosy. No, it's the sheer brutality of the acceleration which sends you hurling towards threatening bends and crests with massive built-up energy. Savour the full-out performance when you can; it won't be often.'

   *Motor* at last managed to provide a comprehensive set of performance figures on a standard Plus Eight injection—registered C636 SWP—in April 1986, returning an average top speed, hood up, of 122 mph with a best one-way run of 127. The acceleration times were equally impressive, gradually improving on the 1977 road test car (fitted with the same 3.31 rear axle ratio) as they progressed up the scale: 0-30 mph 2.2 secs, 40 3.5, 50 4.5, 60 5.9, 70 7.9, 80 9.9, 90 12.7, 100 16.6, 110 22.1 with an overall 25.8 mpg reflecting the high ratio final drive and more efficient fuel injection. Editor Howard Walker enthused over the engine, and grip of the Pirelli P6 tyres, but commented on the rack-and-pinion:

   'Less impressive is the steering . . . While it's now much lighter at parking speeds, there's little in the way of feel at speed and the small degree of castor angle means that the wheel has to be almost wound

Side by side with older Morgans, the latest Plus Eight injection on the right.

back from lock. But at least it's got rid of the couple of inches of free play in the system that was always tolerated as part of the Morgan's character . . .'

And of the rear suspension he pointed out:

'Over bumpy lanes, the latest Plus Eight seemed to cope far better at retaining its composure than did the last Mog we sampled. While no suspension modifications have been made, Peter Morgan did explain that spring suppliers were now tempering the rear leaves to a more consistent standard than before. The new car certainly pitched far less and was thrown off line less often than the previous car.'

## Modified Plus Eights

The combination of the relatively understressed Rover V8 engine and the lightweight Morgan chassis soon made the Plus Eight an attractive car in club competitions, with Chris Lawrence continuing his association with the marque by running Brian Haslam's example during the model's early years. When *Motor* tested the Haslam Plus Eight at Silverstone in July 1971 its solid lifter engine had been bored out to 4 litres and fitted with transistorized ignition, four downdraught Weber carburettors and a special exhaust system although the standard camshaft was retained. In this form, 176 bhp was claimed at the rear wheels.

It also had wider-than-standard wheels fitted with Firestone racing tyres which, despite the hard rubber components prevalent at the time, made the

*Above and left:* Brian Haslam's Plus Eight was developed by LawrenceTune from its 1971 form to run with a spoiler and Robin Grey at the wheel by 1976.

sliding pillar front suspension flex. Lawrence countered this problem by stiffening the pillars with steel centres and stronger mountings, resetting the geometry to give 1 degree negative camber at the same time. A rack and pinion was also substituted for the normal steering box. *Motor's* resident track tester, Michael Bowler, who lapped the grand prix circuit in 1 min 55.5 secs, reported:

'The steering was incredibly light and showed none of the tendency of the standard car to get stiff and bound up under hard cornering . . . the big V8 barked out a healthy growl and really accelerated the car very quickly up to 120 mph or so on the straight to Stowe: 6,000 rpm seemed the useful limit although it will safely go further. The brakes pulled the car down well and on the smooth corners you could brake quite deep before powering through with a trace of oversteer. On the Maggots and Abbey bumps it lurched sideways and dug into the track in a series of sidesteps, but it never felt unstable.'

Another member of *Motor's* test staff, Gordon Bruce, then tried a Plus Eight, registered 4 KYD, owned by tuning shop proprietor and club racer Adam Bridgland, in December 1972. The modifications were confined almost entirely to the engine, which had a Sig Erson camshaft kit with special hydraulic tappets and double valve springs which allowed it to be extended to 7,000 rpm. A four-barrel Holley carburettor, Offenhauser inlet manifold, Janspeed exhaust and Mallory transistorized ignition completed the engine changes, with a Bendix high-pressure fuel pump. Koni adjustable telescopic dampers were fitted to the rear axle and Avon radial ply tyres all round on the standard wheels.

Bruce was disappointed in not being allowed to try full bore starts—in the interests of the final drive's life—but still managed similar acceleration times to a standard car up to 60 mph, after which the Bridgland Plus Eight forged ahead, taking 1.3 secs off the 0–100 mph time towards an estimated top speed of 140 mph. Fuel consumption was down to 14 mpg, however. Of the handling, Bruce commented:

'The conditions could hardly have been worse when we picked up the car . . . and we treated the right pedal with great respect. Later we discovered that the tail was very reluctant to break. Eventually when it did it was in a gentle, controllable, way that was nothing but fun and certainly no cause for alarm. In the dry—at least on smooth roads—it was superb.'

*Motor* then combined their test of the Chris Alford 4/4 in May 1976 with sessions in Plus Eights raced by John Britten and John Atkins. The Britten Plus Eight production sports car racing machine was an early narrow-track car converted to the wider track specification, while retaining the original 3.58:1 final drive ratio. The blueprinted engine, prepared by Racing Services, used Mallory ignition and suspension modifications were confined to Koni dampers at the front and adjustable Armstrongs at the back, with the Pirelli CN36 radial-ply tyres popular on Porsches at the time. Rex Greenslade who returned 61.5 secs for the Brands Hatch club circuit—only 2.5 secs quicker than the 4/4—found the Plus Eight, which normally raced on Michelin XWX tyres, a handful:

'Rush into a corner a mite too quickly and it understeers . . . and understeers . . . and understeers. A little bit more throttle accentuates this attitude until, when your arms have twisted themselves into a knot and you're least expecting it, the limited slip locks up with a jerk, the car

surges forward with a great belt up the back and you're piling on the
opposite lock like there's no tomorrow. And with the amount of lock
you've already applied in the other direction to counteract the
understeer it's no mean feat to get that opposite lock on cleanly and
accurately.

'I soon learned that the best method was to negotiate most of each
corner on a trailing throttle and only squirt when the corner opened up.
Hardly the most sophisticated technique though the car can still be
hustled round at very respectable rates.'

Understeer was not a problem with the Atkins' Plus Eight, registered JA
11, which had wide Woolfrace alloy wheels, Dunlop SP Sport tyres,
decambered front suspension and Koni rear shock absorbers. It was also
much modified mechanically, with a five-speed gearbox from an Alfa Romeo
2600, Holley carburettor and inlet manifold, Janspeed exhaust, Richardson
camshaft and Ryder cylinder heads. Greenslade commented:

'How does it drive? Superbly . . . the Atkins Plus Eight hangs on
much better than any I've tried before and in almost any situation the
amount of available power exceeds grip by such a large amount that the
car can be steered with the throttle . . . When it's warm, the Alfa gearbox
gives a slick precise change, and perhaps even more importantly endows
the car with a fifth gear ratio that makes 90 mph cruising quite relaxed.'

In March 1979, Michael Bowler, then editor of *Thoroughbred and
Classic Cars,* was able to renew his acquaintanceship with MMC 11, or at
least a Plus Eight bearing the same registration number as the demonstrator
he had tested for *Motor* in 1968. The chassis had been changed following an

MMC 11 as tested by Michael Bowler.

accident and, after a career in classic trials, it had been modified for production sports car racing in which Charles Morgan took it to third overall in the 1978 championship. In this form, the original Moss-type gearbox and 3.58:1 rear axle was preferred to the later Rover five-speed because the ratios were more suitable for competition, and the engine had been blueprinted to give another 35 bhp—a total of 150 bhp at the rear wheels. The suspension had been lowered to give a 4 in ride height and Minilite magnesium wheels had been fitted with Michelin XWX 195/70-14 tyres. Bowler reported:

'I drove the car first in its prodsports form with the full-width screen and a hood—hood down adds a second to lap times. The club Silverstone track was a bit greasy, but the tyres hung on extremely well; you couldn't feel a lot through the steering at this stage. You realised that you were understeering in mid-corner and applied power; the resultant fairly sudden change to oversteer required some practise to catch cleanly, but it was quite possible and there was no lurch as it returned to an even keel . . . as the track dried out the steering began to provide more feel with the higher grip and you could flick it into the corner knowing exactly what was happening at the front end . . .

'Later the Plus Eight was converted to modsports form, which meant substituting an aero screen and changing the road tyres to Dunlop low-profile slicks, still on 6 in rims. The effect of this is quite dramatic and particularly so bearing in mind that the suspension is standard Morgan apart from firmer damping . . . the steering was now transmitting good feel of initial understeer and you could put down the power a lot earlier with a much more gradual transition to oversteer, it was much more controllable.'

Bowler, who had lapped at 1 min 9 secs in the damp in prodsports form (against Morgan's 1 min 7 secs best) quickly recorded 1 min 4.2 secs on the Dunlop 195/600-14 slicks and estimated that they were worth 3.5 secs to the normal driver.

*Road & Track* then managed to test one of the turbocharged propane-powered Plus Eights built by Bill Fink of Isis Imports in August 1980. This example was also fitted with optional aluminium bodywork and decambered front suspension, for ultimate performance, which, in effect, made up for what the Americans would have lost over a European model. Nevertheless, the occupants had the benefit of a 170 mph speedometer and 7,000 rpm rev counter. The American testers found the turbocharged Plus Eight to be capable of 128 mph flat out and said: 'At this speed the car will redline fourth fairly easily, and things get very busy indeed . . .'

Acceleration was substantially the same as European Plus Eights, the turbocharged car returning 6.8 secs for the 0–60 with a 15.1-second standing quarter mile.

Publisher Terry Grimwood then took the opportunity to test a Morgan Plus Eight, registered 1 MOG, driven by Grahame Bryant in the Road-Going Sports Car Championship sponsored by his magazine, *Sporting Cars International*, which had taken over from *Sporting Cars*. This 1977 car had a claimed 330 bhp from a 3.9-litre JE Motors Rover V8 engine running

Grahame Bryant's MOG 1 at speed . . .

on four 48-mm Dellorto carburettors with big valve cylinder heads, a Crane 248 camshaft and Janspeed exhaust. The clutch from a Triumph TR7 V8 rally car harnessed the power to a five-speed gearbox with straight-cut gears. The suspension was essentially as standard with the substitution of Koni shock absorbers and addition of a Panhard rod to help locate the rear axle, which had a 3.7:1 final drive ratio. At the front, negative camber was used with 10.75-inch ventilated disc brakes and four-pot calipers. Revolution wheels of 15-inch diameter with 7-inch rims were used at the front with 8 x 15-inch wheels at the back in the wet and 9 x 15 ins in the dry. B F Goodrich Comp T/A tyres were fitted all round, of 205/50 section at the front and 225 section at the back.

Grimwood, a former prodsports champion, reported after a fast session at the Goodwood track:

> 'The car's behaviour at high speed is quite disturbing until old memories of driving prodsports Morgans return, and the white-knuckled grip on the steering is relaxed to allow the car to assume its own unique form of directional stability—wandering vaguely from side to side like a great animal following an elusive scent. This seems to be the secret of driving the Morgan at least safely if not that quickly; to work with it, not against it; to give it its head and hope to God it knows what it's doing. Try to wrestle with the car and it could turn savage, although the occasional discreet prod at the accelerator in corners can be used to suggest that understeer has now reached unacceptable proportions and could we now get the tail out a bit, please.'

This Plus Eight then obliged by winning the *SCI* Road-going championship in 1986 before Jeremy Walton drove it with a variety of other road-going cars on the Silverstone grand prix circuit for *Autocar* in January 1987. By then it had a claimed 340 bhp which gave it an indicated 135 mph with timed runs of 4.9 secs for the 0–60 and an 11.5-second 0–100.

Paul Chudecki then tried the same car in February 1987, for *Sporting Cars International*. After a fast drive on wet roads, he reported:

> 'Quick bursts up to 110 mpg between bends demonstrate the car's enormous acceleration and considerable flexibility in any gear, such is the mallet-like torque, almost 300 lb/ft, and Grahame talks of recently-recorded figures of 0–60 in 4.8 secs and 0–100 in 11.2. Quite believable, but figures that neither Grahame's Porsche Carrera RS or 512BB Ferrari can cope with . . .'

# VII

# The Four-Wheeled Morgan in Competition

Morgan sales had always been inspired by competition successes, so it was only logical that H.F.S. Morgan should launch his new four-wheeler, as soon as the prototype was ready, in the London-to-Exeter Trial. These events, which are called classic trials today, had a far higher profile before the war. There was little circuit racing in Britain at the time, so such trials attracted an enormous following as the forerunners of modern special stage rallying. Major manufacturers, like Austin, Morgan and Singer, entered works teams in these events, which comprised long road sections linking observed sections. Road racing was illegal on the British mainland, so the road sections had to be covered at only a modest average speed that did not not upset the law. As a result, the observed sections, off the road, were fearsome, to ensure that only a few competitors won an award. Deep mud was one of the favourite obstacles, combatted by the use of 'knobbly'-ridged tyres, which wore out quickly on normal surfaces but were capable of hauling cars through the most amazing quagmires. As a result it became popular to carry two spare wheels, equipped with knobbly tyres, to replace the normal rubber on the rear axle during a trial. The additional weight of an extra spare wheel also helped traction, and as a specialist sports car, the 4-4 Morgan was fitted with twin spares. Great pains were taken also to make the underside as flat as possible to avoid projecting parts being damaged on rough tracks. Nevertheless, the 4-4 had a relatively low ride height to give it good handling on the road, and H.F.S. did well to gain a premier award with the Ford-engined prototype model in the Exeter, held late in December 1935, followed by a similar success in the next major trial, the Land's End at Easter 1936.

By the following month, three cars had been completed, which were entered by the works in the Edinburgh trial, a premier award going to service manager Harry Jones, with a Climax-engined example, before privateer E.G. Boutle took a first-class award with a similar car in the Junior Car Club's evening trial at Guildford, Surrey, in June.

When more cars were available in 1937, the Morgan success rate increased. Five 4-4s took premier awards in the Land's End Trial before three

## The Four-Wheeled Morgan in Competition

cars were entered in group one of the RAC Rally. Road rallies of this nature were far more laid back than they are today, and certainly less stressful than event such as the Land's End. The RAC was made up of very long road runs converging on a seaside resort for some gentle tests to sort out the winners. Typically, such tests involved driving as slowly as possible over a set course on the promenade, followed by as quickly as possible for, perhaps, 100 yards, then braking hard into a box marked on the road. The 1937 event, with its finish at Hastings, was made far tougher than normal, however, by heavy snow, sleet, ice, torrential rain, and dense fog, so works manager George Goodall did well to fend off opposition from MGs and HRGs, to win his class with a 4-4. Team members E.D. Bownan and H.F.S. Morgan took eighth and tenth places. Peter Morgan then made his competition debut in the Edinburgh Trial, taking a silver award. It is worth remembering, however, that the overall atmosphere of such events remained delightfully informal, no matter how important the outcome to small works teams such as that from Morgan.

Although road racing was banned on the British mainland, it was possible to close the roads on the Isle of Man and in Northern Ireland for established events, with the result that Morgan's first circuit success came in the 1937 Ulster Trophy race. Purpose-built competition cars, such as Maseratis and Bugattis, were very rare and expensive, so these road races were run on a handicap basis to encourage as many entries as possible. Belfast garage mechanic Robert Campbell was one of the slowest entrants in

Morgan's success rate in the Land's End Trial increased as soon as the 4-4 was in full production in 1937, with L.H. Coney's car pictured here at Bluehills Mine on the way to a premier award, followed by C.H. Richardson's M.G.

H.F.S. Morgan halts before tackling the non-stop section at Costerton in the 1937 London-to-Edinburgh Trial with the proto-type 4-4 drop-head coupé, which was fitted with special rear bodywork cut away to accommodate twin spare wheels. As a revered elder statesman among trials enthusiasts, H.F.S. had been appointed a travelling marshal to deter over-enthusiastic drivers from bringing the sport into ill-repute.

a 4-4s, so he enjoyed an eight-lap advantage over the scratch cars. The circuit based on Ards was through tortuous lanes, however, and several potential winners were eliminated by accidents, leaving Campbell to lead the nine survivors at an average of 53.73 mph for the two-hour race. Soon after, two more 4-4s arrived in Northern Ireland to make up a team in the Leinster Trophy race. A Riley led most of the way before crashing, letting through D.C. McCracken's 4-4 to win from team-mate F.D. Smythe, with Campbell fifth following engine trouble.

Until 1934, apart from a round-the-houses circuit at Douglas, Isle of Man, the only British motor racing venue was Brooklands, a massive concrete track built in 1906 'for the good of the nation' by Hugh Locke King on his estate at Weybridge, Surrey. But, then, private estate roads at Donington Park, near Derby, were adapted to form a very narrow and twisting course, and Britain's oldest road race—the Tourist Trophy—was transferred to it from Northern Ireland. Former Morgan three-wheeler star Henry Laird was entered in 1937 by the works in their 1,098-cc lightweight prototype, running well up the field in the 1,100-cc class until he was sidelined by a broken stub axle.

This highly-successful season was then wrapped up by no less than 12 4-4s taking nine awards in the London-to-Exeter trial. Much the same story continued in trialling the following year, with George Goodall repeating his success in the RAC Rally, but the undoubted highlight was provided in June by 25-year-old Prudence M. Fawcett, who decided to make her competition debut in the world's most famous, and daunting, race, the Le Mans 24-hour, using a 4-4! Morgan prepared a 1,098-cc lightweight along the lines of the TT car for Miss Fawcett to drive with a Mr G. White. The Fawcett Morgan duly lined up with Simcas, MGs and Singers in the 1,100-cc class—and despite the daunting spectacle of Delahayes, Talbots and Alfa Romeos overtaking at nearly double their speed along the Mulsanne straight—managed to stay out of everybody else's way long enough to finish 13th out of 15 finishers. They averaged a creditable 57.2 mph against the winning Delahaye's 82.36. Sadly nothing more was heard in motoring circles of Miss Fawcett after that . . .

But another lightweight, 1,098-cc 4-4 was outstandingly successful the following month in the three-wheelers' old stamping ground at Brooklands. The Light Car Club had decided to replace their classic relay race, which had been poorly supported in recent years, with a three-hour sports car event over the Campbell Circuit. The regulations stated that the cars had to be in standard trim and run fully equipped—but there was some room for manoeuvre, as Allard showed when their V12-cylinder car, which had four more cylinders than normal, was accepted because, as a prototype, it was not expected to finish! Other formidable entries included a Le Mans-style Delahaye. Nevertheless, the 4-4, wagging its tail vigorously on the rough concrete bankings, impressed everybody by leading on handicap at one stage, and lapping steadily to take eighth place overall by E.P. Huxham and T. Bryant. It averaged 52.73 mph against the winning Delahaye's 63.46, but managed to lap the 4.3-litre Allard.

Campbell then took his 4-4 to second place in the Limerick Grand Prix before Peter Morgan joined a team of four 4-4s, including Huxham's car, which qualified for premier awards in the Baddeley Trophy one-hour trial. It is worth noting that Morgan averaged 80.7 mph, against the winning Bentley's 110.

Laird was out of luck again in the TT at Donington, however, his works 4-4 retiring through overheating after impressing the crowds with its stability on a soaking circuit. The 4-4's versatility was emphasised, also, by continuing success in trials, with both Peter Morgan and H.F.S. winning coveted gold medal triple awards for gaining premiers in the three classics, the Land's End, the Edinburgh and the Exeter, in one season.

George Goodall then provided Morgan with even more publicity by winning his class for a third time in the 1939 RAC Rally, H.F.S. and Peter Morgan winning group two with the prototype coupé. Goodall's son, Jim, then won the Scottish Rally outright in a Le Mans Replica while Dick Anthony used the works Le Mans cars that he was to drive with White in June to win the Almond trophy in the Lawrence Cup Trial!

In this case the engine was bored out to 1,104 cc to take it out of the class dominated at Le Mans by the 1,087-cc Simca. Despite fuel feed trouble, Anthony and White increased the car's race average to 64.53 mph, but could manage only 15th place from 22 finishers. The winning Bugatti recorded 86.85 mph and Amedee Gordini's 10th-placed Simca took the Index of Performance. But it was a considerable feat just to finish.

The last recorded Morgan competition success before the Second World War then fell to Peter Morgan who took second place with a 1,098-cc Le Mans Replica in a Donington race meeting run by the MCC, the trials-organising club, and the first one after the war went to Ken Burgess who used a 1,122-cc 4-4 to win his class in a hill climb at Portishead, near Bristol, in October 1945.

The immediate post-war era provided boom times for most sports as young men and women came out of the armed services or continued to be called up, but it took motoring several years to recover, chiefly because of fuel restrictions, which included rationing. Some trials were held, however, on a much more modest scale than before the war, with a severe curtailment of mileage in the case of the classics. But Jim Goodall managed a third-class award in the Colmore, and best overall performances in the Sunbac and Midland trials in 1946 with a special short-chassis 4-4, registered BWP 47, which had been built before the war specifically for trials work. This car was fitted with a Ford 10 engine after the war before receiving a Standard engine to continue successfully in 1947 as Dick Anthony and Peter Morgan competed in 1,098-cc lightweights. Much the same story continued through 1948 and 1949, C. J. McCann—in the ex-Goodall short-chassis car—joining the honours list with R. Hellier in a normal Standard-engined 4-4 as more new cars became available.

Mainland Europe was also recovering slowly from the war with the result that major rallies, such as the Monte Carlo, could once more be organised. By 1950, this classic event had been joined by the Dutch-organised Tulip Rally, which proved every bit as tough. Briton Ken Wharton won in a Ford V8 saloon, but the Dutch brothers Wim and Roger Verhey van Wijk managed a second place in the 1,500-cc class with their new 4-4.

As petrol became readily available again in Britain, it became more practical to think of organising motor races. From this point of view, Britain was lucky in that it had been left with a legacy of redundant airfields which had quite good concrete surfaces constructed within the previous 10 years. These included Silverstone, in Northants, Snetterton in Norfolk, Goodwood in Sussex, Thruxton in Hampshire and Castle Combe in Wiltshire. Perimeter rods were duly turned into motor racing circuits, with control towers as race headquarters. Then, with a ready supply of new tracks, other venues were encouraged to stage motor racing as well to complement a rapidly expanding series of hill climbs. As a result, Morgans began to appear in all sorts of competitions.

One of the most prominent early Morgan drivers was Bournemouth motor trader Jeff Sparrowe, who would become the first president of the Morgan 4-4 Club, using a much-modified Le Mans Replica. During 1950, he led all the way to win the Woodberry Chilcott Cup at Lulsgate, near Bristol, before the organising club moved to Castle Combe, where he averaged 62.5 mph to beat Arthur Mallock in the first of what would become a series of very fast Clubmen's cars. Sparrowe then went on to beat Dave Price's HRG convincingly in the 1,100-cc class of the production car race at Silverstone during the International Trophy meeting, mixing it with such aristocrats as Alberto Ascari in a Barchetta Ferrari and the works Jaguar, Aston Martin and Frazer-Nash teams.

The ending of petrol rationing also meant that the Exeter Trial in December 1950 could return to normal for the first time since 1938. It was based on two 150-mile road sections (ending in Bournemouth!) which had to be covered at the then-formidable average of 26 mph, including observed sections. Sports cars among the 256 entrants included MGs, HRGs, Healey Silverstones, Jaguar SS100s, supercharged Dellows, Singers, Bentleys, Lea-Francis, a 2.3-litre Alfa Romeo and the inevitable Morgans. Two Plus Fours were entered by the works, for Peter Morgan and Jim Goodall, winning first and second-class awards, in company with four 4/4s.

Morgan and Goodall then took the works Plus Fours to first-class awards in the 1951 Land's End Trial, backed by McCann's 4-4, as Sparrowe continued to campaign his Le Mans Replica. But he usually had to give best this season to, first, Leslie Hawthorn, and then his son, Mike, in a highly-tuned Riley TT Sprite. The younger Hawthorn, of course, became world champion racing driver seven years later. Sparrowe did manage one top-line win, however, in the 1,100-cc production car class—in which the Riley did not qualify being a pre-war works special—at the International

Trophy meeting, in which Peter Morgan and former HRG exponent Dave Price aroused the crowds with their cornering in Plus Fours on a soaking track.

From the Morgan point of view, however, the most important event that year was the RAC Rally, which had been revived with international status to lift it towards classics like the Monte Carlo, Tulip and Alpine. Despite its new-found status, few overseas competitors were attracted because its route still appeared to be something of a promenade, from four starting points—at Brighton, Cheltenham, Skegness and Harrogate—converging on Bournemouth. But in every other respect, the first RAC International Rally was much different from its pre-war predecessors. It was held in June, which meant the weather would not be too severe, and to make up for this far tougher tests were introduced en route, particularly over really rough Scottish roads and lapping the new track at Silverstone. But the star performer in speed tests at Blackpool was Peter Morgan in his Plus Four. He came close to beating Britain's top rally driver at the time, Ian Appleyard, in his works Jaguar XK120. Morgan and Jim Goodall then pressed the Jaguars hard again at the Eppynt military firing range, a course which was the forerunner of the special stages which would make the RAC Rally one of the world's greatest. The needle match in the final test was again between Appleyard, on 36.03 marks, and Morgan, on 37.58, but the Jaguar driver stayed ahead to win the over-1,500-cc open sports car class, the Morgans having the consolation of taking the team prize. Although there was no general category, it was readily calculated that Appleyard had won the rally from Morgan, with Goodall third and Dr W.D. Steel completing the winning team.

At that point, apart from T-series MGs, XK Jaguars were by far the most popular cars in top-line British rallies, 37 being entered on the RAC. So the Plus Four received a tremendous sales boost because it cost less than half the price of an XK120 and was a good deal less expensive to maintain, with convert Price taking his example to a class win in the Evian-Mont Blanc rally immediately after the RAC. Goodall then followed up with a class win for his Plus Four in the *Daily Express*-sponsored MCC National Rally with the works Morgans—supported by McCann's glorious old 4-4—winning the team award in the Exeter and the MCC's overall championship.

The 1952 RAC Rally was then brought forward to March in the hope that tougher weather conditions would provide a greater test. Blizzards certainly led to problems, with the Silverstone stage being cancelled, but Goff Imhof, in a stark open Allard J2X, held off all the XK120s to take the *Daily Telegraph's* award for best performance in the open car class—the unofficial general classification. Peter Reece was the highest placed Morgan driver, number six in class, one place in front of Peter Morgan, with Jim Goodall's 12th-placed Plus Four and 20th-placed Dr Steel's car making up the winning team, beating 24 others in the process. Morgan's increasing popularity in this branch of motor sport was emphasised by their seven finishers, including the

Former HRG exponent Dave Price became one of the Morgan front-runners in 1951. He is pictured here in the over 2,000 cc production car race at the *Daily Express* Silverstone meeting in which team mate Peter Morgan also performed well.

C.J. McCann is seen in action during the 1952 Exeter Trial with BWP 47, the ex-Goodall special short-chassis works 4-4 built for the 1939 Land's End Trial, which subsequently used a Ford Ten engine after the war before reverting to Coventry Climax power for McCann.

Dr W.D. Steel became one of the leading Morgan Plus Four exponents in the 1950s, pictured here at Rest and Be Thankful in the 1952 RAC Rally in which he was a member of the winning team.

Plus Four of Ken Bancroft, which had been leading third-placed Appleyard at one point before a blowing head gasket relegated it to 11th in class. Five Plus Fours then took first-class awards in the Land's End Trial with Morgan, Goodall and McCann's 4-4 taking the team award, Reece and 14th-placed RAC driver Jimmy Ray then supporting Morgan for the team award in the Edinburgh Trial before Bancroft won the Morecambe Jubilee Rally from Reece.

The Plus Four also proved to be a competitive car in international rallying in Europe, which despite being run on far more professional lines

Morgan Plus Fours were sufficiently competitive to contest international rallies in 1952—D. Howard's example being seen here in the Alpine.

than rallying in Britain was still delightfully sporting in its nature. Don Magalhaes won the 3-litre class and took fifth overall in the Lisbon Rally, won by a Porsche. The event attracted a strong British contingent, taking advantage of a London starting point. W.K. Stewart also managed a class win with his Plus Four in the Scottish Rally, although it was not yet the major event it would become in following years.

A Plus Four entered at Le Mans by Bob Lawrie and Ray Isherwood went out after only 23 laps with water pump trouble in what had been visualised as a demonstration of high-speed reliability in a class including Ferraris, Aston Martins, Mercedes, Gordinis and a supercharged Peugeot.

Peter Morgan also emphasised his ability in a Plus Four—KUY 387 (*The Autocar* road test machine)— by beating top club racer Peter Gammon in a similar car at the MCC's Silverstone meeting in September. Gammon, who had been a prolific winner in a much-modified MG TC, switched next season to one of Colin Chapman's new Lotus Mark 6 cars with great success.

Then a Plus Four crew at last managed to beat Appleyard's Jaguar in the London Rally in September when Ray and Jimmy Dixon capitalised on an unpenalised road run as Appleyard faltered during the final tests in Wales. But the Morgan team of Ray, Goodall and Reece was relegated to second place in the team section when Reece lost time after being locked in a shed by an irate farmer!

Morgan's strength in depth was never more evident than when Peter and Doreen Reece had to retire in the *Daily Express* National Rally when their Plus Four lost a wheel, but Goodall, Morgan and Steel were still able to win the team award—and P.F.M. Silcock annexed the concours d'elegance prize with his Plus Four!

The Exeter Trial—which, like all other MCC events, continued to be run on pre-war lines—was then moved to a January date in 1953, but still counted for the Triple Award with the Land's End and Edinburgh events from 1952. Once more Peter Morgan showed his ability by gaining a premier award in the Exeter to take the coverted triple, with Goodall and McCann—this time in a works Plus Four—backing him for the team award.

*Above left:* Jimmy Ray won the London Rally two years in succession with his Plus Four, pictured here in the 1952 event.

*Above:* Three semi-works Plus Fours were built in 1952, the first registered KUY 474 for Jimmy Ray, the second, KUY 475 (pictured here at Silverstone in 1967) for Peter Reece, who finished fifth in the 1952 RAC Rally with it, and the third, KUY 476, for Bob Dixon.

*Above left:* Peter Morgan had a highly-successful season in 1952, seen here taking a first-class award in the Land's End Trial.

*Above:* He then went on to repeat the trick in the MCC's Edinburgh Trial.

*Left:* Dr W.D. Steel is pictured storming Buttertubs in the 1952 Edinburgh Trial.

Mixed luck afflicted the Morgans during the rest of the 1953 season, however. Heavy penalties for anything other than a perfect road run put them well down the finishing order in the RAC Rally—won by Appleyard's Jaguar—with only Scots girl Andy Neil winning anything for the Plus Four brigade: third place in the ladies' class. Peter Reece switched for a time to one of the potent new Austin-Healeys after winning his class in the Measham Rally with his Plus Four in February, but few other rally drivers followed his example at this point because the Austin-Healey lacked ground clearance.

This was one of the reasons McCann was able to exploit his old 4-4 to take a premier award on the Land's End. Ray stuck with his Plus Four, however, to win the Rhyl Rally in April. Then dentist Roy Clarkson and *Autosport* editor Gregor Grant took Clarkson's special-bodied fixed-head coupé Plus Four, VNO 600—which had been commissioned to contest the saloon car classes of international events—to the Tulip Rally for one hill-climb win before finishing off the leader board.

Driving tests—this one at Thruxton in June 1953—formed a major part of rallies in the early 1950s, and provided an ideal battleground for the talents of Peter Morgan, seen here in the works Plus Four, and Ian Appleyard.

The Edinburgh Trial was then turned into a rally from which the Morgan team of Plus Four drivers Goodall and Morgan, and 4-4 mounted McCann, took the team award. Ray then won his class in the Morecambe Rally—another Appleyard benefit—with George Turnbull taking a 4-4 to victory in the Ilfracombe Rally.

It was at this point that the Scottish Rally emerged, in June, as a major event with international status, Ray taking his Morgan to a class victory before winning the London Rally—a major feat of map reading which took 318 competitors all round the country—in September. Then Clarkson's special-bodied car beat all the works Plus Fours to finish second to Frank Downs's Sunbeam-Talbot in the MCC's *Daily Express* National Rally in November. Ray's class win gained him the British Trials Drivers' Championship, while Andy Neil, partnered by her sister Chris, won the equivalent ladies' award.

By now, however, Morgans were thoroughly outclassed in normal one-day trials, for which highly-specialised machines were being developed to cope with tortuous off-road courses. But they continued to be competitive in trials run to the classical formula of long road sections with a scattering of off-road tests.

Nevertheless, thick fog and sheet ice on the roads relegated the Morgan team to second-class awards in the 1954 Exeter Trial, although similar conditions failed to deter Plus Four driver Barry Moore, when he won the Cat's Eyes Rally in February.

The emphasis in such areas was still more on the crew's ability than on the outright performance of the car, so Morgan were not outclassed in rallying when the higher-powered Triumph TR2 became more readily available in 1954. Two of these cars dominated the RAC Rally in their debut at the event in March, but it was largely because they also had top-line drivers in the winner, Johnnie Wallwork, and runner-up, Peter Cooper. Various problems hit the Morgan team, but Ray, who was on his honeymoon, managed seventh place and Alec Newsham eighth.

The increasing specialisation of trials had also led to the emergence of a new sport—autocross—to attract the owners of sports cars which were now no longer competitive in other off-road events. Such events were typically organised as a time trial on a circuit in large fields made up of fairly-smooth grass. As such they proved attractive to Morgan owners, especially as regulations had been developed to include classes for series production cars, which allowed reasonable modifications. Plus Four driver Mike Warner lightened his car by fitting cycle-type front wings and became one of the first autocross winners, setting best time of the day in the Eastern Counties event in March before going on to win a handicap race at Snetterton in April.

Morgan's renewed potential in circuit racing was also demonstrated when Laystall engine tuning ace Basil de Mattos took Peter Morgan's Plus Four, KUY 387, which had been fitted with a TR2 power unit, to an overall win in a handicap event at the Goodwood Members' Day meeting in the same month. He was supported by farmer John Moore, fresh from the RAC Rally in his drop-head coupé, who then went on to break two class records at the Lydstep hill climb in Wales as an example of the Plus Four's versatility—which was emphasised by the fact that it was classed as a saloon!

The official Plus Four team of Peter Morgan, Jim Goodall, and A.T. Hall came to grief on the Land's End, however, when the executive director stalled on Hustyn Hill. And Clarkson was going great guns in the Highland Three-Day rally with his Morgan 'saloon' until he put himself out of the running for overall victory by arriving early at one checkpoint. But Andy Neil won the ladies award and another prominent Scottish Plus Four driver, Howard Sturrock, his class.

As Morgan drivers were successful in numerous minor events, Ray's skill at handling a Plus Four then stood him in good stead as he outdrove the TR2s of D.W. Watkin and Lord Bruce to win his class in the Scottish Rally.

*Below:* P.W.S. White is pictured at Bwlch Y Groes on his way to second in class and the team award for the Morgan Plus Fours in the 1954 MCC Redex Rally.

*Below right:* Typical night scene in the 1954 Redex Rally as Les Yarranton checks in at Harrogate with his second-placed Plus Four.

*Bottom:* All-rounder Tiny Lewis tries his hand at Bluehills Mine in the 1955 Land's End Trial.

Peter Reece also managed to beat the TR2s by setting best sports car time in the Clerk hill climb in Lancashire—showing that a well-driven Plus Four (one of the first cars with the interim radiator grille) could still outgun the more powerful TR2s with the aid of its lighter weight.

Ray tried hard for a hat trick in the London Rally in September, but lost marks on the road and only the top women's rally team of Nancy Mitchell and Doreen Reece in a Plus Four brought any reward for Morgan with the ladies' cup.

Then the works Morgans contested the Birmingham Post Rally later that month, but had to give second best in class to Plus Four driver Les Yarranton, who had proved equally at home in autocross. Yarranton then went on to take second place overall in the MCC Rally—now sponsored by

the Redex lubricant firm. The event was won by Jaguar Mark VII driver E.R. Parsons, but Yarranton had the consolation of relegating TR2 exponent Peter Cooper to third place. Jim Goodall won the under 2,600-cc open sports car class with his Vanguard-engined Plus Four and Peter Morgan the closed class with the TR2-engined drop-head coupé, taken straight from the London Motor Show!

Meanwhile 'Dinger Bell', director of the Royal Observatory in Hong Kong had fitted his Plus Four with a TR2 engine to lead the first Macau Grand Prix before losing a wheel.

The 1955 Exeter Trial which followed was an outstanding success for Morgan in that all 13 cars took awards—almost the only standard cars to do so—with Jim Goodall winning a Triple Award and racing drivers Horace Gould and Tiny Lewis making up the winning team with prolific rallyman Doc Spare.

Despite heavy snow, Ken James then won the Liverpool New Year

Rally with his ex-Ray Plus Four before Spare beat TR2 exponent C.M. Seaward to win the Maggi Carlo Rally in the West Country.

Ray had switched to a highly-tuned works Standard Ten saloon for the RAC Rally in March and used it to great effect to win from Harold Rumsey's TR2. Jim Goodall did well in many of the tests with his Plus Four, but was eventually defeated by appalling weather conditions in which Peter Morgan crashed.

In stark contrast, America's Sebring 12-hour race in the same month was run in a heat wave which caused many problems on a circuit that was tough on brakes anyway. The two American-entered Plus Fours of East Coasters Mike Rothschild and Charlie Kunz, Weitz and MacKenzie, were initially outclassed by the more aerodynamic and powerful Arnolt-Bristols, until the leading Arnolt, driven by former grand prix ace Rene Dreyfus, slowed with brake trouble. Rothschild caught him and nearly overhauled the other two Arnolts to finish 27th overall with the Weitz car in 30th position in a race won by Mike Hawthorn and Phil Walters in a works D-type Jaguar.

By 1955, autocross was becoming a highly-popular sport, attracting huge entries with—despite the rough nature of the courses—many drivers using brand-new cars. These included Hugh Denton, who narrowly beat an XK Jaguar to win the Amersham event in April with his Plus Four—one of the first cowled radiator cars.

Meanwhile Scots Plus Four driver Francis Dundas started well in the Circuit of Ireland (Britain's oldest motor rally made up of fast road sections, off-road sections over mountain passes and rough tracks, with a collection of driving and navigation tests, hill climbs and circuit races thrown in), but eventually fell behind the Triumph TR2s of local experts Robin McKinney, Desmond Titterington and Barry McCaldrin, who took the first three places. But fellow Plus Four drivers Barry Phipps and Angela Palfrey had better luck, taking second place overall in the Welsh Rally, which would be elevated to international status nine years later.

Moore then celebrated the opening of the new Aintree club circuit by beating 10 TR2s to win the 2-litre production sports car race. He then lost a rear wheel after winning a handicap race at Silverstone two weeks later, but simply jacked up his trusty drop-head coupé, fitted the spare, and took second place to an AC Ace in a following scratch race! This event was typical of the enthusiasm of the period for club motor racing. A massive crowd watched no less than 16 events—most of them 5-lap races—which attracted a total entry of 184.

Ray Meredith's Plus Four leads M.G. and Alvis opposition in the 750 Motor Club's Six-Hour Relay race at Silverstone in 1955.

In the meantime, the nimble Renault 4CV saloon—with tuning equipment—was emerging as a new threat to Morgans and Triumphs in rallying, B.W. Furson's example winning the Plymouth National Rally in June, although Lewis's Plus Four was the best Bristol starter and J.B. Banbury won the final test.

But now the Plus Four was using the TR2 engine, it began to perform well in Sports Car Club of America (SCCA) races, Gaston Andrey's example winning the Production E class from Rothschild at Beverley Airport, New England, with Gunnard Rubini and Andrey later taking first and third at the Watkins Glen Grand Prix, the chief opposition coming from AC Aces. Rubini and Rothschild then dominated a combined class D and E race at Fairchild, Maryland, beating the Austin-Healeys on handling. The Plus Four was then threatened with upgrading to Class D production, with Ed Hebb's car actually being placed in the higher class to perform well in taking third place at the Giant's Despair Hill Climb behind two very costly Gullwing Mercedes 300SL coupés—which were duly upgraded to Class C against the XK Jaguars! Meanwhile, on the West Coast, Bob Oker emerged as the best Plus Four driver against opposition made up chiefly of Arnolt-Bristols and Porsche Speedsters, before switching to an AC Ace.

Back in Britain, Peter Reece, in the works Plus Four KUY 387, managed to win the 30-lap production sports car race at Oulton Park's Gold Cup meeting, beating Standbridge's Ace and numerous TR2s, after two leading Austin-Healeys had overturned. This race was, in fact, the forerunner of what would become the *Autosport* Production Sports Car Championship the following year. In this series the new series 11 Morgan with its 1,172-cc engine was placed in class one (up to 1,200-cc) against such potential rivals as the Porsche 356, Lotus Mark 6 and 1,100-cc HRG, with the Plus Four occupying class three (1,501-cc–2,500-cc) against, chiefly, the Ace, TR2 and the new TR3, and various Frazer Nashes. A wide variety of engine modifications were allowed and special bodies, but other changes had to be as catalogued by the makers. But sadly, the Oulton Park race was to be the last for Reece, who was killed in a road accident soon after.

In more light-hearted vein, the Morgan 4/4 Club organised a night rally in the Midlands during December which proved so tough that Rumsey's TR2 was able to win by a narrow margin from Barry Phipps and Angela Palfrey, in a Plus Four owned by the organiser, Hugh Denton, from the only other unpenalised competitor, John Shove in a Renault. Palfrey had won the ladies award in the MCC's National Rally, with Spare, Yarranton and Peter Morgan taking first three places in their class.

In the first major rally of 1956, Doc Spare did well to finish third overall and win his class with a new TR3-engined Plus Four, behind Lyndon Sims's Aston Martin and the Appleyard Jaguar, in the RAC Rally, with Yarranton taking third in the production sports car class.

But once the *Autosport* championship got under way it became the major event in which a Morgan could compete. Interest was so high that the

Barry Phipps and Angela Palfrey charge through the snow with their Plus Four in the Morgan 4/4 Club's December night rally in 1955.

events—at race circuits and hill climbs—were often televised because tragic accidents involving outright sports racing cars at Le Mans and Dundrod, where the T.T. was held, had led to severe curtailment of this form of sport. Entries for the *Autosport* championship were often restricted to less than 20 cars on circuits far narrower than they are today—with the result that only John McKechnie managed to race a Plus Four against heavy opposition from Sid Hurrell's TR2 and Ken Rudd's AC Ace. Despite the availability of an extensive range of tuning equipment for the new series II Morgan, this class was dominated by even-lighter and better handling Lotus Mark 6 cars, which had drivers of the calibre of future world champion Graham Hill. Bearing in mind the increasing professionalism that this series attracted, it can be seen that McKechnie did well to finish fifth in the three-hour championship final at Oulton Park, which had been promoted as a replacement for the cancelled TT. In the championship itself, Rudd scored the greatest number of points, but the trophy went to the class two MGA of Dick Fitzwilliam and Robin Carnegie by dint of their performance on handicap in the final, with McKechnie 11th overall of 26 qualifiers, one place in front of Hill.

In more light-hearted club events, McKechnie, Phipps and Ray Meredith won the Aston Martin Owners' Club relay race at Silverstone with their Plus Fours with J.L. Parker-Eaton debuting what would become a famous Plus Four (registered TOK 258) for third in class behind Meredith at the Silverstone Sunbac meeting.

Meanwhile, in America, Rubini and Rothschild finished first and second in the combined class D and E production race at Fairchild before switching to the new TR3. But Andrey fitted his Plus Four with a TR3 engine to win class E production in the 3,800-ft climb of Mount Equinox in Vermont. He had to be content with a string of third places after that as the Porsche Speedster became available with a full-race four-cam Carrera engine for Lake Underwood and his business partner Bengt Soderstrom to finish in that order at Beverley and Thompson raceway. In the end he gave up the unequal struggle and changed to a Corvette before being hired to drive a Testa Rossa Ferrari as SCCA circuit racing also became ever more professional despite an acclaimed amateur constitution.

But in real road racing at Bryfan Tyddyn, near the Giant's Despair hill climb at Wilkes-Barre, Pennsylvania, H.B. Williamson's TR3-engined Plus Four came closer to beating the Porsche and Arnolt-Bristol opposition with a third in Production E.

Subsequently Lew Spencer emerged as a great crowd-pleaser on the West Coast with a Plus Four owned by Los Angeles importer Rene Pellandini. At Laguna Seca, Spencer snatched third place in the over-1,500-cc production class from Ray Steyr's Jaguar XK140. Not only did he win his class, but he also left the class D winner, Hugh Pryor's Austin-Healey, standing in an event won by Bill Love's AC Ace—also imported by Pellandini—from Lloyd Gray's fuel-injected 5-litre Corvette.

*Above:* Peter Morgan gives the series 11 4/4 its competition debut by winning a first-class award in the 1956 Derbyshire Trial.

*Above right:* KUY 387 eventually wound up with cowled radiator bodywork for this rally in 1956.

The Plus Four was then barred from racing for a while on the West Coast following a spate of wheel losses as the steel centres pulled over the nuts of the securing studs. The Morgans were eventually re-admitted when they were fitted with reinforced wheels.

In Britain, Morgan's best chance of success against increasingly more professional opposition came in club competition where Jim Goodall set best time of the day in the Worcester autocross, with Phipps and J. Looker winning their classes and sharing the team award with Goodall. In fiercely-contested Northern events, Alec Newsham took first class awards in the Lancashire Cup and Lakeland Rallies with his Plus Four while Peter Morgan gave the series II Morgan its competition debut to take a first-class award in the Derbyshire Trial, followed by a class win in the MCC's National Rally. Phipps won his class, too, in a Plus Four, Goodall and Yarranton making up the winning team with Morgan.

The Suez crisis then hit fuel supplies to Britain, with rationing and little motor sport, so there were no major events for the Morgans until a much-shortened Land's End Trial at Easter in 1957 during which Peter Morgan's series II and Goodall Plus Four took first-class awards.

In this period more events were being organised for grand touring cars—(which had to have a roof)—in the belief that they would be slower than open sports cars, which had gained a bad reputation following Le Mans and the T.T. But there was nothing in the rules which said that an open sports car with a detachable hard top could not compete as a GT—rather than in the same class as outright sports racers—so the works Triumph TR3s and Austin-Healeys took advantage, especially in international rallies. A Morgan Plus Four crew, Bob Grier and Bob Kennedy, followed suit for the Sebring 12-hour race in 1957 to take them out of the E production class inhabited by Ferraris and AC Aces, to compete instead against the TR3s and similarly-equipped Arnolt-Bristols. Their car ran with great regularity to finish 28th and third in class behind Oker and Rothschild in the works hard-top Triumphs, in a race won by Juan Fangio and Jean Behra in a fearsome Maserati 450S lapping 25 per cent faster.

Morgans were now becoming less competitive in the production classes of SCCA racing as more AC Aces appeared and the Triumph TR3s had disc brakes. But Anthony Zuckert, and Al Sands, in Canada, still managed placings. Much the same applied in Britain during 1957, with Meredith managing only two points in the *Autosport* championship, run to three classes, divided at 1,500-cc and 2,500-cc, and dominated by Rudd's Ace; even the works-supported MGAs in class one ran with disc brakes by then. The works Plus Fours of Peter Morgan and Goodall were confined to less-serious club events, in company with McKechnie's car.

Birmingham garage owners Lionel and Pauline Mayman started to do well with a Plus Four in rallying and the odd circuit race, however, Mrs Mayman taking eighth place overall in the Plymouth National Rally. She then repeated this feat with co-driver Valerie Domleo to win the Coupé des Dames in the London Rally.

During the next season, Pauline Mayman continued to compete in rallies in one Plus Four, while her husband, Lionel, was the only competitor to register a Morgan for the *Autosport* championship, facing fierce opposition from a Jaguar XK120, four Triumph TRs and four Frazer Nashes, six Austin-Healeys and nine AC Aces in the over-1,600cc class; the emergence of lightweight aerodynamic glass-fibre-bodied cars, such as the Lotus Elite, made it impractical to enter a 4/4 in the smaller class. In the events, Lionel Mayman had little success against much faster opposition.

As the *Autosport* championship developed into a series for increasingly-fast cars built purely for racing, although technically to road specification, the old-established British Automobile Racing Club started a new series for the drivers of the more standard road-going cars which were becoming outclassed. Initially, entries were confined to AC-engined Aces (rather than the more powerful and expensive Bristol racing-engined variety), Triumph TRs, Austin-Healeys, MGAs . . . and Morgans. It was in this series, for the Freddie Dixon Trophy, that a young aeronautical engineer, Chris Lawrence, realised that he stood a chance of success in his newly-acquired, second-hand, Plus Four, registered TOK 258. Other Plus Four Morgan drivers in this series included John Looker with a four-seater, Don Pacey and Meredith. By the end of the season, however, Lawrence had emerged as the fastest, finishing as high as third in one race at Goodwood as Mayman could only manage a fifth at Mallory Park, the new six-port six-cylinder Austin-Healeys taking over from the Bristol-engined Aces as front-runners.

In rallying, Les Yarranton won his class in the RAC event from Jim Goodall before the works Plus Four, TUY 875, was lent to former Aston Martin exponent Lyndon Sims to run with the hood raised in the Tulip Rally as a GT car. Major European rallies, like the Tulip, were totally different events at that time to the British variety. The RAC would not allow point-to-point averages of more than 30 mph, placing an emphasis on driving tests and map reading ability on intricate minor roads to sort out the fields, whereas the Continental events often amounted to flat-out road races up and down tortuous mountain passes, with circuit racing thrown in for good measure. In the circumstances, Sims did well to take second place in the 1,601 cc–2,000 cc GT class, splitting the works TR3As—(which were the top rally cars of the period)—although he could manage only 37th place overall.

*Above:* The works Morgan HUY 982—pictured here on the 1959 Exeter Trial—was subsequently fitted with a long-range fuel tank which increased the weight over the rear wheels.

*Above right:* Chris Lawrence wins his first race in TOK 258 at Goodwood in March 1959.

Meanwhile, Pauline Mayman, partnered by Valerie Domleo to qualify as an all-female crew for ladies' awards, began to star in British national rallies, winning the women's prize in the Midland event in April ahead of Yarranton, before repeating the trick in the Morecambe Rally, in which fellow Plus Four driver Brian Harper also won his class. Mayman and Domleo then continued winning ladies' awards, in the Liverpool, Worcester and Bournemouth Rallies, at the start of a career which would take them into the BMC international works team with the world's best women's crew, Pat Moss and Ann Wisdom. By the end of the season they were established as the top national women's crew, winning the BTRDA's silver garter as well as third place in the unrestricted Gold Star awards.

In the less serious club races, hill climbs and trials, Plus Four drivers Frank Livingstone and J.S. Parry were moderately successful with Peter Morgan—in TUY 875—being backed up by Brown, Meredith and Looker to take second place to an MG team in the Aston Martin Owners' Club relay race at Silverstone.

Initially, only Bill Belcher competed in the 1959 *Autosport* championship with a Plus Four although the classes had been restructured to include a 1,600–2,000-cc category. This made a Plus Four marginally more competitive, facing opposition chiefly from Bristol-engined Frazer Nashes and AC Aces, plus Triumph TRs, the larger capacity Austin-Healeys having been moved up a class. Chris Lawrence aimed at the easier Freddie Dixon Trophy races in which the biggest threat came from the Triumph TRs of Bill de Selincourt and Sid Hurrell, and the AC-engined Ace of Bob Staples. MG

Peter Morgan in TUY 875 prepares to receive the sash in the 1959 Six-Hour Relay race at Silverstone from the Morgan Plus Four team manager as Bill Belcher's car waits in the pit lane behind one of the rival M.G. Car Club's MGAs. Morgan helped hold off challenges from the Triumph TRs in the foreground and the Jaguar Drivers' Club entries to his left while leading the winning team.

had introduced a new 1,588-cc twin cam-engined MGA, but this proved marginally slower in the battles for overall placings.

Lawrence started on a high note by winning his first two races at Goodwood and kept it that way, de Selincourt emerging as the most consistent opposition, beating him once at Goodwood. The Morgan and TRs were very evenly matched, however, and Lawrence had to keep up a frantic pace of development, fitting disc front brakes as soon as Morgan listed them in May, and replacing his steel wheels soon after with wider wires. Eventually, however, he won the Dixon Trophy, entering his first *Autosport* event in August as soon as his lead in the alternative series became unassailable. Lawrence's impact in that *Autosport* race was immense as he led the Jaguar XK120 of champion Dick Protheroe at Snetterton until his brakes wilted. He failed to win enough points to make the prestigious three-hour race which ended the *Autosport* calendar, however, and Belcher gained only one sixth place all season.

In non-championship events, the Plus Fours of Lawrence and Belcher teamed up with those of Peter Morgan, Meredith, Jim Goodall and A J Blair to win the 750 Motor Club's classic Six-Hour Relay Race at Silverstone by only 19 seconds from the rival TRs. Lawrence also managed to land a drive in one of the new single-seater Formula Junior Elvas at Brands Hatch in October as a result of his spectacular displays in the Plus Four—which he took along to harry Graham Warner's winning Lotus Elite before finishing second in the supporting GT race.

The Mayman-Domleo duo also started the year well, winning the ladies' class in the Highland Rally, followed by the Midland Rally in which they were second in the over-1,600-cc class to Jim Goodall (who also took second place overall), with fellow Plus Four driver Brian Harper third in class. A crash while hill-climbing at Prescott then put Pauline Mayman out until August when she re-appeared in a new Plus Four, registered EPM324, to win the ladies' awards in the Bolton-Le-Moors Rally, followed by the Liverpool, London (won by Harper's Plus Four) and Bournemouth events. Val Domleo then signed up for the works Triumph team, with Doreen Freeman joining Pauline Mayman in the Plus Four for the RAC Rally, which had been switched to November to give it more status as the final event of the international calendar. Peter Morgan emerged once more as the star Morgan driver, however, winning his class and taking sixth overall in TUY 875, despite handicaps like deep snow which hardly favoured the Plus Four.

Meanwhile Lionel Mayman took over Belcher's Plus Four registered VON 777 to contest the *Autosport* championship in 1960 although it faced heavy opposition from Austin-Healeys, Frazer-Nashes and AC Aces in the over-1,600-cc category. Apart from the odd appearance by Robert Duggen's Plus Four, Mayman's car was the only Morgan registered for the Championship as Lawrence continued to concentrate on his Lola-Climax in international sports car racing. But he found time to lap the entire field with TOK 258 in a marque race at his favourite Goodwood circuit in May as

Mayman managed to win one round of the *Autosport* championship at Mallory Park. This qualified VON 777 in 15th place for the season-ending three-hour race at Snetterton, which he finished to take third place in class in the championship.

But no matter what Mayman did, he could not match Lawrence's performances with a Morgan and devoted his energies to other projects in the following year. Lawrence, meantime, found that there was good business to be had in tuning the Morgan's Triumph TR engine now that his car was established as the front-runner, and Peter Morgan realised that there was little point in spending a great deal of time and money trying to develop an alternative works car—so the deal was struck whereby Lawrence provided his engines for the new Plus Four Super Sports project. TOK 258 was then entered by the works for the Tourist Trophy race at Goodwood in August, sharing the track with Ferrari and Aston Martin GT cars as well as class opposition from works Porsches, Elvas and MGAs of far more modern design.

The wildest dreams of Morgan and Lawrence were fulfilled as the Plus Four caused consternation among Porsches in particular to run as high as 11th place before a 17-minute delay with starter motor trouble in the pits relegated Lawrence to 24th place at the end. It was a sufficiently impressive drive, however, to make it worth launching the Super Sports line. Lawrence was more than happy because he now had the income to develop his own small grand touring car, the Deep Sanderson 201.

In rallying, works teams were starting to get really serious, the British Motor Corporation working to a budget the equivalent of £1 million as they came to the fore with their Austin-Healey 3000s. On lesser planes, Morgans were still good enough to win national events, Brian Harper and Ron Crellin taking the Welsh Rally, with Pauline Mayman winning her class. But the works Plus Four drophead—in theory a GT car—of Welsh wizard Lyndon Sims, could manage only 125th place when the chips were down in the Monte Carlo Rally. Consolation for this very fast and hair-raising driver

Tommy Bridger in one of Dick Jacobs's semi-works MGA Twin Cams leads Chris Lawrence's Plus Four—now with a home-made aluminium hardtop—and Mike Parkes in Sir Gawaine Baillie's Lotus Elite in the Wrotham Trophy race for GT cars at Brands Hatch on August Bank Holiday 1960, won by Jack Sears in the Equipe Endeavour Aston Martin DB4GT. Lawrence eventually took second place in the 2,600-cc class, with Bill Moss chasing in the 1,000-cc Marcos, eighth overall, followed by Peter Lumsden's Elite.

followed in the Tulip Rally as he won his class from Alfa Romeo and Triumph opposition.

Back in national events, there was still a chance of outright victory for a Plus Fours driven by Robert Duggen and Hugh Willmore. Lawrence set his finishing second in the Wolverhampton Rally while winning the ladies' prize, with Harper and Crellin taking the over-1,300-cc class before the Harper car won its class in the Birmingham Rally from Mayman and Domleo. All told it was a good season for Harper and Crellin as they won the BTRDA's Gold Star.

Two of the new Super Sports were entered in the 1961 *Autosport* championship by Peter Marten and Hugh Braithwaite, backed up by tuned Plus Fours driven by Robert Duggan and Hugh Willmore. Lawrence set his sights on international events with a new Super Sports, bearing his old registration number, TOK 258, the original car being retained as a spare and for his new team-mate, former Alfa Romeo driver Richard Shepherd-Barron. A further Super Sports, registered XRX 1, was built for Triumph TR exponent, Philip 'Pip' Arnold. Part of the attraction of such events was that the heavy cost of participation could be more than offset by starting money for foreign entrants, especially if the cars were crowd-pullers like the gloriously 'old-fashioned' Morgans!

The speed of Lawrence in the new TOK 258 astounded his chief opposition—Porsche Carreras, some of which had ultra-lightweight highly-streamlined Abarth bodywork—so much so that he received a special award for setting a new 2-litre GT lap record of 10 mins 31 sec in the Nurburgring 1000 kilometres race, although he did not finish the event. Shepherd-Barron managed second overall in a three-hour production sports car race at Spa soon after, however. Lawrence and Shepherd-Barron then took TOK 258 to Le Mans for the 24-hour race in June but were turned down at scrutineering because the car looked 'too old-fashioned' despite its performances earlier that season.

They then managed to split two Porsche Carreras for second place in the Coppa Inter-Europa at Monza—in which they competed with Arnold— before returning to Britain to attempt to qualify for the *Autosport* championship three-hour finale. But here they found the lighter works Lotus Elites, and AC Aces in their class, too fast in short distance races for what was essentially a car built to a long-distance specification. Shepherd-Barron won his class with Lawrence second in the non-championship Peco trophy marque race at Brands Hatch in August, however.

Hopes were high for the Tourist Trophy at Goodwood the following month as Lawrence battled mightily with world champion-to-be Graham

*Below left:* Brian Harper and Ron Crellin emerged as two of the star Morgan rally drivers, pictured here on their way to victory in the 1960 Welsh Rally.

*Below:* Chris Lawrence in his new Plus Four TOK 258 chases David Dixon's ex-Sebring Austin-Healey to second place in class during the Peco Trophy race at Brands Hatch in 1961.

Hill in a works Porsche Carrera Abarth in practice, team mates Shepherd-Barron and Marten also running well. But in the event, won by Stirling Moss's Ferrari 250GT, Marten suffered engine trouble and Shepherd-Barron's car broke a half shaft, leaving Lawrence 11th overall and third in class behind Hill and fellow Porsche driver Fritz Hahn.

Braithwaite, meantime, had emerged as the most successful of the Morgan drivers in club events, putting in some stirring laps during the 750MC Relay to show great promise, qualifying half-way up the field for the *Autosport* three-hours, in which he won his class. Marten had some reward, however, winning a marque race at Mallory Park in September while on his third engine of the season . . . and Shepherd-Barron and Braithwaite managed to beat BMC works rally driver David Seigle-Morris in an Austin-Healey 3000 at the Brands Hatch Boxing Day meeting, Lawrence being kept fully occupied by the launch of his new Deep Sanderson racing sports car.

The year also marked the last in which the stiffly-sprung Morgan would be competitive in national rallying, with Harper and Crellin winning the Welsh and Wolverhampton events on Harper's way to the BTRDA Silver Star award before switching to an Austin-Healey Sprite.

Firm suspension was not necessarily a handicap on smooth surfaces, however, and more Morgans were seen in circuit racing than for many years—especially because there were so many classes in international events that opposition in the 2-litre GT category was reduced. This meant that it might be only necessary to finish to win an award, as the faster Porsches were in the 1,600-cc class. A. Rogers and J. Bailey took advantage of this situation to win their class at Sebring with a hard top Plus Four, finishing in 35th position overall in a race won by a Ferrari Testa Rossa sports racing car.

In Britain, Bill Jones took over the Marten Plus Four to support Lawrence, Arnold, Braithwaite and Duggen's Plus Fours in the 1,300–2,000-cc class C of the *Autosport* championship. John McKechnie also entered a 4/4 now that it could be made competitive with a 977-cc Ford Anglia engine in the under 1,000-cc class A. Overall victory in the championship looked as far away as ever, though, as new classes were formed for outright racing cars such as the Testa Rossa-engined Ferrari 250GTO, which was to win the first of three world championships in 1962!

The opposition in Europe could be severe, however, in that the Porsches were often put in the same class as Morgans, but, nevertheless the Lawrence team planned another works-backed assault on international events because the publicity they could gain was so attractive. The Spa production car race became their first event, Shepherd-Barron managing second in class behind the inevitable Porsche with Arnold fifth after Braithwaite crashed on the notoriously difficult Belgian road circuit. Braithwaite then teamed up with Arnold for the Nurburgring 1,000-kilometre event, Shepherd-Barron and Lawrence driving TOK 258, supported by another Plus Four driven by Parisienne Morgan agents Jean and Claude Savoye. In the race, the two

British cars were well on the pace, but succumbed to starter motor trouble, leaving the French car to take third place in class.

Le Mans was the big event of the year, however, and this time the Morgan's entry could hardly be refused after being eighth fastest of the limited number of cars present at a special practice weekend in April. High hopes were also held for a success in the event, chiefly because the French circuit had an exceptionally smooth surface, far less taxing than that of Spa and the Nurburgring. They were happy to note, however, that the only opposition in the 1,600–2,000-cc GT class came from an AC Ace. Lawrence took the first three-hour stint, resisting the temptation to over-stress the Morgan's highly-tuned engine by trying to maintain the same pace as the Ace. The policy paid off as soon after Shepherd-Barron took over, the Ace retired with transmission trouble and then the Morgan crew had only to drive for a finish to ensure maximum publicity. Throughout the 24 hours, the only trouble experienced with the car was a broken exhaust pipe, although there was some worry that the main reason for its 130-mph top speed along the long Mulsanne Straight, a very high-lift camshaft, might not last the full distance—2,255 miles in the case of the Plus Four for 13th place overall of 18 finishers. The race was won, almost inevitably, by a Ferrari, with small-engined Porsches and Lotus Elites and an Alfa Romeo GT ahead of

*Top left:* Morgan stalwarts Peter Marten (leading the duo) and Don Jones, battle with Bob Olthoff's semi-works MGA Twin Cam at Crystal Palace in 1962.

*Top right:* Pip Arnold leaves the pits in the 1962 Nurburgring 1,000-kilometre race in his Plus Four Super Sports shared with Hugh Braithwaite.

*Above left:* Chris Lawrence sweeps beneath the Dunlop Bridge in the 1962 Le Mans 24-hour race.

*Above:* Pip Arnold at speed in the 1962 Goodwood TT race.

the Plus Four, but the Morgan captured everybody's hearts because it presented such a nostalgic appearance. For this reason, as much as any, the performance was the most important in Morgan's history, even though the Fawcett/White car had also finished 13th 24 years earlier.

Lawrence's efforts in the *Autosport* championship were also rewarding in that by mid-season he was leading class C for 1,300–2,000-cc GT cars against opposition from works TVRs, Porsches, Triumph TRs and a supercharged Austin-Healey Sprite, followed by a class win in the Peco Trophy race (with Arnold second) at Brands Hatch on the return from Le Mans. Hopes were high for a team win in the TT at Goodwood as Shepherd-Barron held third in class, from Lawrence fifth, and Arnold seventh, before Shepherd-Barron was sidelined by a blown piston. Arnold ran into trouble, too, but Lawrence hung on to finish eighth overall and second in class behind a Lotus Elite.

But Lawrence managed third overall behind Mike Parke's Ferrari 250GTO and Mike Beckwith's Lotus 23—both outright sports racing cars—in the *Autosport* championship. This gave Arnold the class C win because Lawrence already had an award . . .

Morgan's best-ever year in competition was concluded by a second placing in the 750MC's Relay race for the 4/4 Club's team of Meredith, Duggen, Chris Pickard and grand prix-star-to-be Brian Redman in Plus Fours, with McKecknie's 4/4.

For the last race of the season, at Brands Hatch on Boxing Day, 24-year-old Adrian Dence took over Shepherd-Barron's place in the LawrenceTune team, finishing second to Arnold in the GT race. Dence then emerged as the front-runner among the Morgans in the 1963 *Autosport* championship, supported by the Plus Fours of Lawrence—on occasions when he was not occupied with the Deep Sanderson in long-distance racing—Meredith and Chris Dormand-Stewart. But he had to give best to Alan Hutcheson's more aerodynamic works-supported MGB, proving faster than the earlier MGA now that it had an 1,800-cc engine.

In international racing, Arch McNeil and William Clarens managed fourth in class with their Plus Four behind three works Triumph TR4s at Sebring before Lawrence, Arnold and new driver Bill Blydenstein—who had become involved in Vauxhall VX4/90 rally car preparation with LawrenceTune—ran in the 2,001–2,500-cc class of the Spa Grand Prix for marque cars. Lawrence and Arnold took the first two places in class but failed to take the team award as Blydenstein retired with throttle trouble. Lawrence was racing the Deep Sanderson in the Nurburgring 1,000

Adrian Dence flashes out of Paddock Bend in his first drive with the Le Mans Plus Four Super Sports—still bearing the registration number TOK 258—at Brands Hatch on Boxing Day 1962.

kilometres so his place was taken by Braithwaite, partnered by Rob Slotemaker, who ran out the class winner with Arnold—and former MGA exponent Robin Carnegie—as runners-up.

Then, in the best stiff upper lip tradition of Englishmen performing the most amazing feats in remote parts of the world, Super Sports driver Pat Kennett won the 1963 Panamanian Grand Prix! The 100-mile race was held on a very rough and stony circuit that took in a stretch of jungle . . . and amounted to a war of attrition between the Morgan, a Jaguar E-type, a Triumph TR4, an Austin-Healey 3000, a Porsche 356 and sundry other sports cars. Kennett, service manager of the local agents for Morgan, Jaguar and Triumph, slipstreamed the Jaguar until its brakes faded, then took the lead as cars—and drivers—wilted under intense heat and showers of stones thrown up all round the course. Eventually the Morgan ran out the winner at 77 mph with a failing back axle, as the Healey limped in with exhausted dampers, the brakeless E type on three tyres, the TR4 having lost its exhaust pipe . . .

Lawrence's Deep Sanderson, racing for the lucrative Index of Thermal Efficiency prize at Le Mans, performed reasonably well before retiring, but he was back in a new Super Sports for the TT at Goodwood later in the year, backed by Arnold and Dence—now driving the 1962 Le Mans car. Lawrence and Arnold's works machines had special new LawrenceTune cylinder heads which gave trouble, but Dence hung on for 17th place overall in the earlier car.

Dence had become one of the stars in British club racing as he battled with the lighter and better-streamlined glass fibre-bodied works TVRs in his seemingly-ancient Morgan, winning the *Motor Sport* Brooklands Memorial Trophy for his performances at Goodwood. Other notable club performers with Super Sports Morgans were Gordon Spice (later to become an endurance racing ace), Brian Kendall, Don Jones and Terry Sanger. Tommy Entwistle's TVR proved too fleet, however, for Dence's Morgan, winning the Fred W Dixon Trophy championship they had been contesting.

Club racing had never been more popular in Britain than in the early 1960s, but the cars being used were becoming far more sophisticated than Morgans. Rules for marque racing were being stretched to their limit, with numerous freak 'special GTs' appearing—typically sports racing cars, such as a Lotus 11 or Merlyn Mark 1V, with a flimsy lid attached.

Ultra-lightweight GT cars built purely for racing by Diva, Tojeiro and and Ginetta—and, at first, Marcos—were also rendering Morgans uncompe-

*Above left:* Pip Arnold passes a stricken Alfa Romeo Guilia saloon in the 1963 Nurburgring 1,000-kilometre race.

*Above:* Adrian Dence leads a Volvo P1800 at the Nurburgring 1,000-kilometre race in 1963 with the previous year's Le Mans Super Sports, now re-registered 170 GWP.

*Below left:* Ray Meredith proved to be the star member of the Morgan 4/4 Club's team in the 1963 750 Motor club relay race at Silverstone with his Super Sports—but, sadly, his colleagues were off the pace and could not bring the team into contention with the winning Tornado Talisman cars, one of which is pictured on the left.

*Below:* Adrian Dence hung on for 17th place in the 1963 Goodwood Tourist Trophy race with the Le Mans Super Sports.

*Opposite page top left:* John Maclay battles with Ken Baker's Jaguar E type in the 1965 Guards 1,000-mile race for production sports cars at Brands Hatch.

*Opposite page top right:* The Thurston/Terry Morgan SLR overtakes with House/North Plus Four Super Sports bearing the registration number MOG 1 in the 1965 Guards race at Brands Hatch.

*Opposite page left:* The Lawrence/Spender SLR—pictured passing Ken Colley's Daimler SP250—easily won the second part of the Guards race at Brands Hatch in 1965 after trouble on the first day.

*Opposite page right:* The new TOK 258 SLR car is refuelled in the pits during the 1965 Guards race.

*Opposite page left:* Spartan cockpit of the SLR TOK 258.

*Opposite page right:* The SLR TOK 258—now owned by Edgar Wallace and Tony Howard—as it is today, re-registered 581 DOK.

*Opposite page bottom left:* Alan House, who won his class in the 1965 *Autosport* championship with his Plus Four Super Sports is pictured here holding Lionel Mayman's ex-works Austin-Healey 3000 at Silverstone.

*Opposite page bottom right:* Alan House continued to do well in the AMASCO production sports car racing championship in 1967 with Roy North's left-hand-drive Plus Four Super Sports. He is pictured here in June at Brands Hatch.

titive, especially as their traditional body lines mitigated against a high top speed. Against such opposition there was no point in using the better streamlined Plus Four Plus either because it was still a heavy road car. Peter Morgan put the prototype Plus Four Plus to good use in Morgan's traditional domain, the Exeter Trial, however, and Claude Savoye, accompanied by his brother-in-law, Etienne Girard, defied logic and nature to drive a Super Sports, hood down, in extreme cold, into second place in class in the Monte Carlo Rally! Their task, in splitting two hardtop Alfa Romeos, was made only slightly easier by the fact that international rallies were changing also, to a format that mitigated heavily in favour of saloon cars against GT machinery.

Touring car racing was becoming ever more popular also, now that modern techniques of unitary construction made family saloons no heavier than traditional sports cars, giving them a similar performance. This showed itself in events like the Sebring 12 hours, where there were no Morgans in 1964, just Lotus Cortinas driven by the likes of world champion Jim Clark . . .

In events for pure production cars, however, such as trials, Harry Rose and Ami Lefevre won first-class awards with their 4/4s and Ray Meredith won easily at the new Llandow circuit in Wales with his Plus Four. The small Ford engine used in the 4/4 was also being developed to a high state of tune for everything from single-seater racing to touring car events, to the benefit of Morgan drivers: McKechnie's car performed notably well with Cosworth power.

Club racing was also changing in the United States with locally-produced V8 engines being inserted in lightweight British sports racing cars originally built for four-cylinder Coventry Climax units. But there were still categories for pure production cars, which Super Sports driver Earl Jones exploited to win class C in SCCA racing in 1964.

Lawrence also teamed up with BMC works rally driver John Sprinzel, who had been building special-bodied Austin-Healey Sprites, to form Sprinzel Lawrence Racing running four special GT cars—called SLRs—in international events. These were based on three LawrenceTune Plus Four chassis and a Triumph TR chassis provided by Neil Dangerfield, who helped finance the project. The lines of their handsome aluminium bodies bore a strong resemblance to the contemporary Ferrari and Jaguar GT cars and a far higher top speed was anticipated. The first two cars completed were entered for Dangerfield and Spice (in the Morgan variant) at Silverstone early in the year, but did not race. Lawrence then took his example—using his 1963 chassis but bearing the registration number TOK 258—to Spa to finish third in class behind two of Porsche's exotic new 904GTS cars. But the project went no further at that point as Lawrence was still fully occupied with his Deep Sanderson Le Mans cars and was also put out of action by a road accident for several months.

The SLRs could not take part in the TT either, because although it was

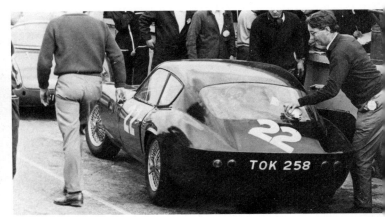

still part of the world championship for GT cars, entries in 1964 were confined to large-capacity cars to present a special spectacle! In a similar manner, the *Autosport* championship was moving more and more towards sports racing cars, with the Fred Dixon Challenge providing basic competition for production sports cars. By now, however, unitary construction had also been honed to a sufficiently light degree to make cars more modern than Morgans thoroughly competitive: in 1964 it became a duel between John Sharp's MGB and Bernard Unett's Sunbeam Alpine, which won the title with no Morgan in contention.

A record 166 entries were received for the *Autosport* championship in 1965, ranging from traditional sports cars such as the Morgan Plus Fours of Alan House, Brian Weatherley, James Tucker and Bill White to Ferrari 250GTOs and AC Cobras. Most of the Plus Fours raced with 2.2-litre TR4 engines but Basil Feilding took full advantage of the 1,600—2,500-cc GT class's capacity limit by fitting the ex-Pip Arnold car, XRX1, with a 2.5-litre Daimler V8 engine. House, Weatherley and Feilding performed sufficiently well in 12 qualifying races—averaging 10 laps—to get an entry in the Snetterton grand finale.

Snetterton was—and still is—the only circuit in Britain to have planning permission for night racing, so a 24-hour event like Le Mans had been organised. The RAC, however, decided that the circuit was too short for accurate all-night timekeeping, and many potential competitors realised that they could not afford such a long event: so two two-hour races—one in daylight and one in the dark—were run as a compromise. House paced himself well for third in class in the first race, then came through in the second to win his class as numerous competitors suffered blown engines in cars which had been prepared for 10-lap spring events. This was enough to make him *Autosport* class B champion.

Meanwhile six Morgans were entered for the longest race in Britain since the war—the Guards 1,000-mile production sports car event at Brands Hatch, made up of two 500-mile races on consecutive days. Lawrence and John Spender shared the new TOK 258 using a 2,196-cc engine, with House running his normal 2,136-cc Plus Four with Roger North. Kendall shared Tucker's two-litre Plus Four, supported by J.C. Thurston and J.V. Terry in another Plus Four. Jones, who had sold his Plus Four to John Maclay, shared the car with him and, although they were reserves, got a drive because there were two non-starters; the sixth Morgan, of Charles Blyth and Mrs. J. Bond-Smith was left out in the cold, however.

Lawrence was an early leader on the first day until he lost nearly 30 laps with a broken chassis tube and brake trouble, then outran all the survivors to win the second race—although the time lost on the first day kept him well down on aggregate.

The following season, Lawrence managed to get his SLR accepted as a marque racer, despite protests, winning easily at Goodwood twice before writing the car off in a crash. Jim Donnelly then took over one of the remaining Morgan SLRs to race in company with Neil Dangerfield's Triumph SLR, winning again at Goodwood from Gordon Miles's Super Sports. Miles then enjoyed a reasonable amount of success as his car, like many others racing in the Fred Dixon Challenge adopted far wider wheels. These wheels—exotic Borrani alloy-rimmed wires in the case of Miles—offered a lot more grip when running with the front tyres from Formula One cars all round. More standard Plus Fours, such as those driven by Andy Pugh and Kendall, Tucker and Blyth, continued to be successful, however, taking eighth and tenth places overall in the Ilford Films 500-mile race at Brands Hatch. Lefevre also continued to do well in trials with his 4/4, winning a gold triple award for gaining first-class awards in the Land's End, Derbyshire and Exeter events.

Peter Morgan also made a re-appearance in trials in 1967, winning his class with the Plus Four Plus in the Exeter before performing well in the Land's End.

It would also be the last year of marque events before the relative championships were renamed Special Sports in company with the fast-developing Special GT series for outright racing cars. Roger Thomas started well in the Fred Dixon Challenge in the Plus Four Super Sports he shared with Roger Bonsall, but it soon became apparent that the 2,000–3,000-cc class in which most of the Morgans ran would be dominated by John Chatham's Austin-Healey 3000, so House—driving Roger North's left-hand-drive Super Sports—stayed well clear in the AMASCO Challenge. In this way he managed five class wins, plus other class placings, which gave him a championship class win.

By 1968, Special Sports—now called Production Sports Car racing—featured even more highly-developed vehicles which had to retain a more-or-less standard body profile but little else. Fuel injection and crossflow cylinder heads were banned from winning cars, but special alloy cylinder blocks and five-speed gearboxes were frequently allowed, to the detriment of any challenge from a Morgan. A Plus Eight might have been competitive, but nobody who had bought one at that time fancied racing it . . .

As a result, Big Healeys dominated the 2,000–3,000-cc classes in which Super Sports ran, although the Stapleton brothers—John in Dence's former Le Mans Super Sports (which had been re-registered JHX 142B when Lawrence transferred the number TOK 258 to his SLR), and Bruce in a similar car—had some placings along with Miles. But, in the main, Morgan circuit racing successes were confined to non-championship club events. The Morgan club had a hard core of racing enthusiasts, but not enough to run a meeting of their own, so the Bentley Drivers' Club—which had been running an event at Silverstone for around 20 years—began organising a race confined to the Morgan marque. This handicap event was won in 1968 by Robin Brown's 4/4 from the Plus Fours of Brian Jenkins and Rose.

A different situation arose in the United States, however, where saloon car racing organiser Bill France decided to run a 24-hour race at his headquarters, Daytona Beach, to rival Le Mans. Although this event was part of the world sports car championship, it failed to attract a full field of sports racing cars because of the expense of travelling to America. The only European teams which could afford it were run by manufacturers and were outstandingly fast as a result. But France decided to admit almost any car to fill out the field for maximum spectacle, despite the inherent dangers of having cars racing together with vastly differing speed potentials, which resulted in a lone Morgan Plus Four entry for George Waltman. In the event, the Morgan ran at the end of the field—averaging only 54 mph—as Porsche 907s, Ferrari 275LMs, Alfa Romeo T33s and Ford GT40s flashed past at more than double the speed. Somehow the Morgan managed to keep out of everybody else's way to finish 30th and last to rapturous applause for the underdog.

In the less rarified climes of traditional trials, Roger Bricknall began a brilliant career by winning a Triple Award with his Plus Four for cleaning every section in the Exeter, Land's End and Scottish events.

As 'production' sports cars became ever more modified—front-running MG Midgets now featured Formula Three racing car chassis with a glass fibre Midget-shaped body—Morgan's chief stamping ground became hill climbs, with David Way taking his 4/4 to third place in the 1969 Castrol/BARC championship behind two Minis. Other successful Morgan drivers in Andy Duncan, Harvey Postlethwaite (who later went on to become a Ferrari Formula One car designer), and Adam Bridgland emerged as a strength in club racing with one of the first Plus Eights to be seen in action, taking second place at the Bentley Drivers' Club meeting to Jim Tucker's full-race Plus Four despite running in road-going trim.

Prodsports (for production sports) became Modsports (for modified sports car racing) in 1970, with a tighter rein being kept on modifications in that it was no longer permissible to remove any metal from between the wheel centres. This effectively outlawed the spaceframe Midgets, but rendered the Lotus Elan, TVR Tuscan and AC Cobra, with their light weight, good aerodynamics and powerful Ford-based engines, highly competitive in the 1,150–2,000-cc, 2,000–3,000-cc and over-3,000-cc classes in which Morgans might have had some success. Nevertheless Michael Ashley-Brown had five class wins in XRX1—the Daimler-engined Super Sports, which had passed through James Henderson's hands since being sold

*Below:* Roy North's left-hand-drive Plus Four Super Sports was subsequently raced by John Stapleton—seen here at Crystal Palace in 1969—before passing on to Bob Stuart and, later, Aubrey Brocklebank.

*Below right:* Claude Savoye gives the Morgan Plus Eight one of its first competitive outings in the 1969 Tour de France—a combination of races, rally stages and hill climbs.

by Feilding. Brian Haslam also started to campaign a Plus Eight, and managed one class win in events dominated by Cobras. Bridgland largely stuck to sprints and Way, Duncan and Meredith to hill climbs with John Day's 4/4 winning the Bentley Drivers' Club race from Peter Binder's 4/4, a Ferrari Dino taking third place in a field which had to be filled out with all-comers, so few Morgans were racing on circuits at the time.

But Peter Morgan kept the marque's traditions alive with another triple award for performances in the Exeter, Land's End and Edinburgh Trials in 1971 with John Stapleton and Haslam taking class placings in modsports racing with their Plus Eights. Haslam proved to be the front-running Morgan driver, also, at the Bentley meeting, finishing third behind two Cobras in the combined AC-Morgan handicap.

Morgan's competition career took an upturn in 1972 when Robin Gray, who had been racing a LawrenceTune Ford Escort saloon, managed to get a drive in Haslam's Plus Eight, which had been prepared by the same firm. He promptly gained a spectacular second and then a first place in rounds of the Fred Dixon modsports championship which had been receiving sparse entries, such was the dominance of TVR's Tuscan in the 2,000-3,000-cc category. Otherwise competition activities were confined to the odd success in sprints and hill climbs by Haslam, Bridgland and Alex Robinson.

Lawrence then bought the Haslam Plus Eight for Gray to continue racing in modsports and the Super Sports (which he re-registered TOK 258) that he had used at Le Mans. This proved ideal for a new form of historic racing for Thoroughbred sports cars built between 1946 and 1959 and prepared to a specification very much like the former *Autosport* marque machines. Meanwhile declining grids in modsports racing had led to the STP championship being reorganized as a new form of Prodsports racing along the lines of a recent Group 1 Production Saloon Car championship—called Prodsaloon, of course! In the new Prodsports championship the early regulations catered only for cars of which a minimum of 1,000 had been made and were currently available in the United Kingdom. They were split into price categories of up to £1,200; £1,625, £3,000 and over £3,000—and Morgan suffered by being excluded due to a rule saying that at least 500 of any one model must be made in a year, which was really aimed at the TVRs, Davrians and Ginettas which had led to the decline of Modsports. But as the year went on the organisers found that they had not allowed a sufficient number of cars to be eligible for the new championship and struggled to provide any sort of spectacle!

*Below left:* Robin Grey in Brian Haslam's Plus Eight, leads Brian Hough's TVR Tuscan in the modsports race at Silverstone in April 1972.

*Below:* John Stapleton had joined the Plus Eight ranks by 1972, pictured here at Brands Hatch in July.

It was a different story, however, in the new Thoroughbred championship. The classes were split at up to 2,000-cc, 3,000-cc and over 3,000-cc so Lawrence fitted a 1,991-cc engine to TOK 258 to win the 2-litre class from MGB opposition in such a convincing manner that he was able to let his associates, Gray and Escort V8 racer Brian Cutting, have a go on odd occasions as well! And just to prove that it was not just a case of a superior driver, they battled for overall wins with TOK.

Morgan's revival in circuit racing was emphasised by several successes for the 4/4s of David Rutherford and John Berry and the Plus Eights of Alex Robinson, John McDonald and Bridgland at the Bentley Drivers' Club meeting and a handicap win for the Libra Morgan Grinders' team of Malcolm Hayward and Bill Hopkins (Plus Eights), Aubrey Brocklebank and Nigel Sill (Plus Fours).

Modsports continued to thrive in 1974, despite the promotion of Prodsports, with Gray in his Plus Eight battling with the Jaguar E types of John Burbidge and Guy Beddington for the over three-litre class until John Pearson returned to his plastic-bodied XK120 to dominate the class; Gray, nevertheless, managed one overall win at Silverstone against the normal front-runners in Lotus Elans and Porsche Carreras. Other modsports Plus Eights were driven by Patrick Keen (in the ex-Stapleton car) and McDonald, who experimented with supercharging and won the Bentley Drivers' Club race and at Croft.

The Prodsports organisers had to allow entries from more cars to expand their grids, to Morgan's benefit, and that of dealer John Britten whose Plus Eight battled with Lotus Europas, but could not match the winning E type of Peter Taylor.

Gray drove TOK 258 again in Thoroughbred racing with considerable success despite engine problems, finishing second in the championship to the redoubtable Triumph TR3 of Reg Woodcock. Other successful Morgan drivers at this time included Wells with his 4/4, and John Berry and Andy Duncan who hill-climbed similar cars.

Morgans really began to come into their own in 1975 as Gray won his

class in the premier modsports championship with his Plus Eight, frequently getting on terms with the Elans which usually won overall; and this was despite having to use a standard engine at one point when his 3.8-litre racing unit had blown up.

John Britten continued to drive successfully in Prodsports with his Plus Eight but was completely upstaged by his salesman, Chris Alford, who won the championship outright in a 4/4—running in the £1,401–£2,250 class! Britten won two races, but Alford managed 15 class wins out of 15 starts against chiefly MGB and Triumph TR6 opposition, attributing his success to the fact that he could outbrake any of the opposition.

In one-day events, the Morgan team of Rob Wells and Bryan Harvey in 4/4s, Bill Hopkins, and Peter Morgan's son Charles, in Plus Eights, won a rain-truncated Six-Hour Relay and John Berry's lightweight 4/4 won the Bentley Drivers' Club Morgan scratch race, Brocklebank winning a handicap event at the same meeting in the ex-Lawrence SLR.

Alford won the £2,001–£3,000 class in Prodsports again in 1976—but in another car sold by Britten's garage, a TVR. His closest rivals were 4/4 exponents Chris Hampshire and Anthony Brewer, however as Chris Meek's very special Lotus Europa ran away with the championship. Plus Eights driven by Britten, Bill Wykeham, Bob Stuart and Charles Morgan (in MMC 11) also performed well with Morgan gaining one second place.

Gray tried hard in Modsports with his Plus Eight, winning once, and eventually gaining third place overall, despite missing part of the season after crashing at Oulton Park, as John Cooper easily took the title with a Porsche Carrera RSR. But Gray had the consolation of winning the Bentley Drivers' Club's Morgan scratch race with the Plus Eight before retiring the following season.

Prodsports developed into a savage battle during 1977 as Meek used every trick in the book to vie for two titles with his Europa—with his chief opposition, Colin Blower in a TVR3000M and the Plus Eights of Wells and

*Above left:* Zakspeed and Tyrrell grand prix driver Jonathan Palmer, then a medical student, leads the modsports field at Brands Hatch into the first bend in November 1976, followed by Bob Jarvis's Davrian and Gordon Dennis in Robin Grey's Morgan Plus Eight.

*Above:* Andy Garlick's Morgan leads a Thoroughbred field dominated by Porsche 356s at Brands Hatch in 1977.

*Below left:* Swansong for Robin Grey as he leads the field in his last race at Brands Hatch in May 1977.

*Below:* Bruce Stapleton became one of the front-runners in 1977 Prodsports racing with his Rola Shipping-sponsored Plus Eight, pictured here at Brands Hatch.

Wykeham (who both won once), Charles Morgan (one second place) and Chris Stapleton generally suffering . . . although Meek eventually missed out on both titles to a Ginetta and a Midget due to lack of reliability and the Morgan drivers distinguished themselves by treating racing as a sport and refusing to protest. Keen also won one non-championship modsports race with Chris Cooke's 4/4 winning the Bentley Drivers' Club Morgan scratch race.

After a slow start, Prodsports was developing into a high-successful formula, with two championships in 1978, sponsored by Aleybars and DB Motors. Charles Morgan won six races in the works Plus Eight MMC 11, battling chiefly with Wykeham and Blower's TVR, to take the DB title as Wykeham also took on Meek, now in an MG Midget, for the Aleybars championship. Once again Meek won, but Wykeham was well satisfied with second place. Other Plus Eights proved competitive in the hands of Anthony Palmer, Bruce Stapleton, Stuart, Peter Garland, Norman Stechman, Mary Lindsey and Keen with Cooke's 4/4 again winning the Bentley Drivers' Club scratch race. And Wells, who prepared MMC 11, took it to four more wins in non-championship events for good measure . . .

There were also enough Morgans racing to make up two teams in the 750MC Relay, temporarily moved to a new parkland circuit at Donington. In a good old-fashioned way, they were named Anglemog Saxon—made up of Garland, John Millbank, Bob Chaplin and Duncan in 4/4s, Peter Evans's Super Sports and Dave Saunter's Plus Eight—and Anglemog Vikings—consisting of Mary Lindsey, Keen and Stechman in Plus Eights, MacDonald and Garlick in Plus Fours and Andy Kennedy's 4/4. In the event the two teams both covered 264 laps with the Saxons winning the handicap award by three seconds from the second-placed Vikings . . .

Snetterton also staged a new version of the old *Autosport* Three-Hour race, with a second part run in darkness which gave a Prodsports class victory to the Plus Eight of Wykeham and Stapleton (third overall) from the similar car of Palmer.

The following season, 1979, as Charles Morgan concentrated on the CAV Prodsports series, Wells borrowed MMC 11 for the DB Motors/*Cars and Car Conversions* championship, both having to borrow other Plus Eights to complete their series when it needed engine work! But Morgan won class A in his series, finishing third overall behind Meek's MG Midget, with Wells also winning his class A and taking second place overall behind Alison

Davis's Ginetta. At the same time, Wells began designing a works-sponsored Plus Eight project to make Morgan competitive again in Modsports now that Gray had quit . . .

Meanwhile Morris Stapleton Motors had been involved in an equally-ambitious attempt at recapturing some of Morgan's glory in international endurance racing. This lightweight Plus Eight was specially-adapted for long distance events, making its first appearance in the Brands Hatch Six Hour—one of the British rounds in Le Mans-type racing—against Porsche opposition in group four plus a BMW M1 and a works turbocharged Lancia for overall positions. For this event, Wykeham was joined by John Spero and Brian Classic, who drove steadily to finish with a highly-creditable 18th position overall and eighth in class.

In distinct contrast, Askew won the Bentley Drivers' Club Morgan scratch race with his modsports 4/4 . . .

*Collector's Car* editor Phil Young started the 1980s valiantly with a Rob Wells-prepared factory Plus Eight on the Monte Carlo Rally (with Tony Ambrose) before they were misdirected by a gendarme in a snowstorm!

Malcolm Paul and Steve Cole became front-runners in the CAV and DB Motors Prodsports series as Wells and Charles Morgan concentrated on preparing MMC 11 for the first of what would become the classic of British production car racing, the Willhire 24-hour race at Snetterton.

Wykeham and Stapleton also persisted with the Group Four Plus Eight in British rounds of the World Endurance Championship, finding more power to take seventeenth place with Classic in the Brands Hatch Six Hour (despite oil pump problems), before having to retire in the Silverstone Six Hour where Richard Down had taken Classic's place. Wells and Wykeham competed sporadically in Modsports and the Inter-Marque Challenge (at that time for Porsche, Aston Martin, Morgan and Alfa Romeo cars). But their main effort was centred on the Willhire race with Wells joined by Charles Morgan, Stechman and Paul in MMC 11 and Wykeham aided by Bruce Stapleton, Down and Spero in a Morgan-loaned Plus Eight. These cars competed for the Commander's Cup while a separate class was run for team entries along the lines of the 750MC Relay rules in which the Morgan Sports Car Club entered Plus Eights driven by Mary and John Lindsey, Keen, MacDonald, Garland and Duncan. The Morgans were immediately among the front runners until MMC 11 lost 1$\frac{1}{2}$ hours in the pits with final drive problems, leaving the Morgan club relay team to take third place overall and the Stapleton's single car entry fifth behind the winning Opel team, but taking the Commander's Cup. Wells, however, had consolation: he

*Below left:* The Stapleton/Wykeham/Classic Morgan Plus Eight charges on as Eddie Cheever flashes past in his Lancia Beta Monte Carlo to second place in the 1980 Brands Hatch Six-Hour race.

*Below:* Malcolm Paul is pictured finishing fourth to Chris Meek's Panther Lima in a CAV Prodsports round at Brands Hatch in May 1980 after spinning his Plus Eight while in second position.

won the Bentley Drivers' Club Morgan scratch race!

Prodsports was re-organised in 1981 to provide one national series with CAV sponsorship, DB Motors having switched to Special GT. Only Group Three —series production cars—would now be eligible to Prodsports, eliminating the Ginettas, Panthers and Lotus Europas. But in Class A, Tony Lanfranchi ran a Porsche 911SC to great effect, against the Plus Eights of Paul, Cole and Stechman. Early races showed them to be equally matched, resulting in Lanfranchi—who had been racing for more than 25 years— taking the lead on experience. Then in mid-season Cole began to close up in the Class A title race, losing out to take second place only in the last round, with Paul fifth and Stechman tenth, Trevor Lewis's MG Midget having run away with the overall championship. Blower, for once, was well down, having run a heavier new TVR Tasmin, Meek moving to Special GTs with a Europa.

Wells, meantime, had come on to form with the new Modsports Morgans carrying the number MMC 3, its ultra-lightweight construction and British Leyland works-assisted Rover V8 making it such a consistent class winner that it beat Steve Roberts's 1,340-cc Davrian for the STP series title, Wells also winning the Bentley Drivers' Club race again from Charles Morgan and Grahame Bryant's Plus Eight. Keen also took the Le Mans TOK 258 to the Thoroughbred championship in the last round at Silverstone.

*Below:* Norman Stechman and Steve Cole race side by side with their Plus Eights in the CAV Prodsports round at Brands Hatch in May 1981.

*Below right:* Steve Cole's Plus Eight charges into the lead of a CAV Prodsports round at Mallory Park on his way to second place in the 1981 title race.

*Bottom left:* Andy Simm contests the over-1,300-cc class for GT and modsports cars with his 4/4 at the Bugatti Owners' Club hill climb in April 1982.

*Bottom right:* Hectic pit stop for the works Plus Eight in the 1982 Willhire 24-hour race.

Stechman's Plus Eight, shared with Malcolm Harrison, Mike Ridley and Francois Duret, also staged a repeat win, taking the Commander's Cup in the Willhire 24-hour race, leading the event at one point, as did the sister car driven by Wells, Paul and Charles Morgan until that lost a wheel. But Morgan and Paul avenged their Willhire disappointment by taking a clear victory over the Opel Commodore of Martin Carroll and Syd Fox in a new Three-Hour Race at Brands Hatch.

Finally Stapleton, Wykeham and Down gave the endurance racing Morgan its last race before new regulations took over by finishing fifteenth in the Silverstone Six Hours.

The Willhire 24-hour became the premier event in the production car racing calendar for 1982 with sufficient entries to eliminate the team relay system and allow only single cars to run. The works Plus Eight of Wells, Alford and Paul won easily by 11 laps from a BMW 323i, before both were excluded due to technical infringements and the Opel Commodore won again. The Prodsports series itself was won by Cole, who drove his newly-sponsored Plus Eight with flair and consistency throughout the season. Paul was able to match him on his day but never frequently enough to challenge Cole for the CAV title. In general, however, the CAV grids were pitifully thin and it was decided to combine the series with Prodsaloons the following year. As a result, sports cars in near-standard trim started appearing in the Donington Production GT series and the 750MC's Garelli

*Below left:* Jim Deacon's Plus Eight is pictured heading for eighth place in the 1982 Willhire 24-hour race despite losing time with fuel pump trouble.

*Below:* Frank McClain storms Prescott with his Morgan Plus Four in the classic car class of the Bugatti Owners' Club hill climb in April 1984.

*Bottom left:* Dawn halt in the 1984 Land's End Trial organised—as ever—by the MCC (or Motor Cycling Club), hence the two-wheeled competitors.

*Bottom right:* Typical end to a section of the Land's End Trial . . . on the end of a rope in 1984.

Works development engineer Maurice Owen thunders up the Bluehills mine track in the 1984 Land's End Trial.

*Below:* Steve Cole races to second place in the Cheshire Cats' Hundred Mile race at Oulton Park in April 1984, won by the Porsche Carrera RS of Josh Sadler and Chester Wedgewood.

*Below right:* Kevin Donnelly contests a round of the Thoroughbred championship at Silverstone in July 1984 with his Flat Rad Plus Four.

Sports Car Championship. Peter Garrod's Lotus Europa took the major honours in the Garelli series, but had a hard time seeing off the Morgan 4/4 of Richard Casswell and the larger class stayed open until the final round when Bill Taylor's Porsche Carrera RS was content to follow home Bryant's alternative car—an MGB GT V8—to scoop enough points to demote Fred Campbell's Plus Eight to third position. In the Bentley Drivers' Club race, the first of three consecutive results was recorded: Well's Plus Eight from those of Bryant and Campbell!

Meanwhile, in the Donington Production GT series, there were several fine scraps between TVRs and Plus Eights, with three wins by Cole securing his class from Kent's turbocharged TVR.

The parallel Donnington GT series for modified sports and saloon cars developed into a championship dominated by old single-seater chassis—such as those used in Formula Two racing—clothed in plastic bodies resembling production cars, with the result that Jeff Wilson's 'BMW M1' (a Chevron Formula 5000 car with a 440bhp 3.4-litre Ford GAA Group Two saloon car racing engine) proved too rapid for Wells's more conventional and less aerodynamic Plus Eight, which withdrew after a couple of outings. A one-circuit championship at Castle Combe saw Tom Hind's Plus Eight win its class, however. Keen also managed to win his class in the Thoroughbred championship with TOK 258 despite a decision to run modified and unmodified cars together in a series which had fallen into decline following rule changes which favoured some makes of cars against others.

Declining grids in Production car racing led the organisers to abolish the upper price limit on eligible cars, with the result that a works Porsche 928S won the Willhire 24-hour event with the Bulldog Team's Plus Eight of Mary and John Lindsey, Jim Deacon, Leigh Sebba, Saunter and Tim Sissons finishing fifth, the Allied Rubber Products Plus Eight of Stechman, Paul Everett, Mike Ridley and Duret taking fourteenth. The strongest of the multi-class sports/saloon series became the Donington Production GT in which Cole failed by only one point to wrest the overall title from Bob Buttery's Alfasud, although he won the large Class A. He also had one win in the 750MC's series, with Casswell's 4/4 having another victory in a series dominated by Taylor's Porsche. Paul and fellow Plus Eight pilot Jeff Stow scored points in the former CAV series, now sponsored by Uniroyal, but could not match the Caterham Seven of overall winner Maynard Soares.

Problems between the Caterham Sevens—very light small sports cars which could out-corner almost anything but lacked straight-line speed—and big saloons, such as BMWs, which were slow through the corners but fast along the straights—culminated in a potentially serious accident in 1984 in the even more popular Willhire 24-hour race and led to the rules being

*Below left:* Tom Hinds takes fourth place with his Plus Eight in a round of the Castle Combe Special GT championship in 1984 won by Rob Cox-Allison's Lotus Elan Black Bullet.

*Below right:* Caroline Tarry's Plus Eight battles with Fergus Oakley's Lotus Super Seven in the Road-Going Sports Car championship at Brands Hatch in September 1984.

*Bottom left:* Driving tests are great fun . . . particularly when you are blindfolded in a Morgan 4/4.

*Bottom right:* Morgan line-up at a Wiscombe Park hill climb in 1984.

You have to be tough to drive a Morgan in mid-winter . . . Barry Sumner on the 1985 Exeter Trial.

*Below:* R.M. Comber gives the 1939 Land's End special 4-4 an outing on the 1985 Exeter Trial.

*Below right:* Richard Casswell takes seventh place with his Morgan 4/4 in the road-going sports car race at Brands Hatch in March 1985.

changed to ban sports cars in 1985. As a result that race became the last for the Morgans in which Wells, Alford and Charles Morgan led with MMC 11 before being eliminated with electrical trouble. The Bulldog Plus Eight of the Lindseys, Duncan and Bob Cook survived to finish twelfth from a record 36 starters. Morgans were also rendered less than competitive for front-running honours by the admission of Ginettas to help fill the grids. Interest was also declining fast in Modsports, although Wells did manage one win with the Plus Eight in an STP series won by Rob Cox's Caterham and Hinds took third place in the Castle Combe series.

Keen made a comeback in 1984, however, to take his class in Thoroughbred racing with TOK and come a close second to former Grand Prix driver Mike Wilds in an Aston Martin DB4.

During 1985, the 750MC's road-going sports car series developed into one of the chief areas of interest for Morgan circuit racing followers with

Bryant, who also drove a Carrera RS in the Porsche Challenge, winning the top class in his Plus Eight from Porsche opposition and taking third place overall to a Triumph Spitfire and a Caterham as Cole appeared among the regular winners in the BRSCC's Ronnie Scott sports car series taken by a Porsche Carrera. Cole then switched to a works TVR 420SEAC for the series in 1986, regularly leading Bryant's Plus Eight until it became apparent that only one of these TVRs had been built, leaving Bryant as the undisputed winner. Stechman won the Bentley Drivers' Club race from MacDonald and Stuart, however, Bryant winning at last in 1986 from the Plus Eights of Garland and Tony Morgan-Tripp.

*Top left:* Morgans everywhere, including on the grass, at Becketts in the Bentley Driver's Club meeting in August 1985.

*Top right:* Grahame Bryant trails a smokescreen in the Morgan scratch race at the Bentley Driver's Club meeting in August 1985.

*Above left:* John MacDonald takes second place in the 1985 Bentley Driver's Club Morgan scratch race with his ex-Marten Plus Four Super Sports.

*Above right:* Steve Spencer takes over for his stint with the Daimler-engined Plus Four for the Morgan Sports Car Club's team in the 1985 Six-Hour Relay race at Silverstone.

Pat Kennett in action with his London Motor Show interim Plus Four in the M.G. Car Club's Kimber Trial in November 1985.

*Top left:* Mary Lindsey lifts a wheel of her Plus Eight in the 1985 Kimber Trial.

*Top right:* Barrie Taylor storms the Wiscombe Park hill climb in 1986 with his 4/4.

*Above left:* Morgans to the fore in the unique 1986 John O'Groats to Land's End Trial.

*Above right:* K. Morton regularly contests Vintage Sports-Car Club events with his 4-4, pictured here at Silverstone in June 1986.

*Right:* Kevin Laidlaw's Plus Eight contests the over 1,600-cc mod-sports class at Shelsley Walsh hill climb in July 1986.

*Below:* Peter Askew prepares for blast off in the 1986 Brighton Speed trials with his modified 4/4.

*Below right:* Morgans everywhere in a demonstration run at Silverstone in 1986.

Throughout club racing, one-make series had also emerged as an ideal way of providing close racing at—hopefully—reduced cost. This trend led to the establishment of a Morgan Challenge, with not only Bryant, but Deacon, Sebba, and Charles Windridge and Morgan-Tripp as the front-runners with Plus Eights and Barrie Taylor with his 4/4, giving hope for a secure future for Morgans in competition.

# VIII
# Buying a Used Morgan

Most of the problems associated with buying a used Morgan centre around the fact that these cars have always been built to a tight budget to keep down the price when new. As a result, until recently, the bodies—for instance— were assembled first at the factory and then painted as a complete unit, rather than having each panel painted before assembly. The chassis also flexes and with stiff suspension the body has a hard life. The result is that after a few years' use, corrosion is to be expected. The exact extent of the body's deterioration depends on how and where the car has been used and how well it has been maintained.

After checking that the car stands squarely on a flat surface, look for rust bubbles on steel sections of the body, especially around vulnerable areas such as the beaded seams. As the body flexes with the chassis, the bridge of paint across these seams can crack, letting in road spray—which often contains highly-corrosive salt in winter—as the joint is attacked simultaneously from the underside. The inside faces of these joints are likely to be covered only with primer, because the body was painted as a unit assembled from primed panels: and the problem with primer is that unlike a top coat of paint, it is porous. Thus, even where the primer is not worn away, it does little to delay corrosion.

If such corrosion—the first outward signs of which are bubbling at the seams—is allowed to continue for long, the corrosive solution penetrates the Morgan's wooden frame. The frame then starts to rot leading to the need for even more extensive repairs. Heat from the exhaust system also dries out onto adjacent wood too fast. Two-seater cars made before 1976 are also especially vulnerable at the back because the rear panel was held on by tacks and aluminium beading—which, in turn, corrodes in contact with steel and cracks when weakened.

Further typical corrosion traps include the piping around the cowl and the joints between the headlamp nacelles on interim and curved-radiator cars, with special emphasis on the most exposed part—the point directly under the headlamp rim. Cracks in the wing are also likely to radiate from the sidelight housing if it is not kept securely fastened. This is because the

Rust attacks a Morgan's steel body everywhere if it is neglected.

sidelight mountings are also the sole means of attachment for the end of the wing supporting bracket and are subject to a lot of strain and vibration. At the same time it is wise to check the body's means of attachment to the chassis, particularly at the back: on hard-used and ill-maintained cars it can be anything but sound.

A general idea of the quality of the ash frame can be gained by checking

Steel wings are especially prone to corrosion.

for any softness in the area of the scuttle, door frames, pillars and rear panels. The portion that suffers most in the entire body is around the chassis under the doors because water finds its way into the padded trim and is held there to provide an ideal starting point for rust. As a result, chassis have

Once the wings are removed, renovation is far more practical.

Impacts can crack the wings.

Sometimes it is only practical to fit completely new bodywork.

often been found to have rotted almost completely through at this point in little more than 10 years. The lower and trailing edges of the doors also suffer from road spray and debris and can mean that the entire door has to be re-skinned if not replaced.

Morgan chassis are extremely strong, but partly because they are bolted up during construction rather than welded, they flex more than normal and are more prone to cracking during old age or as a result of heavy use and a lack of maintenance. Exhaust mountings, shaken loose by hammering over rough surfaces, are frequent causes of this condition, which can also occur at the point where the exhaust passes through the chassis. Heavily-stressed parts include the area around the crossmember behind the engine, particularly in early cars and especially in Plus Fours with the heavy Vanguard or TR2 engine, which did not have reinforcing gussets. The early Plus Eights with metal floors also suffer from a lot of rust which can spread

The remotely-mounted gearbox of this series 1 4-4 is in good condition, but the chassis siderails betray their age.

New siderails have been fitted to this series 1 4-4 during its restoration.

to the scuttle support. Cracks are also likely to be found around the engine mountings, particularly of the Plus Eights which have to withstand a lot of torque. Early cars are also subject to chassis cracking around the front frame, although later ones were strengthened at this point and last a lot longer. If the diagonal tie rods are not kept tight, trouble can also be generated around the elongated holes through which their cast brackets pass.

Radiators can also suffer badly from jolts and vibration, especially on early cars with the hardest suspension.

It is inevitable with extremely hard suspension that wear will result fairly rapidly in its components—the first of which will be the centre pins and bushes at the front which are likely to need replacement every 15,000 miles. Shock absorbers need to be functioning efficiently—check by bouncing the car as well as driving it—and damper blades need periodic attention as well. Their deterioration is one of the prime causes of a Morgan's notorious wheel wobble. Loose spokes and worn splines (through wheels not having been secured tightly enough) are typical of any wire-wheeled cars, but beware also of out-of-true steel wheels on Morgans which have had a hard life. Check also for any signs of cracking around the stud holes of early steel-wheeled cars.

The back axle should show no more than two inches of backlash, measured at the rim, keeping in mind that many early axle parts are by now unobtainable or are likely to be expensive if remanufactured because of the small quantities involved. Play of around 1.5 inches at the wheel rim is permissible in a Cam Gears steering box, however, providing it is operating smoothly. Wear in other steering parts should be easy to detect although it should be noted that the bushes of the later collapsible columns are not available as replacements, which means that the entire unit has to be changed if they are worn.

Apart from problems associated with overheating in modern traffic

Bad vibrations can lead to leaking radiators especially on the early 4-4s and Plus Fours.

*Below left:* Shock absorber mountings need vigilant attention.

*Below:* Access to a Morgan's rear axle is good

Steering box mountings and
chassis siderail bolts need to be
kept tight.

What it should look like . . . the
engine bay of a series 1 Coventry
Climax-powered 4-4.

conditions if an auxiliary fan is not fitted, the Coventry Climax engine used
in the earliest 4-4s suffers from an insufficiently-rigid crankshaft. This can
result in trouble with the overstressed centre main bearing. The construction
of the rocker arms can lead to a lot of trouble if they do not receive careful
maintenance. This is because they were drilled to allow oil to reach the pads

in contact with the inlet valves and also the push-rod cap ends. The oil flow was restricted to the lower parts of the arm by a piece of string inserted in the top of the oil holes—which, inevitably becomes clogged and stops the oil flow, with the result that the rocker shaft wears. The only solution, apart from replacing the string regularly, is to remove it and replace it with a proper restrictor in the pipeline. Oil also forces its way out of the timing case and into the chain-driven dynamo of early cars, a fault shared with the contemporary overhead camshaft MGs.

The Standard engines used in later 4/4s gave little trouble if they were maintained carefully and the small Ford power trains used from the series II 4/4s onwards have always been exceptionally long-lasting units. The only

Leather upholstery suffers badly if it is neglected and it costs a fortune to replace.

normal problems are high-mileage wear which manifests itself first in blue smoke from the exhaust on the over-run, and later if the engine is revved hard after ticking over for a while. Fumes are also emitted from the oil filler's breather, generally after about 75,000 miles, when the engine needs a rebore or new oil scraper rings.

While the gearboxes give little trouble, the Morgan-made changing mechanism on early models can be decidedly eccentric. The first arrangement relied heavily on the quality of its rubber bushes for precision, and obviously they deteriorate with age and wear, and the later push-pull mechanism had a habit of coming out in the driver's hand! Clutch life is generally around 40,000 miles.

While the Standard Vanguard and Triumph TR units used in Plus Fours may be amongst the toughest units ever made, they are not entirely foolproof. Their main attribute is that they seem to be able to go on for a tremendous mileage without overhaul, and seemingly run well when, in fact, they can be in an extraordinarily worn state. The result is that components have a tendency to break without warning because they have run for an uncertain time without attention. Timing chain tensioners are a typical example. Bearings can also give unexpected trouble, which is not surprising when it is realised that one of the first signs of a worn engine can be manifested in the piston rings and it is quite easy to replace the rings, pistons and liners without touching the bottom end of the engine. As a result, a seemingly healthy power unit can be running on bearings of great antiquity.

In addition, camshaft knock on earlier engines can be disastrous. They do not have replaceable bearings which means that a new cylinder block is needed unless it is possible to cure the damage by surgery—which will be very expensive.

Clutches are as strong as those of any similar car, and have only one inherent weakness: the release fork is located on its operating shaft by a pin which can shear inside the bellhousing. It should be wired on for security in case it falls down and damages something else. In some cases, the fork snaps next to the pin—and in either case, the unfortunate owner or driver is left without means of disengaging the clutch at the very least. If the car is travelling fast, it is wise to try to stop it by use of the ignition key if you cannot change gear without a clutch.

The Moss gearbox is a very strong unit and can last a long time in its typically noisy and obstructive state. Synchromesh varies from weak to non-existent, but the actual gearchange should be positive—if slow—and it should not jump out of engagement. Beware, however, spares are likely to be expensive if re-manufactured. Plus Four clutches last, on average, 40,000 miles, like those of 4/4s.

The Rover engine used in the Plus Eight is an extraordinary one: it rarely runs at more than 45 psi hot and frequently drops to 5 psi on take-off and tick-over with no seeming ill effects! Be wary of anything resembling the tick of a loose tappet on this engine, or any misfiring. A ticking from a hydraulic tappet can be the cam follower tapping the camshaft, with resultant expensive repairs being needed if this condition does not receive immediate attention. Leads frequently fall off the side-mounted plugs on the V8 and cause it to misfire; it's easy enough to replace the offending plug lead, but if the misfire persists, check everything, including the compression. The high-compression V8 that I used for two years ran with a slight misfire for 1,000 miles before it was discovered that this condition was caused by a broken piston (which, in turn, was caused by enforced running on inferior-grade fuel). Oil level is also of crucial importance in this engine, which, in common with similar low-pressure American V8s, has an exceptionally small sump. It is also essential to change the oil diligently if bearing wear is to be minimised.

The Rover gearboxes used in the later Plus Eights are generally reliable although the four-speed version is at the limit of its capacity such is the torque produced by the V8, and will initially give trouble on the change from second to third. Tuned examples of the Plus Eight using the SD1 gearbox can suffer from similar problems with bearing wear. The SD1 gearbox should also be treated extremely gently when cold, especially when attempting to change into second gear, because of its taper roller bearing design. A problem with the stress concentration on fifth gear also manifests itself with heavy use, especially in competition with uprated engines.

The old Moss gearbox can be considered quiet, however, compared to the Salisbury limited-slip differential used in the Plus Eight. The limited-slip friction pads clatter a lot when they are hot, producing the most noise in tight turns. In fact, the owners' manual carries a warning to expect dramatic sound effects . . . but they mellow with age and rarely spell disaster on standard cars! Excessive wear on one rear tyre—so much that its rolling radius is greater than that of its opposite number—or the mixing of different tyres, can also lead to a rear-wheel steering effect on a Plus Eight as the limited slip plates go into action and disengage.

# IX
# Maintaining a Morgan

Keeping a Morgan on the road or track can be more demanding than a more modern machine, but more rewarding at the same time because the process can go on indefinitely. No four-wheeled Morgan ever need be written off because basic spares such as chassis frames and body parts can be bought from the factory. Items such as axles for earlier models may be no longer available but, such is the strength of the Morgan clubs, there is always the possibility that they might be re-manufactured, so it is worthwhile substituting other parts temporarily to keep a car in action.

While the long-term future for any Morgan is more secure than with mass-produced machines where it will never be economical to re-make obsolete bodies and chassis, all models need immediate attention in the short-term. Instant attention is needed to any cracks that develop in the paint around the wing beading, and the rear panel seams of pre-1976 cars, to prevent corrosion. The readily-available water repellant called Waxoyl can be invaluable in this context when applied to such areas. But it is inevitable that at some time the body will need to be completely refinished. At such a time, there is no doubt what should be done: the wings must be removed from the body, whatever corrosion that has developed in the body and wing flanges repaired, or the panels replaced—and then everything should be painted properly before re-assembly using new piping, cadmium-plated or stainless steel nuts and bolts and brass screws.

It is also essential to keep the sidelights screwed down tight to stop cracks developing around their mountings and it is a popular exercise with steel wings to weld in plates on the underside to strengthen the metal and give added support to such an over-stressed area. It also helps to make sure that the front wing-supporting brackets do not touch the wings at any place other than the actual mounting because the vibrations that result if they do can also cause extensive damage.

The doors and their surrounding areas are equally vulnerable. Wise owners dry them off after using the car in wet weather, leave them open to let air circulate around them when garaged, and keep the paint around their flanges in good order. It also pays to keep the frames well protected and to

Chassis can rot badly, particularly around the door area.

*Above and left:* All chassis are basically the same, although detail changes can be expected, like those found between the pre-war 4-4 frame, pictured first, and that of a 1951 Plus Four, pictured second.

dry off the interior as much as possible when it becomes soaked.

Morgan body timbers last well, but it is usually around the door areas that rot sets in first. Good-quality ash is hard to find, but happily the factory still makes replacements which are relatively easy to fit during a major renovation of the body.

Because the chassis is a bolted-up affair, it pays to keep a close check on

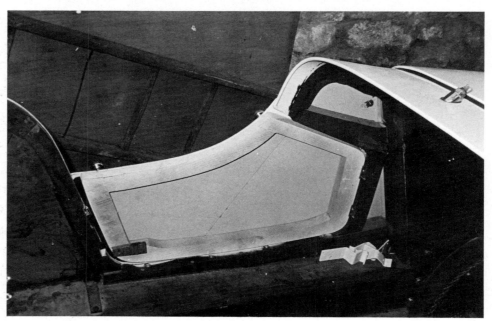

Typical cracking around the base of a sidelight.

Doors suffer from corrosion, especially around the bottom rail.

New door frames look simple affairs, but they are difficult to make because of the vertical curvatures that are needed.

the tightness of all bolts such is the extent of flexing; with the same stricture being applied to the exhaust pipe mountings—to prevent further damage to the chassis—and the engine mounts. Underseal can cause more problems than it prevents with a chassis because it seals in any corrosion—which then carries on with impunity—if applied at any other time than when the chassis has just been shotblasted to perfection during a total rebuild. By far the best policy is to keep the chassis well cleaned and painted—but if corrosion develops in just one side, it is better to take advantage of the bolted construction by fitting a new rail rather than to have a plate welded in. The problem with repairs by plating—which were popular many years ago when most cars had separate chassis—is that the thicker section which results is less flexible than the rest of the metal, leading to further problems with stress. If a minor crack develops in otherwise good metal, it is better to weld it up than to plate it. During a total rebuild it is also worth considering having the chassis galvanised to lengthen its life, although the very flexibility of the metal means that the galvanisation will not be so effective as with more rigid modern unitary construction bodies.

Hinges also benefit from good lubrication, particularly on the bonnet where the metal can be overstressed by a stiff joint. The small triangular rubbers sold by accessory firms can also be invaluable for protecting paint that is likely to be damaged around the bonnet's corners.

It is also essential to keep moving parts in the suspension well greased, especially the sliding axles at the front. Morgan's one-shot lubrication system helps but is inadequate on its own, and over-enthusiastic use—especially when the engine oil is hot—can coat everything at the front, including the brakes. The notorious Morgan wheel wobble which tends to make itself felt

Scuttle assembly of an early Plus Four.

between 50–55 mph can often be alleviated by careful attention to the damper blades, which should be kept well-adjusted in any case. The front suspension also needs overhauling frequently—around every 15,000 miles— at which time the kingpins should be replaced as well as the bushes. This is because, for obvious reasons, the kingpins wear more in the central positions than the top or the bottom, so it is not enough to simply ensure that the bushes are a good fit at the extremities. Wheel balance, uneven tyre and steering gearwear, can be other contributory factors to wheel wobble along with more serious problems such as a distorted chassis. The rear trunnions also need to be greased regularly on early cars and all leaf springs benefit from being sprayed with oil for lubrication and to prevent corrosion. In

The classic Morgan front suspension.

common with any other car, shock absorbers need replacement from time to time, but in the case of four-wheeled Morgans, the car benefits a great deal in ride and handling from conversion to telescopic dampers (such as those made by Koni) at the back.

Obviously it pays to keep brakes well adjusted, especially the linkages of the handbrake and the cables on early cars. It is also essential to use the recommended brake pads or linings, especially with the early cars which relied on a high-friction material. Brake components do not last forever, either, with corrosion-resistant Kunifer lines being recommended against the standard pipes which are especially prone to rust at the back; competition pipes of the type made by Aeroquip are expensive, but far safer for the flexible parts.

Handbrake linkages need to be kept well lubricated.

# X
# Competition Preparation

Preparing a Morgan for competition varies widely because of differing regulations for individual events. In essence, the closer a car is to its original specification, the better chance it stands in concours events, whereas far more modifications are acceptable on the race track or in trials. There seems little point in modifying a Morgan too far, however, because it simply would not be a Morgan . . .

The ultimate was undoubtedly achieved by Rob Wells with his 1981 modsports championship car MMC3 in which the chassis was strengthened by a tubular space frame and the front suspension changed to a wishbone type so that it could use very wide racing tyres. The extremely rigid frame also allowed far softer spring rates to be used to make the car handle like a conventional modern competition machine. The Rover V8 engine was also set back 18 ins to give a better balance, with—initially—rear-mounted water radiators, although these were changed later for a lighter and more efficient frontal system. This car also achieved fame by having a very light one-piece glass fibre body which hinged up from the back for access!

It could be argued, of course, that this car was hardly a Morgan even if it did look like one, with the equally-obvious answer that the scale of these modifications were no more than what was being carried out on other cars which still came within modsports regulations.

But, in most cases, chassis modifications are confined to fitting extension plates to the bottom of the front suspension posts to give 1–1.5 degrees of negative camber, or altering the front bulkhead to achieve the same object. A lesson learned from the Morgan three-wheeler drivers, fitting a strut from the top of each kingpin, diagonally backwards and down to the chassis rails, to stiffen up the front suspension, is also popular. Many drivers also remove the front suspension's one-shot oiling system and replace it with grease nipples so that the brakes are not inadvertently oiled. Telescopic shock absorbers at the back and adjustable ones all round also prove far more effective than the standard items, and glass fibre bonnets and wings can be used to reduce weight.

Trials drivers also raise their chassis as far as possible, although the rear

Four-branch manifolds not only liberate extra power, but they look great . . .

axle's movement limits this. Six, or even seven-leaf springs are also fitted to raise the ride height at the back as far as possible, an even harder ride being preferred to scraping or snagging the underside on rough tracks. Underbody projections, such as exposed nuts, are also removed or countersunk as far as possible and exhaust systems routed as far out of the way as possible—frequently along the underside of the front wing.

But apart from fitting the stickiest or grippiest tyres that are allowed by individual competition regulations, and getting them to work properly by suspension adjustments, the most mileage for modifications comes from engine tuning.

The main problem with the Triumph TR engine used in Plus Fours has been crankshaft failure due to sheer old age, the damper being a particularly vital component. If possible, the crankshaft should be nitride hardened, although an efficient oil cooler can render this unnecessary. Screening for cracks, and careful checking on the condition of the bearing journals is essential. Micro-polishing the journals to not more than 1 micro inch as an aid to lubrication is also to be recommended. It is important also to check the end-float of the crankshaft and adjust it as necessary for a final fit of 0.004 ins to 0.006 ins. Then the crankshaft must be balanced with the vital front pulley and polished or shot-peened to remove any surface cracks.

There is not much you can do with the cylinder block. Just check the camshaft bearings and cam followers carefully, with particular emphasis on the oil drain holes from the cam follower section. These must be absolutely clear. The camshaft end plug must be very tight or a lot of oil will be lost. It is best to seal this plug in position with epoxy adhesive. Early engines before the number TS9095E can be line bored for the later thinwall camshaft bearings.

If more than 0.125 ins is to be milled from the cylinder head face, there may be interference with the top edge of the block on the manifold side when a competition exhaust is fitted. To overcome this, the edge of the block can be filed or ground off at about 45 degrees so that the manifold will fit without fouling. The block surface has to be checked where the liners seat at the bottom to make sure there are no rough edges.

The rear main bearing needs a great deal of care in fitting. The packing must be driven home well or there will be big trouble. The connecting rods need to be crack tested: they can be lightened considerably, but only in the right places. About 75 per cent of the metal can be removed from the stiffening rib at the bottom, and the rib over the top of the big end can be reduced by half. The flash marks can also be removed. The beam of the rod should be shaped so that the face has a slight curve with the high portion in the centre. The same profile can be maintained for the small end, with the sides sloping off to the bush opening. The small end should be ground with an old gudgeon pin bush in position. Then the entire rod should be polished before shot-peening and balancing in company with the other three rods. Needless to say, new bolts and locking tabs must be used during reassembly.

The standard pistons are perfectly suitable unless the engine is overbored, in which case it is best to use Powermax components. Standard rings tend to seat poorly in a race engine, so competition ones are recommended. The piston should be polished all over to minimise skirt drag, and it is vital that all the crowns should be at the same height in relation to the block face. If one of the piston crowns is slightly higher than the others,

*Below:* Concours detail for the eagle-eyed . . . in the early days of Morgan history, wheels were balanced by having lead strips wrapped round their spokes, not by having weights stuck or clipped to their rims.

*Below right:* Original rubber spare bulb holder for the series 1 4-4.

the face can be ground until it lines up perfectly. Finally, everything should be balanced.

When building an engine with a TR2, TR3 or TR3A cylinder head, it is necessary to check the clearance between the water outlet portion of its casing and the water pump body after milling the face. The problem does not arise with the larger-bore heads used on the TR3B and TR4 engines unless a very large amount of metal is removed—more than 0.141 ins— because they have a special flat on the bottom of the water outlet. If there is any difficulty with the early head, it is best to take off some metal from the water pump casting. Should the engine have been taken from a Triumph TR, it may be discovered that there are two heads for the later four-cylinder cars, depending on which carburettors were fitted. They can be told apart because the SU head had 1.625-inch manifold intake ports and Stromberg heads had ones of 1.5 ins.

Extreme care must be taken when milling the early cylinder head face because the margin for error is far less. The classic suggestion is to cut in careful stages, with frequent checks to make sure that the operator does not break into the water jacket or weaken the 'squish' area around the combustion chamber to the point where it can collapse.

For maximum performance, the compression ratio needs to be raised as far as practical, depending on what type of fuel is available. At one time these engines were taken up to 13.4:1, although maximum power without detonation was usually achieved at 12.6:1. Now, with lower octane rating petrol being the order of the day, something like 11.7 is better. This can be achieved by grinding off about 0.15 ins from the cylinder head face, and the use of 87-mm pistons and liners with a steel shim head gasket.

When the cylinder head has been milled, the shape of the combustion

*Below left and right:* Series 1 twin spare wheel clamps were drilled for lightness, but proved fragile, so a solid casting was used on the Plus Four pictured second.

chamber will, of course, be considerably altered. The inlet valve shroud may be removed completely—which is a good thing. By removing the shroud, the fuel is allowed to enter the cylinder faster, and this is able to fill more of the combustion chamber in the same length of time. In other words, it increases the volumetric efficiency and at the same time the effective compression.

Great care must be exercised in inspecting the edge of the combustion chamber for sharp ridges. These will glow hot and cause detonation and perhaps pre-ignition, so it is necessary to smooth off a 0.0313-inch radius. The sparking plug relief in the combustion chamber floor has to be blended in and the sharp edges around its hole should be smoothed off. During the milling, the chamfer opposite the hole should also be completely removed. This should be replaced by grinding off the edge of the combustion chamber. Increases in compression tend to promote turbulence in the mixture as the piston nears top dead centre. This turbulence is vital for complete combustion. With a normal compression ratio, the 'squish' area provides a jet of fuel into the flame front which does the job very easily. With a higher compression ratio, there is no need for such a large squish area which only absorbs heat and drains off power. By replacing the chamfer, and radiusing the edge of the squish area, the turbulence is reduced slightly, but it does not matter because of the increase in compression ratio. But there is a slight gain in power because the area of metal that can absorb heat has been reduced.

The grinding operation must be taken slowly and easily so that there is no loss of head gasket seal. It is a good idea to use the gasket as a pattern to see exactly where it is possible to grind. The operator is advised to fit two old

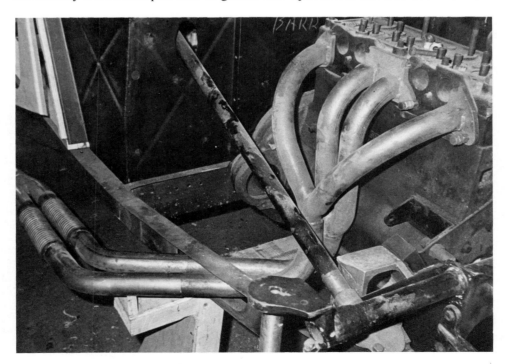

Many exhaust systems have to be specially made to circumnavigate frame members.

valves in place before starting work to avoid damaging the seats. The chamfer opposite the plug hole is ground first, reducing its length as more metal is removed from the face so that the water passages are not penetrated; 0.625 ins can be ground back with about 0.090 ins off the head face, and the chamfer must be radiused into the chamber to a distance of about half the chamber's depth. Then the area next to the exhaust valve should be ground as far as a gasket scribe line and blended in. After that, it is a case of polishing with patience, grindstones and emery cloth.

Then the operator has to get down to the valve seats. The inlet needs to be only 0.02 ins wide, but the exhaust must be 0.032 ins because it has to handle so much more heat. Modifications to the chamber head will have narrowed the valve seats a lot, so the valve throat must be enlarged for maximum use of the seat. For safety's sake, the operation is best done with a side and face cutter in a drill press or milling machine. The seat should be cut to an angle of 45 degrees, and the valve to an angle of 44 to ensure a proper fit with the seat on the centre of the valve. Then the valves are lapped in until the seat is perfect. They can be lightened slightly and polished a lot. Competition valve springs are a must.

There is more scope for constant velocity porting with a late-type cylinder head because the inlets can be cut 1.5 ins throughout their length; the face chamfer on the older head results in a port that has to be tapered from 1.625 ins to 1.5 ins. The larger port gives slightly more top end power, but the smaller is far superior for flexibility.

The valve throat must be blended into the port with no sharp edges and

The best time to detail an engine bay is during a total rebuild.

Replacement body panels are still
made for Morgans.

a fine polish if possible. The golden rule in this area is not to change the cross
section without a fine taper. Exhaust ports can be treated differently because
the gas is moving out under pressure. In this case it is best to taper the port
out of the edge of the manifold face and to match it into the assembly.

The ports of the inlet manifold should be slightly larger at the
carburettor end than at the head face, and the manifold must be polished
internally and then matched up with the carburettor body to each port. The
balance pipe must be checked for cleanliness.

The standard rocker arms can be lightened considerably by grinding
away superfluous metal around the adjustment nut, at the valve end, and
along the top. The whole arm can be polished, but no metal can be cut away
from the sides. The exact area where the rocker strikes the valve stem must be
checked with excess metal ground away without taking off the nose radius.
Competition pushrods with sweated ends that make rocker geometry
corrections easier are to be recommended.

The cam followers can be lightened by paring off 0.375 ins from the top
end in a lathe. The edges must then be radiused and the internal diameter can
be bored out to 0.05 ins. They should then be polished all over with the sharp
edge at the base sanded off. It is essential to always use new cam followers
during a rebuild and a new timing chain and tensioner are to be
recommended.

Camshafts depend on which carburettors are used, with 40DCOE
Webers as the most effective and 2-inch SUs as the next best. The three most
radical camshafts in general use are ones with 39-81-81-39, 42-74-74-42 and
51-79-79-51 timing. The minimum compression ratio in each case is 11.7:1. A

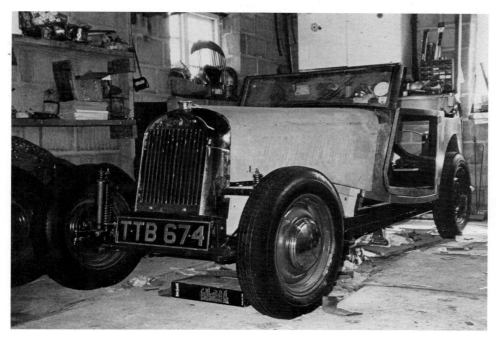

Mounting a Morgan body can be a work of art.

standard distributor can be used, but it is wise never to start a race with a new set of points or fan belt, if fitted. This is because they tend to wear far more in the first 100 miles than later. Full metal wires are recommended for the ignition and the generator mounting plate bolts should be drilled and wired; the bolts run straight through the cylinder block's wall and can produce a giant oil leak if they work loose. The thermostat should be broken open for the best running temperature and a catch tank fitted for the crankcase breather on the distributor side.

A competition flywheel weighing 11 lb against the normal 31 lb is ideal in conjunction with a competition clutch. The TR's standard mechanical fuel pump should be removed and its aperture blanked off to be replaced with an electric pump mounted somewhere cool, such as at the back of the car.

It is not difficult to produce double the power, about 250 bhp, with the Rover V8, however (which is as much as most people can handle in a Morgan) and, with considerable extra expense, 300 bhp or more.

Secondhand Rover V8 engines are easily found and there is still the odd Buick, Oldsmobile and Pontiac engine available in the United States with new low-compression Rover versions available again—after brief sorties with the Rover SD1 saloon and Triumph TR8 sports car—now that the Range Rover is being imported; in Australia the Leyland P76 4.4-litre version of the Rover V8 presents an intriguing proposition. Such applications are made all the more viable by the five-speed gearbox's ability to handle the V8's power, although its long-term durability in road applications is open to doubt. But it has more than enough miles in it initially for a competition car.

*Above:* The place to start mounting a new body is at the scuttle. Everything else hangs around it.

*Above right:* Little and large . . . pistons and gaskets from Plus Four and series 1 4-4.

So far as the Rover engines are concerned, there are two main types: the old pre-1973 ones with rope rear crankshaft oil seals and the later ones, which soon found a home in the Rover SD1 saloon and the Triumph TR8 in the United States, which had a lip seal. A very tightly-packed rope seal will handle extra power, but it is better to have the cylinder block line bored—3.875 ins diameter, 0.4375 ins depth—to take the lip seal if more than 5,000 rpm is envisaged. The early engine's rope seal at the front is in a low pressure area, so it should present no problem. When reboring this alloy block, it is advisable to have the main bearing caps torqued in place to avoid the possibility of bore distortion. New camshaft bearings—available from specialist tuners—are almost invariably essential.

Removing burned oil deposits is a tedious business, but vital, and no more than a total of 0.02 ins should be taken off the cylinder heads and block when refacing: remember that this amount should be identical each side, with similar care taken with the combustion chambers and pistons if equal compression is to be achieved.

High-revving V8s can suffer from oil retention in the block as the lubricant fails to return to the bearings sufficiently quickly; to reduce the chances of this happening, smooth off all the rough edges in the block and fit an extra drain from the back of the vee to the sump. A hole for a 15-mm copper pipe should be drilled above the rear camshaft bearing, with the pipe running back through the left-hand side of the bellhousing flange. A rubber hose then connects this pipe to a further run into the sump, helping to drain off some of the oil that invariably collects at the back of this rearward-inclined application.

The crankshaft, which is good for 8,200 rpm, should be hardened for more than 6,000 rpm, and balanced. The connecting rods are safe for 7,000 rpm, after which special Carillo rods from America are essential—if you have a large enough budget. The early engines had rather weak 10.5:1 compression ratio pistons, with much stronger 10.25 versions being marketed later: it is wise to use the new ones. Very expensive forged pistons are also available, but are in the same price league as the Carillo rods. The combustion chamber volume was increased with the introduction of the SD1 engine, which can also affect calculations.

Rover engines made between 1974-7 had 9.25:1 compression ratio heads of the larger valve SD1 type; engines made after 1977 had 9.35:1, until the Rover Vitesse was introduced in 1982 with 9.75:1; in other applications, the Range Rover and MGB GT V8 used 8.15:1 until 1977, and 8.3:1 for Range Rovers and Land-Rover V8s after that, with further variations on some export models.

In normal applications, a compression ratio of between 10 and 10.5:1 is best. The standard hydraulic tappets are good for 7,000 rpm and are worth retaining unless higher revs are needed because of their maintenance-free virtues and the fact that they do not stress an engine like the ultimate solid lifters.

More than a dozen replacement camshafts have been available for the V8, mostly made by Crane, with Iskendariam and Austin Rover Motorsport alternatives. Crane's H214 is one of the most attractive for economy applications. If it is fitted to a standard Plus Eight engine, with BAF-type needles in SU carburettors, it will give an immediate power increase to 198 bhp. Only a very small amount of flexibility and fuel economy is lost, with performance equivalent to that of the fuel-injected Vitesse engine. The modified unit also lasts as long as a normal one, making this conversion one to be highly recommended.

It is essential to fit new followers with a replacement cam, and to avoid pre-SD1 followers in this case.

The next cam in the range is the H224, originally intended for rallying. In this case, the valve springs and retainers must be used with Crane high-rev lifters to give a maximum of 7,000 rpm although the best range is between 2,500–6,000 rpm, during which torque is abundant. The spring seats will have to be machined to avoid coil binding. There is also a very wild full-race cam, the H234, for use with hydraulic tappets; after that, solid lifters are needed. These require tappets to match and adjustable pushrods or roller

*Below left:* Little and large . . . crankshafts from the Plus Four and the series 1 4-4.

*Below:* Do-it-yourself wheelarch repairs.

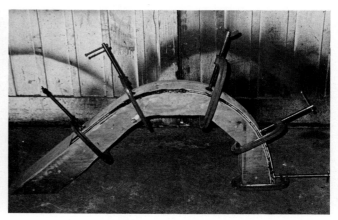

rockers. The first camshaft for use with such equipment is the F228, which is similar to the H224. These cams work well between 3,000 and 7,000 rpm, in which case the engine needs to be built to withstand an excess of their top range. Three more cams are available that need engine speeds of 8,000 rpm to take maximum benefit.

The normal camshaft timing gears give few problems, but if they do, steel gears should be substituted. In the same way, the hydraulic tappets are quite reliable providing the engine's oil—which operates them—is not allowed to become contaminated, in which case bits of dirt cause problems. They are capable of taking up quite a bit of adjustment, but if the cylinder head is skimmed a lot, they will not close properly. At the other extreme, if a very thick gasket is used, they will rattle. In either case, the rocker shaft pillars should be packed or machined, or adjustable pushrods fitted.

Preparation of the early and the later type of SD1 heads is quite simple. The early heads have smaller combustion chambers and use short-reach, 12.7-mm, sparking plugs. The inlet valves are 38 mm and exhaust 33.3 mm. Longer, 19-mm, plugs are used with the later heads, with 40-mm inlet and 34.3-mm exhaust valves. The early heads also have slightly smaller ports which can be cleaned out to SD1 size but no more because their waterways are close at hand. SD1 ports should not be enlarged for the same reason. In some export versions, there is an emission equipment airbleed in the exhaust ports which should be blanked off for high performance. Larger valves are available, but they are only necessary for power outputs beyond 260 bhp.

In normal cases, Oteva valve springs can be used, but if more than 200 bhp is envisaged, it is wise to use a Felpro Permatorque gasket, which is thicker. Ultimately, in turbocharged or supercharged applications, an even thicker Fitzgerald gasket is available. Obviously these gaskets will affect the compression ratio, and in cases where oversize inlet valves are used with high-lifted camshaft and high-compression pistons, the valves may touch the tops of the pistons. The valves are inclined, so there is not a large area of contact and it is quite practical to have cut-outs machined in the pistons for clearance.

Alternative applications are boring and stroking to raise the capacity to 3.9 litres or 4.2, although Traco in the 1960s produced a 4.4-litre version of the Oldsmobile engine for CanAm cars which could be stretched as far as 4.8 litres for Formula A (the American equivalent of the European Formula 5000) racing.

So far as carburettors are concerned, the SUs are the best economy applications, giving a reasonable performance and the most popular alternatives are the carburettors made by Holley. The best Holley carburettor for general competition use in this case is the 600 cfm unit with a mechanical linkage (or double pumper) for instant throttle response.

The next choice upwards is Webers, but these are unlikely to appeal to Morgan followers because they project upwards, far beyond the normal bonnet line.

Chassis are most easily rebuilt on trestles.

Oil coolers for competition work take a natural siting under the water radiator.

An electronic ignition system is to be recommended to cope with high revs and Champion N6Y sparking plugs are essential for more than 200 bhp, with N2Gs and ultimately N84Gs after that.

Alarmingly low oil pressure readings from these engines can be improved by fitting either an uprated pressure relief valve from a Rover Vitesse or a Buick 7-litre oil pump. The sump can also benefit from being enlarged and baffled because the total capacity is rather small. An oil cooler

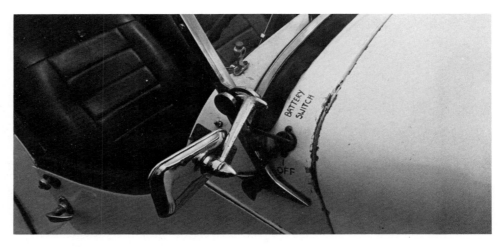

Handy place for an emergency battery cut-off switch as often demanded of competition cars . . . on the scuttle.

is to be recommended in any tuned application and it may be necessary to shroud the starter motor and plug leads with asbestos to counter the extremes of temperature from the exhaust manifolds and pipes.

Tuning the various Ford engines which have been fitted to Morgans could easily fill several books—and has—and seems to have become a never-ending science. The most popular units tend to be either Formula Ford 1600 engines from a wide variety of builders who extract between 100–105 bhp, but whose efforts tend to be put in the shade by those who produce such engines for the British Clubmen's racing cars: these units produce around 185 bhp but tend to be far from tractable, even in long-stroke 1,700-cc form, because they rely on large-valve heads. They are also fragile, needing rebuilds even more frequently than the Formula Ford 1600's average of eight hours' running.

More recent developments in British hot rod racing, in which 1,700-cc forms of the pushrod engine are almost standard fitments, have proved potentially beneficial to Morgan 4/4 owners. The most advanced units, with small-valve heads to make them so tractable they can even be driven on the road, have come from Nick Mason Engineering in Waltham Abbey, Essex, where no less than 192 bhp is being extracted.

In this case, Mason engines use dry-sump lubrication and all-steel components, such as the crankshaft, connecting rods and a very special camshaft, running on twin 45DCOE carburettors with 38-mm chokes. Maximum power is produced at 8,200 rpm with a fluctuation of only 2 bhp between 7,250 rpm and 8,750 rpm on the way to a 9,000-rpm maximum. Alternative long-stroke 1,800-cc Mason engines produce more torque with ultimate twin overhead camshaft BDA versions churning out as much as 275 bhp! The advantage of this machinery is that the pushrod Ford engines are extremely light, whereas the heavier twin-cam units have to resort to an alloy cylinder block to bring down their weight and the old favourite, the Lotus twin cam unit, seems to have reached the zenith of its power at 165 bhp with the attendant weight penalty of its cylinder head.

# XI
# The Interchangeability of Spare Parts

Contrary to appearances, the opportunities for interchanging parts on Morgans are decidedly limited. Because they have always been hand-made cars, every one is a little different from the others—and, in any case, the days are long gone when anybody scrapped a Morgan, so the availability of donor cars is now highly unlikely. This happy situation for the marque is made all the more practical by the continuing availability of chassis, suspension and body parts from the factory. In addition, although Morgans have always shared mechanical parts with mass-produced cars, in the case of the older models, these cars have long since disappeared from scrapyards: in many cases they are more than 50 years old, and supplies have been exhausted in the search for spares or scrap, or, in some cases, they have become quite valuable in themselves.

In the case of the Coventry Climax-engined 4-4s, the power unit was shared with the Triumph Gloria saloons, of which there were a variety made up to 1939. The Standard engine was special to the Morgan, but those used in Standard Eight and Flying Tens will fit.

But often the only avenue for Morgan enthusiasts is to have spare parts remanufactured by firms like Quaife Power Systems, at Tonbridge, Kent (who, for instance, make excellent gears in batches as small as 25 lots). In such cases, it is impossible to tool up for quantity production, Quaife, for instance often machining gears from solid metal. Such processes are, inevitably, expensive, and although The Morgan Sports Car Club has been particularly successful in this field, there is a limit to what can be done. The easiest solution is for Morgans needing vital parts, such as rear axles, or gearboxes, to receive similar components that are available—often from later cars—to keep them running until original-pattern parts become available again. The very construction of an older Morgan, with its separate gearbox and simply-mounted rear axle, makes such measures all the more practical.

The best avenues for interchangeability lie with the Ford, Triumph and Rover-engined cars. In the case of the 4-4s from the series 11 onwards, a bewildering array of parts is available. Not only were the Anglia, Prefect, Popular and 5-cwt van side-valve engine, gearbox and clutch shared with the

*Right and below:* Strong lines in interchangeability . . . the Standard engines used in early Plus Fours.

contemporary Ford saloons, but they enjoyed a tremendous amount of interchangeability themselves! The engines and gearboxes—with period tuning gear—also found their way into a lot of special cars built in the 1950s, which can provide good power units for Morgans, but are becoming less likely sources of supply as such cars become more valuable.

The later overhead-valve Ford engines are still readily available, not only in scrapyards but at low prices in reconditioned or new form. The array of tuning equipment available for these engines is vast, and they can in themselves be readily swopped around, in all manner of capacities from the smallest 997 cc to 1600 cc in standard form, with all manner of developments in larger capacities. The popularity of the Lotus Elan and Europa also

Rover V8 engines are in ready supply in many countries from derelict saloon cars.

ensures a continuing supply of twin cam versions of these engines—which were fitted in basic form to Ford Anglia, Prefect, Classic, Cortina and Escort saloons as well as commercial vehicles.

The Standard Vanguard and Triumph TR engines fitted to Morgans had slightly modified manifolds and water pumps, and the Rover engines in the Plus Eights came, chiefly, from 3500 or SD1 saloons rather than the 3.5-litre, Range Rover and MGB GT V8 cars, which had units built to a different specification. In America, the very similar Buick, Oldsmobile or Pontiac engine made by General Motors between 1960 and 1963 will also fit the Plus Eight, likewise in Australia where the Rover version of the engine was used in capacities up to 4.4 litres.

Numerous Fiat saloons have used the late Plus Four's twin cam engine.

# XII
# The Men Behind Morgan

The man who started it all . . . H.F.S. Morgan.

Not only is Morgan the oldest privately-owned motor company in the world, but the 125 people who work for the firm which started in 1910 are best viewed as one big family. In fact many are related, with son following father in numerous crafts, and mothers and sisters working in the trim shop. But it has always been a member of the Morgan family of Malvern, Worcestershire, that has been in charge.

Local curate George Morgan's son, Harry—later known universally by his initials H.F.S.—had the choice of art or engineering after leaving school at the turn of the century. He chose engineering, using his artistic inclinations to demonstrate ability as a draughtsman and designer while at college in Chelsea, South London. A pupillage followed at the Great Western Railway works at Swindon, Wiltshire, which was so successful that he was offered a job.

But like many budding railway engineers (W.O. Bentley of Bentley Motors and Reggie Hanks of the Nuffield Organisation included) the young Harry Morgan decided that cars had more future. So with backing from his father, he started a garage in Malvern Link that was an immediate success—with George Morgan making sure that the finances were run properly. Morgan's present managing director, Peter Morgan (H.F.S's only son) recalls that his father was an uncommonly good designer and engineer. He could produce something so brilliantly simple that it not only worked well but cost far less to produce than rival products.

H.F.S. Morgan excelled himself when he produced his first car, a three-wheeler, in 1909. Not only was it light and simple, and endowed with a very high performance from its 7-hp V-twin motor-cycle engine, but it had one of the world's first independent front suspension systems. This gave it excellent handling, and has been used, in essence, on every Morgan made since.

Full-scale production started with a two-seater in 1911 that demonstrated its virtuosity in reliability trials—the forerunners of modern trials and subsequently rallies—before going on to great success on the racetrack. The sales of road-going versions also soared to as many as 2,500 a year because of

H.F.S. Morgan—in trilby hat—shows the ropes to his son, Peter, who became the second great personality that kept Morgan alive.

*Far left:* The historic Morgan factory and the man who is now the Morgan Motor Company, Peter Morgan.

*Left:* The young and the old . . . veteran development engineer Maurice Owen discusses the future with Charles Morgan.

*Above:* Charles Morgan—like all his family before him—still harbours an intense affection for the three-wheeler.

*Above right:* The historic workshop where new versions of the Morgan are developed . . . Maurice Owen's hidey-hole.

its simplicity of design: almost any large motor cycle engine could be bolted into a light and efficient tubular backbone frame.

Many rivals fell by the wayside following the introduction of the equally-brilliant and hardly more expensive four-wheeled Austin Seven in 1922. But the Morgan three-wheelers continued to sell reasonably well on their amazingly high performance, so much so that H.F.S. Morgan was able to build up considerable financial reserves.

This essentially conservative approach stood the firm in good stead until ever-declining sales of the three-wheelers forced them to produce the four-wheeled version in 1935, although three-wheeled production trickled on until 1952. As four-wheeled sales prospered—partly on an excellent performance, partly on superb styling (H.F.S. Morgan had never lost his artist's eye), and partly on a refusal to over-produce—the firm's founder spent less time at the works, concentrating on running his investments.

He was far more inclined to leave the administration of his motor company to managers like George Goodall until his son, Peter, was able to take over. The Second World War was survived partly by letting unused production bays to the Standard Motor Company and partly ensuring an income from the machine shop through munitions work. And when the young Peter returned from Army service, his first job was to look for a new engine. Standard-Triumph's chief, Sir John Black, had a notoriously volatile temperament, so the shrewd businessman, H.F.S. Morgan, did not want to be too dependent on any one supplier as he was forced to seek export sales to ensure State steel supplies.

Peter Morgan—who had inherited not only his father's excellent driving ability, but his business acumen—had the brief to find a cheap unit of no more than 1,500-cc capacity. Three-wheeler sales had always survived by means of tax concessions for small vehicles and H.F.S. Morgan saw no reason that the situation should be different with four-wheelers. Peter Morgan was turned down, first, by Leonard Lord at Austin, because he had an Austin A40 sports car in mind, and then by Vauxhall because they had no intention of selling their engines to anybody. Morgan's former suppliers, Coventry-Climax, had an attractive engine . . . but it cost as much as the rest of the car, so that was ruled out. Peter Morgan, therefore, experimented with

*Above right:* Morgan graveyard: here lies a Plus Eight, that gave everything to an impact-testing crash.

*Above:* Chassis assembly begins with welding up small parts.

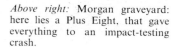

Men in Morgan's machine shop make many special parts for the cars . . .

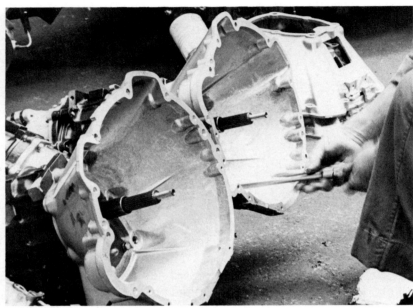

*Above:* And women work the machine tools.

*Above right:* Clutch release mechanisms on the Rover gearbox have to be modified for the Plus Eight.

all that was left: a 1,760-cc prototype of the Standard Vanguard engine, persuading his father that the rise in capacity was acceptable.

'Imagine our horror when the 2,088-cc unit came along and clobbered us for class racing,' he said years later. 'But it was a very reliable unit, and although people always think of us as using it for a long time—18 years—we've had the Rover engine for more than 20 years now!'

Such was H.F.S. Morgan's financial muscle that he was able to rebuff an approach by Black to take over Morgan in 1951. The Standard chief wanted to use the Morgan as a cheap way of developing a car to cash in on the boom in sales of MGs and Jaguars in the United States that was subsequently taken up by Lord with the Austin-Healey 100. 'Father was sure that, when the chips were down, Black would not spend the money needed to make a new sports car, and we would be left high and dry,' said Peter Morgan. 'I said he would, and for once I was right.'

As it was, Black managed to get his Triumph TR built incredibly cheaply, but was put off stopping Morgan's engine supplies in a fit of pique by the fact that the Plus Four's performance in rallies provided an excellent advertisement for Standard.

'The only time in which we were cut back—from about eight engines a week to five—was when Standard-Triumph's competitions chief, Ken Richardson, got annoyed when Triumph owners asked why our cars were faster,' said Peter Morgan. 'That was when we went to Ford in 1955 and started making the 4/4 again.'

By then Peter Morgan, born in 1919, was demonstrating great ability behind the wheel as well as in the forefront of the family business. He recalls: 'When I started driving before the war—you picked up everything you knew

Chassis are erected in an impressive line in one of the 'shops'.

initially on the road rather than at a racing or rally school—father said I had to learn about competition first in trials and then in rallies before going racing. And he banned me from racing down Alps, which is why I never got into the great European rallies. I had the beating of the best rally driver of the time, Ian Appleyard—who had been a consistent winner in Europe—at one

Detail work on the chassis needs many hours of labour.

*Above:* Completed chassis wait for space in the body shop.

*Right:* Ash frames made in the body are erected on the completed chassis.

point, and I think I could have done it if he had not had special high-geared steering . . . but really it was the war which wrecked my competition career.'

Peter Morgan gave up competition when he was made managing director on Goodall's death in 1958, followed by his father dying, aged 78, in 1959. He said: 'I had always done my own final preparation, and now there was not time to do it personally, I quit. Rallies were over by that time and since then I have always been very close to Morgan racers.'

The death of H.F.S. Morgan led to a crisis in the firm's history as Peter's four elder sisters shared the financial reserves, leaving him with just the business as a running concern. He remembers: 'Father was a very fair man. He said he was going to sell the business, but he left it to me because I loved it. So I called the staff together and said: "The holiday is over, we have to make cars now!" '

Throughout the 1950s, Morgan had been dependent on their market in the United States, particularly in the kind Californian climate. Eighty-five per cent of their production was going to Northern America in 1960, until recession hit the west coast aircraft industry. It was at this point that Peter Morgan looked back on his father's experience and cut production from nine cars per week to eight, a course H.F.S. Morgan followed in the early 1920s when the Austin Seven was all the rage. Peter Morgan recalls:

'For a time, we just couldn't sell the cars, until Chris Lawrence's performances with the Super Sports brightened things up in Europe. I thought the shape of the car was a lot of the problem, so that's why we

brought in the Plus Four Plus. But, with hindsight, I'm thankful we kept producing the standard models!

'Management is made easier by being part of such a small team. Many of the people here did not like the idea of going over to glass fibre for the

*Above left:* Door frames are made with great precision to fit individual openings.

*Above:* Once checked for fit, the door frames are skinned in metal.

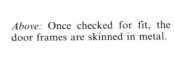

Frequently cars have to be shuttled around as various tasks are completed.

Great care is taken to ensure that the ash frames are symmetrical.

Much of the panel beating is done in the metalworking shop.

body panels. Because you work so closely with each other, you can smell out trouble before it starts . . .'

Happily for the Morgan workforce, which remains delightfully loyal and troublefree, demand picked up dramatically on the vital home market in 1965 when young people with more money to spend than their parents had enjoyed began to feel nostalgic for the traditional sports cars they could no longer buy new from anybody else. 'Perhaps they were stimulated by the sight of the Plus Four Plus, because they all went for the Plus Four and 4/4,' said Peter Morgan with a laugh.

The new impetus in sales came just in time as Rover—like Triumph before them—contemplated getting into the sports car market. Peter Morgan was able to rebuff their approach, which evaporated when Rover, in turn, was absorbed into British Leyland in 1967. 'Peter Wilks, of Rover, had already offered the new V8 engine they were developing from the General Motors' Buick design,' said Peter Morgan. 'I said I wanted to soldier on on my own, but could I have the engine anyway? They said we would need General Motors' permission, and campaigned for us. I also had a good friend, a Morgan racer who was high up at General Motors, to help present our case. In the end, Rover came back and said General Motors did not mind us using the engine, but Triumph could not have it because they made too many cars. At the same time, Harry Webster—I'd known him well since his Triumph days—showed me all the engines he was designing, the Dolomite and Saab's slant four, and the V8 for the Stag. But British Leyland's new chief, Donald Stokes, was not too keen. He didn't want what was to be the

When the frame is clothed in metal, the wings and bonnet are fitted.

Plus Eight against his six-cylinder Triumph TR5. So we got hold of a Buick engine and Webster took our prototype away. When he came back, he said: "You can have the Rover engine provided you don't produce too many cars and you don't change the style." They didn't think it would make any appreciable difference to the sales of Triumphs, or MGs, which were also involved with British Leyland. So far as I can remember, the General Motors' agreement ran for five or seven years.'

The wisdom of Peter Morgan's policy of keeping down the price of his cars as far as possible was never better demonstrated in the long-term than when the waiting list built up to an official 10 years during the 1970s. This

*Below left:* Then the radiator grille is checked for fitting.

*Below:* Windscreen frames are fitted later.

No spare feet are wasted at Malvern Link.

Ford and Rover-engined cars jostle for space.

was despite the loss of the American market between 1968 and 1970, 1972 (the Rover V8 engine being certified for America between 1970-71) and at low key only since 1976. The 1973-75 slump in sports car sales was partly taken up by the increased demand for the Plus Eight in production sports car racing. Then, with Prodsports in decline, sales fell off during the early 1980s as a temporary recession hit what was now the all-important home market. Morgan were able to bite deep into the waiting list until the demand picked up again in 1982.

Peter Morgan says: 'I am never complacent over orders—they change so much. At any one point I can have 2,000-3,000 named orders; if I was to finish them in three months, I'd be lucky to collect the money for 10 per cent! I've always tried to go for a spread of markets. The Japanese, for instance, would like more than their 12-20 cars a year, but we cannot commit ourselves to the detriment of others, when regulations and economies are constantly changing.

'We are hoping to step up production by 10 per cent to 11 cars per week now that the Range Rover, which uses a low-compression version of the V8 engine, is being sold in America. That means that we will be able to increase our presence there from the 40 or 50 propane gas cars a year, but not to such an extent that we are dependent on American sales again.'

The United States' product liability laws—which can be heavily penal and eccentric—are as much of a worry to Morgan as any other, larger, manufacturer. Peter Morgan recalls having to pay legal costs of £150,000 in successfully defending his company's good name after a crash in 1981 which involved a 13-year-old car that had been illegally imported through Canada. 'Luckily we were able to spread that over two years,' said Peter Morgan. 'The profit margins here are far from excessive! Upping the price too much means going for a killing, and you end up killing yourself.'

Plus Eights running on slave wheels are prepared for painting.

Wiring looms are inserted after painting.

When Peter Morgan reached 65 years of age, he was joined in the business by his son, Charles, who has spent his early career as a television cameraman besides racing the works Plus Eight. Peter Morgan says: 'There was no question of co-ercing him into the business. He was free to follow any profession he chose, but I must say that I'm happy he chose Morgan in the

Final assembly takes place with ancient pot-belly stoves for heating.

*Above:* Trim is tacked into place on the wooden framework.

*Above right:* Preparing metal parts for final assembly with beading.

end! Fortunately, nobody wants me to retire yet, so we are working happily together . . .'

Naturally, Charles is looking to the future now that he has an influence on Morgan's destiny. Now that the firm is again on a sound financial

*Above:* Morgan's legendary stuffed owl—in residence since the late 1960s—scares away pigeons which used to roost in the rafters of the dispatch bay to the detriment of new cars' paint . . .

*Right:* 'Peter Morgan practically lives here,' say his oldest employees.

One of Morgan's greatest advocates and life-long supporters, John Orton, with the oldest running four-wheeler example of the marque.

footing, he has been able to work with his father on improved specifications. Since 1986, modern two-pack paint has been used, with cadmiun or zinc-plated body fixings and powder-coating for the chassis, and Cuprinol treatment for the wood used in the bodywork.

The two-litre Fiat-engined version of the Plus Four sold well, but had to be discontinued when the Italian firm went over to a transverse installation and could supply only a gearbox suitable for a steering column gearchange. Since then development had centred on a Rover M16-engined version of the Plus Four with a V8-engined Plus Four for Charles Morgan to race in the 750 Motor Club's road-going sports car challenge. The Knight steering rack is proving highly popular and late in 1987, Morgan was set to return to the United States with a petrol-powered Plus Eight following the introduction of the Range Rover—using a low-compression version of the same engine—in that market.

Future developments could centre on computer-controlled active suspension to improve the ride, experiments with coil-sprung rear suspension and quarter-elliptic springs having failed. In the more immediate future, anti-lock braking is a possibility for the Plus Eight, the chief problem being finding room to locate the extra equipment needed.

Meanwhile father and son are convinced that the basic shape and construction of their cars must not change, and Peter Morgan points out: 'The club people are such great fun. We all share the same punishment!'

# XIII
# The Morgan Clubs

Membership of the various Morgan clubs is around 5,000 worldwide. In company with many other marque groups, the Morgan clubs have enjoyed a relatively rapid rise in membership since the early 1970s when classic cars really came into their own. Before that, people interested in car clubs tended to belong to more generalised organisations. It is notable, therefore, that the Morgan Three-Wheeler Club, founded in Britain in 1944, is one of the oldest marque clubs, having a current membership of around 750, which has remained fairly constant over the years. But the biggest club catering for the marque is The Morgan Sports Car Club (which is devoted to four-wheelers) which has 2,000 members; it was founded (as The Morgan 4/4 Club) in 1951.

In keeping with other organisations for similar cars, the scene in the North American continent is different: there are around 1,200 Morgan-owning members, split into 11 different clubs because the far greater distances involved make it impractical to hold national meetings more than once a year. When viewed as a total, most members are concentrated on the east coast, where the memberships of The Morgan Car Club of Washington DC, The 3/4 Morgan Group Ltd in New York (which also covers New Jersey), Morgan Owners of Philadelphia and Western New York Morgan Owners' Group, total 600. In fact the Washington DC club, formed in 1959 as the Morgan Car Club of America (before it changed to its present name in 1965), is still often referred to as the mother club with 300 members, the New York and New Jersey club having 200.

The oldest Morgan clubs in America are on the west coast, however, reflecting a similar level of interest. The Morgan Plus Four Club of Southern California was formed in 1955 (now listing 200 members) and still shares many activities with the Plus Four Club of Northern California (100 members) which was formed in 1957 from the southern club's San Francisco Bay area chapter. In addition there is the Morgan Owners' Group Northwest, formed in 1976 and covering Oregon, Washington, Idaho and parts of British Columbia, which has 50 well-scattered members. Other organisations catering for the marque in the United States and Canada include the 100-member Morgan Owners' Club Great Lakes, formed in the

Detroit area in 1965, its counterpart, the Morgan Owners' Group of Canada, formed in 1962 in the Niagara area, the Ohio Morgan Owners, formed in 1973, which has 90 members and also covers Indiana, West Virginia and parts of Pennsylvania, the small Morgan Owners' Group South, formed in 1976 in Southern Carolina, which has strong dual membership with the Washington DC club, and the Morgan Motor Club in Texas, formed in 1974.

The strongest areas of interest in Europe are in Germany, where the Morgan Club Deutschland, formed in 1970, has more than 300 members and the Morgan Club de France—formed as part of the British four-wheeler club in 1973 before becoming independent in 1977—has 200 members. Other clubs include the Morgan Owners' Club of Sweden, formed in 1966, with 130 members, the Morgan Club Schweiz, formed in Switzerland in 1977, with 100 members, and the Morgan Sports Car Club of Holland, formed in 1972, and the Morgan Club Italia, formed in Italy in 1981 as one of the youngest Morgan clubs with the Morgan Club Espania, formed in Barcelona in 1984. Slightly smaller European clubs include The Morgan Sports Car Club of Japan, formed in 1972, with 85 members, the Morgan Sports Car Club of Austria, formed in 1977, with 60 members, the 50-member Morgan Club of

Austrian Morgans, like this 1955 drop-head coupé, travel far.

*Above left and right:* Germany boasts many Morgans, from the series 1 to the Plus Eight.

Denmark, formed in 1973, and the Morgan Sports Car Club of Belgium, formed in 1974. In contrast, The Morgan Sports Car Club of Poland has only one owner, Kathi Hoffman, who started it in 1982, but attracts around 40 other cars for social runs driven by people living in Poland who fancy a Morgan!

Further afield, the Morgan Sports Car Club of New Zealand, formed in 1973, has 100 members and the Morgan Owners' Club of Australia, formed in 1958, has 80 members, with the Samog club in South Africa, formed in 1971, enjoying a membership of around 90.

These clubs operate in a broadly similar manner, organising monthly meetings and—usually—a monthly magazine or newsletter under a variety of

Mama Mia Mog in all its finery.

Morgans everywhere for the 1986 jamboree at Malvern.

Concours judges compare notes about this series 1.

*Above:* Long-distance travelling in a Morgan cries out for a luggage rack.

*Above right:* Many hours of concours labour can bring a trophy . . .

names: the British four-wheeler club has *Miscellany*, the Washington DC club *The Rough Rider*, the New York club *The Morganeer*, the Philadelphia club *MOPs Mania*, the southern Californians *Plus-4 Format*, their northern counterparts *Morgan Plus Four Format*, the Great Lakes club *Flexible Flyer*, the Canadians *The Blurb*, the Ohio club *Oh! Moggie*, the Texans *Mog Log*, the Germans *Morgan-Post*, the Swedes *Mog*, the Swiss *Mcs Organ*, the Dutch *Fata MORGANs*, the Italians *Morgan* and a yearbook, the Austrians *The Morganeer*, the Belgians *Belmognews*, the New Zealand club *Rough Rider*, the Australians *Morgan Ear*, and the South Africans *Rapper*.

Apart from social meetings, barbeques, picnics, parties, weekend runs, treasure hunts, rallies, gymkhanas, driving tests, sprints, autocross, racing, hill climbs and concours, most of the clubs—including the Polish—organise international events which prove attractive to members of other Morgan clubs.

The Australian club combines with other organisations catering for similar areas of interest, such as Austin-Healeys, MGs, Jaguars, Lotus and Triumph, to make events—especially racing—more viable with the British club, in particular, doing invaluable work in raising the finance to re-manufacture long-obsolete mechanical spares.

But above all, one of the greatest attractions of belonging to a club specialising in one make of car, such as the Morgan, has been in the shared experiences of running and owning such a machine. It has proved impractical

*The six photographs left and above:* Morgan folk love regalia, particularly badges to denote memorable happenings . . .

*Below:* Typical line-up for a noggin and natter.

Morgans of the world unite . . .
particularly this famous one which
turned up in Moscow. (Picture by
courtesy of TASS.)

to print lists of contacts in various countries, because—as with any amateur
organisation—the people involved change their duties and addresses from
time to time, well within the lifespan of a book. But at the time of
writing—and doubtless for a considerable time after—any necessary
information could be gained from Barry Isles, secretary of The Morgan
Sports Car Club, Hollands Farm, Coombe Green, Birtsmorton, Worcs
WR13 6AB, England, or, of course, the Morgan factory itself at Pickersleigh
Road, Malvern Link, Worcs WR14 2LL, England.

# XIV
# Your Morgan Logbook

## Morgan 4-4 Two-Seater

Introduced 1936, 730 cars built by 1939 with 1,122-cc engine, 59 chassis with 1,122-cc engine, 61 cars with 1,098-cc engine, 29 cars with 1,267-cc engine including 663 cars with two-seater bodies.

### Engine

Four cylinders, in-line, overhead inlet, side exhaust valves CUBIC CAPACITY 1,122 cc; BORE AND STROKE 63 mm x 90 mm; MAX POWER 34 bhp at 4,500 rpm; MAX TORQUE 52 lb/ft at 2,500 rpm. Optional 1,087 cc: BORE AND STROKE 62 mm x 90 mm; MAX POWER 46 bhp at 4,500 rpm; MAX TORQUE 56.5 lb/ft at 2,500 rpm. Optional 1,098 cc: MAX POWER 55-60 bhp. Optional 1,267 cc: BORE AND STROKE 63.5 mm x 100 mm; MAX POWER 39 bhp at 4,200 rpm; MAX TORQUE 62 lb/ft at 2,500 rpm.

### Chassis

WHEELBASE 7 ft 8 ins; WEIGHT 1,500 lb; FRONT TRACK 3 ft 9 ins; REAR TRACK 3 ft 9 ins; LENGTH 11 ft 8 ins; WIDTH 4 ft 6 ins; HEIGHT 3 ft 8 ins (4 ft 2 ins with hood erect); FRONT SUSPENSION Independent with sliding stub axles and coil springs on vertical pillars; REAR SUSPENSION Live axle with half elliptic springs; BRAKES 8-inch drums all round; STEERING Reduction gear mounted on column (almost immediately replaced by worm and nut steering box); GEARING (overall) 5, 7, 12, 17.5:1, (22.6 reverse); from 1939 5, 6.7, 11.95, 19.3:1, (22.35 reverse); TYRES AND WHEELS Dunlop 5.00 x 16 ins pressed steel.

## Morgan 4-4 Four-Seater

Introduced 1937, 99 built by 1939. As 4-4 two-seater except WEIGHT 1,642 lb.

### Morgan 4-4 Drophead Coupé
Introduced 1938, 58 built by 1939. As 4-4 two-seater except WEIGHT 1,736 lb; WHEELS AND TYRES 5.50 x 16 ins.

### Morgan 4-4 Two-Seater
Introduced 1946 as per 1939 1,267-cc specification, 249 cars built by 1950, plus 4 1,098-cc models and 54 chassis with 1,267-cc engine.

### Morgan 4-4 Four-Seater
Introduced 1946 as per 1939 1,267-cc specification, 140 built by 1950.

### Morgan 4-4 Drophead Coupé
Introduced 1946 as per 1939 1,267-cc specification, 106 built by 1950.

### Morgan 4/4 Two-Seater Series II
Introduced 1955, built until 1960.

**Engine**
Four cylinders, in-line, side valves CUBIC CAPACITY 1,172 cc; BORE AND STROKE 63.5 mm x 92.5 mm; MAX POWER 36 bhp at 4,400 rpm; MAX TORQUE 41 lb/ft at 4,000 rpm.

**Chassis**
WHEELBASE 8 ft; WEIGHT 1,600 lb; FRONT TRACK 3 ft 11 ins; REAR TRACK 3 ft 11 ins; from 1958 with wire wheels, 4 ft 1 in; LENGTH 12 ft; WIDTH 4 ft 8 ins; HEIGHT 3 ft 10 ins (hood erect 4 ft 4 ins); FRONT SUSPENSION Independent with sliding stub axles and coil springs on vertical pillars; REAR SUSPENSION Live axle with half elliptic springs; BRAKES 9-inch drums all round, from 1959 optional 11-inch discs at front; STEERING cam-and-peg steering box; GEARING (overall) 4.4, 8.25, 15.07:1 (reverse 19.71); TYRES AND WHEELS 5.00 x 16 ins.

### Morgan 4/4 Competition Model Series II
Introduced in 1957, built until 1960. As 4.4 series II except:

**Engine**
MAX POWER 40 bhp at 5,100 rpm.

## Morgan 4/4 Two-Seater Series III
Introduced in 1960, built until 1961. As 4/4 series II except:

**Engine**
Four cylinders, in-line, overhead valves CUBIC CAPACITY 997 cc; BORE AND STROKE 80.86 mm x 48.41 mm; MAX POWER 39 bhp at 5,000 rpm; MAX TORQUE 53 lb/ft at 2,700 rpm. As 4/4 series II except:

**Chassis**
WEIGHT 1,525 lb; GEARING (overall) 4.4, 6.21, 10.54, 18:1 (reverse 23.7); TYRES AND WHEELS 5.25 x 15 ins.

## Morgan 4/4 Series IV Two-Seater
Introduced in 1961, built until 1962. As 4/4 series III except:

**Engine**
Four cylinders, in-line, overhead valves; CUBIC CAPACITY 1,340 cc; BORE AND STROKE 80.96 mm x 65.07 mm; MAX POWER 54 bhp at 5,000 rpm; MAX TORQUE 74 lb/ft at 2,500 rpm. As 4/4 series III except:

**Chassis**
WEIGHT 1,500 lb; BRAKES 11-inch discs at front as standard; GEARING (overall) 4.56, 6, 11, 18.8:1 (reverse 18.1); TYRES AND WHEELS 5.60 x 15 ins.

## Morgan 4/4 Series V Two-Seater
Introduced in 1962, built until 1968. As 4/4 series IV except:

**Engine**
Four cylinders, in-line, overhead valves; CUBIC CAPACITY 1,498 cc; BORE AND STROKE 80.96 mm x 72.74 mm; MAX POWER 59.5 bhp at 4,600 rpm, optional 56 bhp; MAX TORQUE 81.5 lb/ft at 2,300 rpm. As 4/4 series IV except:

**Chassis**
WEIGHT 1,600 lb; GEARING (overall) 4.56, 6.44, 10.92 16.2:1 (reverse 18.1); TYRES AND WHEELS 155-15.

## Morgan 4/4 series V Competition model

Introduced in 1962, built until 1968. As 4/4 series V except:

**Engine**
MAX POWER 78 bhp at 5,200 rpm; MAX TORQUE 91 lb/ft at 3,600 rpm.
As 4/4 series V except:

**Chassis**
GEARING (overall) 4.1, 5.8, 9.82, 14.54:1 (reverse 16.22), optional from 1964 4.1, 5.78, 8.36, 14.51 (reverse 16.22), optional from 1967 4.1, 5.73, 8.24, 12.19 (reverse 13.63).

## Morgan 4/4 1600

Introduced in 1968, built until 1970. As 4/4 series V except:

**Engine**
Four cylinders, in-line, overhead valves; CUBIC CAPACITY 1,597 cc; BORE AND STROKE 81 mm x 77.6 mm; MAX POWER 71 bhp at 5,000 rpm; MAX TORQUE 91.5 lb/ft at 3,600 rpm.

**Chassis**
As 4/4 series V except:
FRONT TRACK 4 ft; REAR TRACK 4 ft; GEARING (overall) 4.1, 5.73, 8.24, 12.19 (reverse 16.22).

## Morgan 4/4 1600 Four-Seater

Introduced in 1968, built until 1970. As 4/4 1600 two-seater, except:

**Chassis**
WEIGHT 1,750 lb.

## Morgan 4/4 1600 Competition model

Introduced in 1968, built until 1981. As 4/4 1600 except:

**Engine**
MAX POWER 88 bhp at 5,400 rpm; MAX TORQUE 96 lb/ft at 3,600 rpm.

## Morgan 4/4 1600 Four-Seater

Introduced in 1970, built until 1981. As Morgan 4/4 Competition model except:

**Chassis**
WEIGHT 1,750 lb.

## Morgan 4/4 Two-Seater

Introduced 1981. As 4/4 1600 except:

### Engine

Four cylinders, in-line, overhead valves; optional 1981-6 CUBIC CA-PACITY 1,585 cc; BORE AND STROKE 84 mm x 71.5 mm; MAX POWER 97 bhp at 6,000 rpm; MAX TORQUE 94 lb/ft at 3,800 rpm; or 1981-3 CUBIC CAPACITY 1,597 cc; BORE AND STROKE 80 mm x 79.96 mm; MAX POWER 96 bhp at 6,000 rpm; MAX TORQUE 98 lb/ft at 4,000 rpm, from 1983 with 1,597-cc engine; MAX POWER 105 bhp at 6,000 rpm; MAX TORQUE 102 lb/ft at 4,800 rpm. As 4/4 1600 except:

### Chassis

As 4/4 1600 except:
Optional from 1984 STEERING rack and pinion or recirculating ball steering box; with 1,585-cc engine, from 1981-6 GEARING (overall) 3.4, 4.1, 5.58, 8.41, 14.8:1 (reverse 13.12); with 1,597-cc engine from 1983 (overall) 3.12, 4.1, 5.73, 8.24, 12.19:1 (reverse 16.22).

## Morgan 4/4 Four-Seater

Introduced 1981. As Morgan 4/4 two-seater except:

### Chassis

WEIGHT 1,750 lb.

## Morgan Plus Four Two-Seater

Introduced 1950, built until 1968.

### Engine

Four cylinders, in-line, overhead valves CUBIC CAPACITY 2,088 cc; BORE AND STROKE 85 mm x 92 mm; MAX POWER 68 bhp at 4,300 rpm; MAX TORQUE 112 lb/ft at 2,300 rpm, from 1954 optional CUBIC CAPACITY 1,991 cc; BORE AND STROKE 83 mm x 92 mm; MAX POWER 90 bhp at 4,800 rpm; MAX TORQUE 117 lb/ft at 3,000 rpm, from 1955 optional (with 1,991-cc capacity) MAX POWER 95 bhp at 4,800 rpm, from 1956 optional (with 1,991-cc capacity) MAX POWER 100 bhp at 4,600 rpm, from 1959 optional (with 1,991-cc capacity) MAX POWER 106 bhp at 5,500 rpm, also optional CUBIC CAPACITY 2,138 cc; MAX POWER 100 bhp at 5,000 rpm; MAX TORQUE 127 lb/ft at 3,350 rpm; 2.138-cc engine standard from 1961, 1,991 cc optional.

**Chassis**
WHEELBASE 8 ft; WEIGHT 1,900 lb; FRONT TRACK 3 ft 11 ins; REAR TRACK 3 ft 11 ins, from 1958 with wire wheels, 4 ft 1 in; LENGTH 11 ft 8 ins from 1959 12 ft 3 ins; WIDTH 4 ft 8 ins; HEIGHT 3 ft 10 ins (hood erect 4 ft 4 ins); FRONT SUSPENSION Independent with sliding stub axles and coil springs on vertical pillars; REAR SUSPENSION Live axle with half elliptic springs; BRAKES 9-inch drums all round, from 1959 optional 11-inch discs at front, disc front brakes standard from 1960; STEERING worm and nut steering box, from 1955 cam-and-peg steering box; GEARING (overall) 4.11, 5.4, 8 and 13.5:1 (reverse 13.87), from 1952 optional 3.73, 4.9, 7.28, 12.28:1 (reverse 12.62); TYRES AND WHEELS 5.25 ins x 16 ins pressed steel, from 1958 5.25 x 15 ins, optional wire wheels 5.60 x 15 ins.

## Morgan Plus Four Four-Seater
Introduced 1951, built until 1968. As Plus Four two-seater except:
WEIGHT 2,050 lb; LENGTH 11 ft 10 ins; HEIGHT (hood erect) 4 ft 6.5 ins.

## Morgan Plus Four Two-Seater Drophead Coupé
Introduced in 1952, built until 1969. As Plus Four two-seater except
WEIGHT 2,140 lb; LENGTH 11 ft 10 ins; HEIGHT (hood erect) 4 ft 5.5 ins.

## Morgan Plus Four Four-Seater Drophead Coupé
Introduced in 1954, built until 1956. As Plus Four two-seater drophead coupé except:

**Chassis**
WEIGHT 2,134 lb.

## Morgan Plus Four Super Sports
Introduced 1961, built until 1969. As Plus Four two-seater except:

**Engine**
CUBIC CAPACITY 1,991 cc; MAX POWER 115 bhp, optional 2,138cc; MAX POWER 125 bhp, from 1962 2,138 cc standard, 1,991 cc optional.

**Chassis**
As Plus Four except:
WEIGHT 1,800 lb.

## Morgan Plus Four Plus

Introduced in 1963, built until 1967. As wire wheeled Plus four except:

### Chassis

WEIGHT 1,850 lb; LENGTH 12 ft 8 ins; WIDTH 5 ft 1 in; HEIGHT 4 ft 3 ins.

## Morgan Plus Four

Introduced 1984, built until 1986. As 1,585-cc 4/4 circa 1984-6 except:

### Engine

Four cylinders, in-line, overhead valves CUBIC CAPACITY 1,995 cc; BORE AND STROKE 84 mm x 90 mm; MAX POWER 130 bhp at 5,900 rpm; MAX TORQUE 130 lb/ft at 3,600 rpm.

## Morgan Plus Eight

Introduced 1968.

### Engine

Eight cylinder, vee-formation, overhead valves CUBIC CAPACITY 3,528 cc; BORE AND STROKE 88.9 mm x 71.1 mm; MAX POWER 152.5 bhp at 5,200 rpm; MAX TORQUE 210 lb/ft at 2,600 rpm; from 1971 160 bhp; from 1974 150 bhp; from 1977 162.5 bhp at 5,250 rpm, 198 lb/ft at 2,500 rpm; from 1983 optional 200 bhp at 5,280 rpm, 220 lb/ft at 4,000 rpm.

### Chassis

WHEELBASE 8 ft 2 ins; WEIGHT 1,950 lb, from 1972 1,935 lb; FRONT TRACK 4 ft 1 in, from 1973 4 ft 3 ins; REAR TRACK 4 ft 3 ins, from 1973 4 ft 4 ins; LENGTH 12 ft 8 ins; WIDTH 4 ft 9 ins, from 1973 4 ft 11 ins; HEIGHT 3 ft 8 ins (hood erect 4 ft 2 ins); FRONT SUSPENSION Independent with sliding stub axles and coil springs on vertical pillars; REAR SUSPENSION Live axle with half elliptic springs; BRAKES 11-inch discs front, 9-inch drums rear; STEERING cam-and-peg steering box, from 1983 rack-and-pinion; GEARING (overall) 3.58, 4.71,. 6.98, 13.49 (reverse 11.96), from 1972 3.54, 4.92, 7.55, 12.83 (reverse 12.14), from 1973 3.31, 4.6, 7.06, 12 (reverse 11.35), from 1977 0.833, 3.31, 4.62, 6.91, 11 (reverse 11.35); TYRES AND WHEELS 185-15, from 1977 195-14, from 1982 205-15.

## Morgan Plus Eight Sport Lightweight

Introduced in 1975, built until 1977. As Morgan Plus Eight except:

### Chassis

WEIGHT 1,835 lb; WHEELS AND TYRES 195-14.

# Index

# Index of Illustrations

# Picture Acknowledgements

**Classic Cars** black and white pages 1, 2, 3, 4 top, 7, 8, top and bottom, 13 top, 19, 20, 21 top and bottom, 22, 28, 29 top, bottom left and right, 31 top and bottom, 32 top and bottom, 33 left and right, 35 bottom right, 36 top, 37 bottom, 38, 40, 41 left and right, 42, 43 bottom, 44 left and right, 49 top right, 52, 53 left and right, 54 left, 57, 89 top, bottom left and right, 93 left and right, 94, 95 left and right, 96 top, centre, bottom left and right, 100 top and bottom, 104 top left and right, bottom left and right, 108, 109 left and right, 110 left and right, 114 left and right, bottom left, 122, 124 top, bottom right, 125 left and right, 126 left and right, 128, 129 top left and right, centre left and right, 130, 131, 132 top left, 137 top right, bottom left and right, 147 right, 166 top and bottom, 171 bottom, 172, 173 centre left and right, bottom, 176 top right, bottom, 177, 178, 184, 185 right, 189 bottom right, 191 bottom left, 212 bottom, 217 top and bottom, 239 top, 240 left.

**Hilton Press Services** cover, back cover, colour plates 1, 2, 3, 4, 5, 6, 7, 8, 9, 10, 11, 12, 13, 14, 15, 16, 17, 18, 19, 20, 22, 23, 24, 26. Black and white, pages 4 bottom, 5, 9, 12 top and bottom, 13 bottom, 14, 15 top and bottom, 16, 17 top left and right, bottom left and right, 18, 23, 24 top left and right, bottom left and right, 26, 34 top, bottom left and right, 35 top left and right, bottom left, 36 bottom, 37 top, 43 top left and right, 46 top left and right, bottom, 47, 48 top and bottom, 49 top left, bottom

left and right, 50 top and bottom, 51, 54 bottom right, 55 top left and right, bottom left and right, 56 top left and right, bottom, 59, 62 left and right, 66, 67 left and right, 68 top left, centre and right, upper centre, lower centre and bottom, 69 top left and right, centre, bottom left and right, 70 top, bottom left and centre, 71, 72 top and bottom, 74 left and right, 75 top left and right, bottom left and right, 77 left and right, 79 top and bottom, 80, 81, 82 top left and right, bottom left upper and lower, bottom right, 84, 85 top left and right, bottom, 86 left and right, 87, 91 top left, centre and right, bottom, 97 top and bottom, 98 left and right, 99 top left and right, bottom left and right, 102 top left and right, centre left and right, bottom, 107 left and right, 114 bottom right, 115, 118, 120, 121, 124 bottom left, 129 bottom, 132 top right, centre, bottom, 133 top, centre left and right, bottom, 134, 137 top left, 140 top left and right, bottom, 144, 146, top right, bottom right, 147 top left, 151 top, centre, bottom left and right, 154, 155, 156, 158, 159 top and bottom, 161, 162, 163, 171 top, centre, 173 top left and right, 174, 176 top left, 180 top left and right, 182 top left and right, bottom, 185 left, 187 top left and right, bottom left and right, 188, 189 top left and right, bottom left, 191 top left and right, upper centre left and right, lower centre left and right, bottom right, 194 left and right, 195 left and right, 196 top left and right, bottom left and right, 197 top left and right, bottom left and

right, 198 top left and right, 199 bottom left and right, 200 top left and right, bottom left and right, 201 top left and right, bottom left and right, 202 top, bottom left and right, 203 top left and right, 204 top, bottom right, 205 top left and right, centre left and right, 206 top right, upper centre left and right, lower centre, bottom left and right, 208 top and bottom, 209 top, bottom left and right, 210 top and bottom, 211 top, bottom left and right, 212 top, 213, 216, 218 top, centre, bottom, 219, 220, 221, 223, 224 left and right, 225 left and right, 226, 227, 228, 229, 230 left and right, 231 left and right, 233 top and bottom, 234, 236 top and bottom, 237 top and bottom, 239 bottom left and right, 240 right, 241 top left and right, bottom, 242 left and right, 243 top and bottom, 244 left and right, 245 top left and right, bottom, 246 top and bottom, 247 top, bottom left and right, 248 top and bottom, 249 top left and right, bottom, 250 top left and right, bottom left and right, 251, 253, 254 top left and right, bottom, 255 top and bottom, 256 left and right, 257 top left, centre and right, centre left, centre and right, bottom.

**London Art-Technical** 142 top, centre, bottom left and right, 146 top, bottom left.

**Morgan Motor Company** black and white 238

**Sully, Alex** black and white 203 bottom left and right, 204 bottom left, 205 bottom, 206 top left

**TASS** 258

**Young, Phil** colour plates 21, 24